The Veil and the Male Elite

The Veil and the Male Elite

A Feminist Interpretation of Women's Rights in Islam

FATIMA MERNISSI

TRANSLATED BY
MARY JO LAKELAND

Addison-Wesley Publishing Company, Inc.
Reading, Massachusetts   Menlo Park, California   New York
Don Mills, Ontario   Wokingham, England   Amsterdam   Bonn
Sydney   Singapore   Tokyo   Madrid   San Juan
Paris   Seoul   Milan   Mexico City   Taipei

Library of Congress Cataloging-in-Publication Data

Mernissi, Fatima.
    [Harem politique. English]
    The veil and the male elite: a feminist interpretation of women's rights in Islam /
Fatima Mernissi ; translated by Mary Jo Lakeland.
    p. cm.
    Translation of : Le harem politique.
    Includes bibliographical references and index.
    ISBN 0-201-52321-3
    1. Women in the Hadith. 2. Women in Islam. 3. Muhammad, Prophet.
  d. 632—Views on women.
  BP 135.8.W67M4713   1991
  297'.12408—dc20   90-47404
                                                            CIP

Jacket design by Marge Anderson
Set in 11/13-point Bembo by Hope Services (Abingdon) Ltd, Great Britain

1 2 3 4 5 6 7 8 9 - M W - 9 5 9 4 9 3 9 2 9 1
First printing, August 1991

Contents

Preface to the English Edition

Is Islam opposed to women's rights? Let us take a look at the
international situation, to see who is really against women.

Is it not odd that in this extraordinary decade, the 1990s, when
the whole world is swept by the irresistible chant for human
rights, sung by women and men, by children and grandparents,
from all kinds of religious backgrounds and beliefs, in every
language and dialect from Beijing to the Americas, one finds only
one religion identified as a stumbling block on the road to true
democracy? Islam alone is condemned by many Westerners as
blocking the way to women's rights. And yet, though neither
Christianity nor Judaism played an important role in promoting
equality of the sexes, millions of Jewish and Chistian women
today enjoy a dual privilege – full human rights on the one hand
and access to an inspirational religious tradition on the other. As
an Arab woman, particularly fascinated by the way people in the
modern world manage and integrate their past, I am constantly
surprised when visiting Europe and the USA, who "sell" themselves as super-modern societies, to find how Judeo-Christian
their cultural atmosphere really is. It may escape them, but to an
outsider Europe and the USA are particularly rich in religious
influences, in myths, tales, and traditions. So much so that I
continually find myself asking questions such as "What do you
mean by St George and the Dragon?" simply so that I can follow
conversations.

Westerners make unconscious religious references constantly in their daily activities, their creative thinking, and their approach to the world around them. When Neil Armstrong and his fellow astronauts walked on the moon on July 20, 1969, they read to the millions watching them, including us Muslims, the first chapter of the Book of Genesis: "In the Beginning God created the Heavens and the Earth . . ." They did not sound so very modern. They sounded to us very religious indeed, in spite of their spacesuits. When I went to the USA in 1986 I was surprised to see preachers – Christian-style mullahs – reciting day-long sermons on satellite television! Some banks and businesses evidently found it worth their while to finance whole days of religious transmissions, poured free of charge into American homes. Here is a clear message for those who doubt Islam's capacity to survive modernity, calling it unfit to accompany the age of higher technology: why should Islam fail where Judaism and Christianity so clearly succeed?

What can we women conclude from the Euro-American situation? First, we see religion can be used by all kinds of organizations in the modern world to promote money-making projects; and second, since Islam is no more repressive than Judaism or Christianity, there must be those who have a vested interest in blocking women's rights in Muslim societies. The cause must again be profit, and the question is: how and where can a businessman who profitably exploits women (whether the head of a multinational or a local bazaar entrepreneur), find a source in which he can dip his spurious rationale to give it a glow of authenticity? Surely not in the present. To defend the violation of women's rights it is necessary to go back into the shadows of the past. This is what those people, East or West, who would deny Muslim women's claim to democracy are trying to do. They camouflage their self-interest by proclaiming that we can have either Islam or democracy, but never both together.

Let us leave the international scene and go into the dark back streets of Medina. Why is it that we find some Muslim men saying that women in Muslim states cannot be granted full enjoyment of human rights? What grounds do they have for such a claim? None – they are simply betting on our ignorance of the past, for their argument can never convince anyone with an elementary understanding of Islam's history. Any man who believes that a Muslim woman who fights for her dignity and right to citizenship excludes herself necessarily from the *umma* and is a brainwashed victim of Western propaganda is a man who misunderstands his own religious heritage, his own cultural identity. The vast and inspiring records of Muslim history so brilliantly completed for us by scholars such as Ibn Hisham, Ibn Hajar, Ibn Sa'ad, and Tabari, speak to the contrary. We Muslim women can walk into the modern world with pride, knowing that the quest for dignity, democracy, and human rights, for full participation in the political and social affairs of our country, stems from no imported Western values, but is a true part of the Muslim tradition. Of this I am certain, after reading the works of those scholars mentioned above and many others. They give me evidence to feel proud of my Muslim past, and to feel justified in valuing the best gifts of modern civilization: human rights and the satisfaction of full citizenship.

Ample historical evidence portrays women in the Prophet's Medina raising their heads from slavery and violence to claim their right to join, as equal participants, in the making of their Arab history. Women fled aristocratic tribal Mecca by the thousands to enter Medina, the Prophet's city in the seventh century, because Islam promised equality and dignity for all, for men and women, masters and servants. Every woman who came to Medina when the Prophet was the political leader of Muslims could gain access to full citizenship, the status of *sahabi*, Companion of the Prophet. Muslims can take pride that in their language they have the feminine of that word, *sahabiyat*, women who enjoyed the right to enter into the councils of the Muslim *umma*, to speak freely to its Prophet-leader, to dispute with the men, to fight for their happiness, and to be involved in the management of military and political affairs. The evidence is there in the works of religious history, in the biographical details of *sahabiyat* by the thousand who built Muslim society side by side with their male counterparts.

This book is an attempt to recapture some of the wonderful and beautiful moments in the first Muslim city in the world, Medina of the year 622 (the first year of the Muslim calendar), when aristocratic young women and slaves alike were drawn to a new, mysterious religion, feared by the masters of Mecca because its prophet spoke of matters dangerous to the establishment, of human dignity and equal rights. The religion was Islam and the Prophet was Muhammad. And that his egalitarian message today sounds so foreign to many in our Muslim societies that they claim it to be imported is indeed one of the great enigmas of our times. It is our duty as good Muslims to refresh their memories. *Inna nafa'at al-dhikra* (of use is the reminder) says the Koran. When I finished writing this book I had come to understand one thing: if women's rights are a problem for some modern Muslim men, it is neither because of the Koran nor the Prophet, nor the Islamic tradition, but simply because those rights conflict with the interests of a male elite. The elite faction is trying to convince us that their egotistic, highly subjective, and mediocre view of culture and society has a sacred basis. But if there is one thing that the women and men of the late twentieth century who have an awareness and enjoyment of history can be sure of, it is that Islam was not sent from heaven to foster egotism and mediocrity. It came to sustain the people of the Arabian desert lands, to encourage them to achieve higher spiritual goals and equality for all, in spite of poverty and the daily conflict between the weak and the powerful. For those first Muslims democracy was nothing unusual; it was their meat and drink and their wonderful dream, waking or sleeping. I have tried to present that dream, and if you should find pleasure in these pages it is because I have succeeded in some small way, however inadequate, in recapturing the heady quality of a great epoch.

Acknowledgments

For sound advice regarding my research for this book I am indebted to two of my colleagues at the Université Mohammed V: Alem Moulay Ahmed al-Khamlichi, and the philosopher 'Ali Oumlil. The latter suggested to me the inclusion of the material concerning the ordering of the suras in the Koran and the dating of them; he also recommended to me some references concerning the traditional methodology as regards the sacred texts. Alem Moulay Ahmed al-Khamlichi gave me much advice and patient assistance, rare among colleagues, especially with chapters 2, 3, and 4, concerning Hadith. His generosity even extended to putting his own books at my disposal and marking the pages for me. I confess that I would have hesitated to be so generous myself, because the number of loaned books that you never see again has increased sharply since the war in Lebanon, which has sent the price of Arabic books soaring. Professor Khamlichi teaches Muslim law at the Faculté de Droit of the Université Mohammed V. In his capacity as 'alim (religious scholar), he is also a member of the council of 'ulama of the city of Rabat and a specialist in problems dealing with women in Islam. It was he who gave me the idea for this book. It was while listening to him at a televised conference at the Rabat mosque, expounding his views on the initiative of the believer with regard to religious texts, that I felt the necessity for a new interpretation of those texts.

I am also grateful for the patience and unflagging aid of M. Bou'nani, director of the Institut Ibn-Ruchd of the Faculté de

Acknowledgments

Lettres of Rabat, who saved me much time with regard to finding and consulting the available documents in the library of the Faculté de Lettres; to the Bibliothèque Générale of Rabat; to Mustapha Naji, bookseller, who turned the bookseller/client relationship into an intellectual exchange and a debate on the future of the Muslim heritage that was sometimes a little too impassioned for my taste, but certainly fruitful; and to Madame Dalili, who took care of all the concerns of daily life during the long months of research and writing of this book.

Finally, I would like to express my gratitude to Claire Delannoy, the first non-Muslim reader of this book, thanks to whom the often problematic relationship between writer and publisher became a veritable dialogue between cultures.

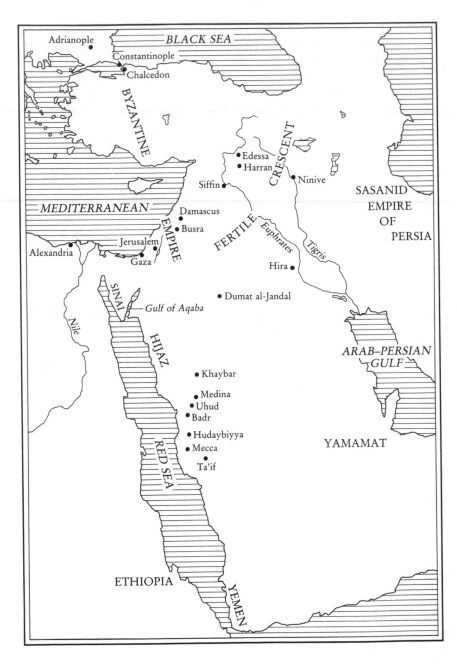

MAP OF ARABIA AT THE TIME OF THE HEJIRA

Introduction

"Can a woman be a leader of Muslims?" I asked my grocer, who, like most grocers in Morocco, is a true "barometer" of public opinion.

"I take refuge in Allah!" he exclaimed, shocked, despite the friendly relations between us. Aghast at the idea, he almost dropped the half-dozen eggs I had come to buy.

"May God protect us from the catastrophes of the times!" mumbled a customer who was buying olives, as he made as if to spit. My grocer is a fanatic about cleanliness, and not even denouncing a heresy justifies dirtying the floor in his view.

A second customer, a schoolteacher whom I vaguely knew from the newsstand, stood slowly caressing his wet mint leaves, and then hit me with a Hadith that he knew would be fatal: "Those who entrust their affairs to a woman will never know prosperity!" Silence fell on the scene. There was nothing I could say. In a Muslim theocracy, a Hadith (tradition) is no small matter. The Hadith collections are works that record in minute detail what the Prophet said and did. They constitute, along with the Koran (the book revealed by God), both the source of law and the standard for distinguishing the true from the false, the permitted from the forbidden – they have shaped Muslim ethics and values.

I discreetly left the grocery store without another word. What could I have said to counterbalance the force of that political aphorism, which is as implacable as it is popular?

1

Introduction

Silenced, defeated, and furious, I suddenly felt the urgent need to inform myself about this Hadith and to search out the texts where it is mentioned, to understand better its extraordinary power over the ordinary citizens of a modern state.

A glance at the latest Moroccan election statistics supports the "prediction" uttered in the grocery store. Although the constitution gives women the right to vote and be elected, political reality grants them only the former. In the legislative elections of 1977, the eight women who stood for election found no favor with the six and a half million voters, of whom three million were women. At the opening of Parliament, there was not one woman present, and the men were settled among their male peers as usual, just as in the cafés. Six years later, in the municipal elections of 1983, 307 women were bold enough to stand as candidates, and almost three and a half million women voters went to the polls. Only 36 women won election, as against 65,502 men![1]

To interpret the relationship between the massive participation of women voters and the small number of women elected as a sign of stagnation and backwardness would be in accordance with the usual stereotypes applied to the Arab world. However, it would be more insightful to see it as a reflection of changing times and the intensity of the conflicts between the aspirations of women, who take the constitution of their country seriously, and the resistance of men, who imagine, despite the laws in force, that power is necessarily male. This makes me want to shed light on those obscure zones of resistance, those entrenched attitudes, in order to understand the symbolic – even explosive – significance of that act which elsewhere in the world is an ordinary event: a woman's vote. For this reason, my misadventure in a neighborhood grocery store had more than symbolic importance for me. Revealing the misogynistic attitude of my neighbors, it indicated to me the path I should follow to better understand it – a study of the religious texts that everybody knows but no one really probes, with the exception of the authorities on the subject: the mullahs and imams.

Going through the religious literature is no small task. First of all, one is overwhelmed by the number of volumes, and one immediately understands why the average Muslim can never know as much as an imam. Al-Bukhari's prestigious collection of traditions, *Al-Sahih* (*The Authentic*), is in four volumes with an abstruse commentary by an al-Sindi who is extremely sparing with his comments.[2] Now, without a very good commentary a nonexpert will have difficulty reading a religious text of the ninth century (al-Bukhari was born in 256 of the Muslim calendar, which begins in AD 622). This is because, for each Hadith, it is necessary to check the identity of the Companion of the Prophet who uttered it, and in what circumstances and with what objective in mind, as well as the chain of people who passed it along – and there are more fraudulent traditions than authentic ones. For each Hadith, al-Bukhari gives the results of his investigation. If he speaks of X or Y, you have to check which Companion is being referred to, what battle is being discussed, in order to make sense of the dialog or scene that is being transcribed. In addition, al-Bukhari doesn't use just one informant; there are dozens of them in the dozens of volumes. You must be careful not to go astray. The smallest mistake about the informant can cost you months of work.

What is the best way of making this check? First of all, you should make contact with the experts in religious science (*al-fiqh*) in your city. According to moral teaching and the traditional conventions, if you contact a *faqih* for information about the sources of a Hadith or a Koranic verse, he must assist you. Knowledge is to be shared, according to the promise of the Prophet himself. *Fath al-bari* by al-'Asqalani (he died in year 852 of the Hejira) was recommended to me by several people I consulted. It consists of 17 volumes that one can consult in libraries during their opening hours. But the vastness of the task and the rather limited reading time is enough to discourage most researchers.

The schoolteacher in the grocery store was right: the Hadith "those who entrust their affairs to a woman will never know prosperity" was there in al-'Asqalani's thirteenth volume, where he quotes al-Bukhari's *Sahih*, that is, those traditions that al-Bukhari classified as authentic after a rigorous process of selection, verifications, and counter-verifications.[3] Al-Bukhari's work has been one of the most highly respected references for 12 centuries. This Hadith is the sledgehammer argument used by those who want to exclude women from politics. One also finds it in the work of other authorities known for their scholarly rigor, such as Ahmad Ibn Hanbal, the author of the *Musnad* and founder of the Hanbali *Madhhab*, one of the four great schools of jurisprudence of the Sunni Muslim world.[4]

This Hadith is so important that it is practically impossible to discuss the question of women's political rights without referring to it, debating it, and taking a position on it. Fu'ad 'Abd al-Mun'im, for example, who has written a book on *The Principle of Equality in Islam*, published in 1976,[5] recapitulates all the debates that have surrounded this Hadith since the ninth century in his chapter entitled "The Principle of Equality in Islam and the Woman Problem," but without elaborating a personal, contemporary critique of the question. All attempts at reflection on the problem of political status are swallowed up by the debate on this Hadith. It is omnipresent and all-embracing.

A recent book by Muhammad 'Arafa, entitled *The Rights of Women in Islam*, maintains not only that a woman has no rights, but that she does not exist in political history:

> At the beginning of Islam, Muslim women played no role in public affairs, despite all the rights that Islam gave them, which were often the same as those accorded to men. When the Companions of the Prophet consulted among themselves after his death to name his successor, at the meeting known as that of *Saqifat Bani Sa'ida*, no women at all are said to have participated. We have no evidence of their participation in the choice of the other three orthodox caliphs. In the whole history of Islam there is no mention of the participation of women alongside men in the direction of the affairs of state, whether in political decision making or in strategic planning.[6]

Then how does this author deal with 'A'isha, the Prophet's wife, who led an armed opposition against the caliph who ruled at that time? He cannot ignore her without losing his credibility, since he is basing his case on the first decades of Islam. The Prophet died at Medina on Monday, June 8, AD 632, when his wife 'A'isha was only 18 years old. At the age of 42 she took to the battlefield at the head of an army that challenged the legitimacy of the fourth orthodox caliph, 'Ali. This took place at Basra on December 4, AD 656. Isn't challenging the caliph by inciting the population to sedition and civil war participating in political life?

'A'isha in fact played a key role in the lives of two caliphs, and she contributed to the destabilization of the third, 'Uthman, by refusing to help him when he was besieged by insurgents in his own house. She left Medina when it was on the brink of civil war to make the pilgrimage to Mecca, despite the protests of many of the notables of her entourage. As for 'Ali, the fourth caliph, she contributed to his downfall by taking command of the opposing army which challenged his legitimacy. The historians called this confrontation "The Battle of the Camel," referring to the camel ridden by 'A'isha, thereby avoiding linking in the memory of little Muslim girls the name of a woman with the name of a battle. Nevertheless, you can't just wipe 'A'isha out of the history of Islam. Our author can't ignore her, so he says:

> It is true that 'A'isha fought 'Ali Ibn Abi Talib at the Battle of the Camel . . . But this individual act of a woman companion cannot be claimed [to legitimate the participation of women in political affairs], given that the voice of Allah and his Prophet is clear on this point. Moreover, it must not be forgotten that this individual act by 'A'isha was denounced as an error by the greatest of the Companions and condemned by the other wives of the Prophet. And in any case, 'A'isha regretted her act. It is thus not acceptable to base claims on 'A'isha's experience, which was considered to be an act of *bid'a*.[7]

And *bid'a* (innovation) in Islam is an act of errant behavior, a scandalous violation of the sacred tradition.

Another contemporary historian, Sa'id al-Afghani, spent ten years on research on 'A'isha in order, according to him, to clarify for the Muslims a question that has become pressing since modernization – the relationship of women to politics. His biography of 'A'isha appeared for the first time in 1946, with a title that makes its aim perfectly clear: *'A'isha and Politics*.[8] We owe to Sa'id al-Afghani the publication of two other major texts on 'A'isha which only existed up to that point in the form of obscure manuscripts. The first is a collection of the refutations and corrections that 'A'isha made to certain Hadith which, according to her, were misreported by the Companions.[9] The second is a volume of *Siyar al-nubala'* by al-Dhahabi devoted to a biography of 'A'isha.[10] In overseeing the publication of these two documents, al-Afghani has unquestionably contributed the historian's perspective in clarifying the personality of 'A'isha. His conclusion, however, is that it is absolutely necessary to keep women out of politics. For him, women and politics are a combination of ill omen. In his eyes, the example of 'A'isha speaks against the participation of women in the exercise of power. 'A'isha proves that "woman was not created for poking her nose into politics."[11] According to him, "the blood of the Muslims was spilt. Thousands of Companions of the Prophet were killed . . . . Scholars, heroes of many victories, eminent leaders lost their lives"[12] – all because of 'A'isha's intervention in politics. 'A'isha was not only responsible for the blood spilt at the Battle of the Camel, which set in motion the split of the Muslim world into two factions (Sunnis and Shi'ites), a battle where she herself was in command. She was also responsible for all the subsequent losses suffered by those who followed her:

> On that day [the day of the Battle of the Camel], 15,000 people were killed, according to the most conservative estimates, and all in a few hours. And you [the reader] would be better off not knowing what happened afterward, at the battles of Nahrain and Siffin and all the other battles where we turned our arms against each other . . . . And to think that, just before, Allah had united the ranks of the Muslims and purged their hearts of hate.[13]

Al-Afghani is convinced that if 'A'isha had not intervened in the public affairs of the Muslim state, "Muslim history would have

6

taken the path of peace, progress, and prosperity."[14] According to him, Allah wanted to use the experience of 'A'isha to teach the Muslims a lesson: "It seems that Allah created women to reproduce the race, bring up future generations, and be in charge of households; He wanted to teach us a practical lesson that we cannot forget."[15] For al-Afghani:

> The Battle of the Camel is a beacon in the history of the Muslims . . . . It is ever present in their minds to put them on guard any time there appears among them a tendency to blindly imitate other nations by claiming political rights for women . . . . The memory of 'A'isha should be pondered more than ever in our day. It never ceases saying to the Muslim: Look how this endeavor failed in the very heart of our Muslim history! We don't have to repeat it senselessly. We don't have to spill blood again and destroy new homes . . . . How can we do such a thing with the example of 'A'isha so fresh in our memory?[16]

The task that al-Afghani took on – to devote a significant part of his life to writing a biography filled with lessons for the future – met with such success that the work was republished in 1971 in Beirut.

But in what sources of Muslim history was al-Afghani able to read that 'A'isha was guilty of fomenting sedition and bloodshed – 'A'isha, that woman who "had no equal among either the women or the men of her century," according to the testimony of her own contemporaries? From what authors did he draw the information making 'A'isha responsible for all the blood spilt in the Muslim world since December 4, AD 656? And above all, from what sources of religious history did he draw the arguments that permit him to generalize, to move from the case of 'A'isha to that of all other women, thus stripping millions of women citizens of their political rights? In what pages of our Muslim history, so copiously recorded, did he, as historian and expert, find the documents that allowed him to exclude women from public life, to relegate them to the household, and reduce them to the role of silent spectators?

Al-Afghani used the works of the great names of Muslim religious history, especially al-Tabari, one of the most unassailable monuments of that literature – "that author who enjoys an unparalleled reputation among historians . . . an author of unquestionable probity and honesty, a major model for all those who followed him as historians."[17] The 13 volumes of al-Tabari's *Tarikh* (*History*) are truly a marvelous source of reference and a dazzling panorama for all who want to learn about the first days of Islam. But the reader is warned on page five that al-Tabari only undertook to write his *Tarikh* as a supplement to his *Tafsir* (commentary on or explication of the Koran), which comprised no less than 30,000 pages to begin with. His historical work is only a summary of his *Tafsir*, which he finally reduced to 30 volumes. You can see what an enormous task faces the person who wants to return to the sources! So, inspired by a fierce desire for knowledge, I read al-Tabari and the other writers, especially Ibn Hisham, author of the *Sira* (biography of the Prophet); Ibn Sa'd, author of *Al-Tabaqat al-kubra* (a biographical collection); al-'Asqalani, author of *Al-'Isaba* (biographies of the Companions of the Prophet); and the Hadith collections of al-Bukhari and al-Nasi'i.[18] All of this, in order to understand and clarify the mystery of that misogyny that Muslim women have to confront even in the 1990s.

The Muslim Prophet is one of the best-known historical personages of our history. We have an enormous amount of information about him. We have details about the way he led expeditions, but also a myriad of descriptions about his private life: how he behaved with his wives, his domestic quarrels, his food preferences, what made him laugh, what irritated him, etc. It is impossible to distort his personality in a Muslim country, where religious education begins in preschool. Nevertheless, a Muslim expert has been able to say that the Prophet Muhammad excluded women from public life and relegated them to the household. But to do this, he had to do outrageous violence to Muhammad as a historical person about whom we have copious documentation. The question then becomes: To what extent can one do violence to the sacred texts?

Not only have the sacred texts always been manipulated, but

manipulation of them is a structural characteristic of the practice of power in Muslim societies. Since all power, from the seventh century on, was only legitimated by religion, political forces and economic interests pushed for the fabrication of false traditions. A false Hadith is testimony that the Prophet is alleged to have done or said such and such, which would then legitimate such an act or such an attitude. In this conjuncture of political stakes and pressures, religious discourse swarmed with traditions that legitimated certain privileges and established their owners in possession of them. This reached such a point that, beginning with the first generations of Muslims, the experts felt a need to create a science for the detection of fabricated traditions. The Hanbali imam Ibn Qayyim al-Jawziya undertook a review of some of them in order to demonstrate a technique for detection of false traditions based on analysis of the content. A large number of them were simply ridiculous and not a matter of political strategy: for instance, the Prophet is supposed to have advised a sterile man to eat lots of eggs and onions, to have said that a believer should eat sweets, that looking at a very beautiful face was a form of prayer, etc.[19] We will see, in the case of al-Bukhari, one of the ninth-century founders of the science of *isnads* (the chains of transmission from the time of the Prophet), how the Muslims developed a science for the authentication of Hadith that resembles interview and fieldwork technique (and that would turn late-nineteenth-century anthropologists green with envy). All of this shows that the present day is no exception when it comes to misrepresenting privileges and interests in the name of the Prophet.

I knew that this journey back in time that I was undertaking would not be without risks. One doesn't journey to the wellsprings of history to drink, but for other more mysterious celebrations, for everything that relates to memory. And "every celebration of a mystery," Genet tells us, "is dangerous; being forbidden, the very fact that it takes place is cause for celebration."[20]

Delving into memory, slipping into the past, is an activity that these days is closely supervised, especially for Muslim women. A passport for such a journey is not always a right. The act of recollecting, like acts of black magic, really only has an effect on the present. And this works through a strict manipulation of its opposite – the time of the dead, of those who are absent, the silent time that could tell us everything. The sleeping past can animate the present. That is the virtue of memory. Magicians know it, and the imams know it too.

To ride alone back into memory with no guardian or guide; to take the paths that are not forbidden, but simply pleasant, agreeable, not heavily traveled, still unexplored (perhaps because power doesn't take that route); to go poking around in the vast areas of the Muslim heritage that is mine – is this a sin for me? Doesn't the Koran, according to the *Lisan al-'Arab* (*The Language of the Arabs*, a prestigious dictionary), command us simply to "read"? But can one ever "simply" read a text in which politics and the sacred are joined and mingled to the point of becoming indistinguishable from each other? It is not just the present that the imams and politicians want to manage to assure our well-being as Muslims, but above all the past that is being strictly supervised and completely managed for all of us, men and women. What is being supervised and managed, in fact, is memory and history. But up until now no one has ever really succeeded in banning access to memory and recollection. Memory and recollection are the dawn of pleasure; they speak the language of freedom and self-development. They tell us about a Prophet-lover who, in the middle of the desert, spoke in a strange language to his mother-tribe and his warrior-father. They tell us of a Prophet who spoke of absurd things: nonviolence and equality. He spoke to an aristocracy fierce with pride and drunk with the power of the bow.

This book is not a work of history. History is always the group's language, the official narrative that is pressed between covers of gold and trotted out for ritual ceremonies of self-congratulation. This book is intended to be a narrative of recollection, gliding toward the areas where memory breaks down, dates get mixed up, and events softly blur together, as in the dreams from which we draw our strength.

This book is a vessel journeying back in time in order to find a fabulous wind that will swell our sails and send us gliding toward new worlds, toward the time both far away and near at the beginning of the Hejira, when the Prophet could be a lover and a leader hostile to all hierarchies, when women had their place as unquestioned partners in a revolution that made the mosque an open place and the household a temple of debate.

So let us raise the sails and lift the veils – the sails of the memory-ship. But first let us lift the veils with which our contemporaries disguise the past in order to dim our present.

PART I

*Sacred Text as Political
Weapon*

I

The Muslim and Time

Muslims suffer from a *mal du présent* just as the youth of Romantic Europe suffered from a *mal du siècle*. The only difference is that the Romantic youth of Europe experienced their difficulty in living in the present as a disgust with living, while we Muslims experience it as a desire for death, a desire to be elsewhere, to be absent, and to flee to the past as a way of being absent. A suicidal absence.

One of the reasons for the success of Moroccan thinkers like Muhammad al-Jabiri and 'Abd al-Kabir Khatibi is that they broke with the funereal droning in which the intellectual scene of the Arab world had been wallowing since the 1967 defeat. They helped us to talk about our time of defeat. Not in order to lament, with eyes fixed on the military superiority of the Western enemy, finding there an excuse to fade into the past, but in order to reflect on ourselves, to find the energy to seek a framework for action. "Memory is a developing thing," explains Khatibi, "it accumulates the progress that world civilization gives it to think about. In exploring new thoughts and new practices, it learns how to better manage space, time, and its life force. The best attitude, the most humble and effective, is apprenticeship."[1] But to advise humility to a humiliated Arab world, where the politicians rely on the grandiose dreams and myths of past glories, is very disturbing to people. We hear a total dissonance between the *khutbas* (sermons) of those in power and the pragmatic analyses of those intellectuals who choose to speak their minds instead of serving as an echo chamber for the delirium of the leaders. Muhammad al-Jabiri is hardly well received when he coolly exposes the fact that those who read grandeur into the ancient texts are hallucinating – simply hallucinating.

The Arab reader, according to him, turns to the past in order to draw from it the strength that the present denies him. "He reads there his hopes, his desires. He wants to find there," explains al-Jabiri in his book *Nahnu wa al-tharwa* (*We and Our Heritage*), "knowledge, rationality, progress, etc.; that is, he looks there for everything that he has trouble mastering in the present. Whether in dreams or reality, he turns to the past for everything that he lacks in the present."[2] In the essays in his most recent book, *Taqwin al-'aql al-'arabi* (*The Process of the Formation of Arab Thought*), he demonstrates with scathing elegance that the most important heritage our ancestors bequeathed us is a system of censorship which is so omniscient and efficacious, in which politics and religion collaborate so closely, that reason (*al-'aql*) comes to be confused with this censorship itself.[3] Al-Jabiri clarifies for us one of the mysteries of the contemporary scene: the incredible presence of religion and the imams in the domain of the production of ideas. Why is it not, one may ask, the scientists who dominate this field and are seen as authoritative by the "politicians"? – since our most urgent problem is mastery of that technology that has fatally turned us into consumers in a state of the most total passivity. Al-Jabiri gives copious historical examples to prove that in Islam the politicians quickly realized that they could only authoritatively manage the present by using the past as a sacred standard. According to him, the famous *'asr al-tadwin* (the era of putting the religious texts into writing) was the beginning of an institutionalization of censorship. It began in year 134 of the Hejira (eighth century AD) when the Muslim savants began to make a catalog of Hadith (the recorded deeds and sayings of the Prophet), *fiqh* (religious knowledge), and *tafsir* (explication of the Koran) "at the express order of the Abbasid state and under its supervision."[4] This took place during the reign of the Abbasid caliph al-Mansur, who ruled from year 136 of the Hejira to 158. Leafing through al-Jabiri's book, one sees the Muslim present emerge in an extraordinary light. The infatuation of modern politicians with the men of the past in an Arab tradition which linked the cult of the ancients to the institutionalization of authoritarianism becomes extremely suspect at a moment when we have greater need than ever to pay careful attention to the use of our present energies. Why is there this desire to turn our attention to the dead past when the only battle that is important to us at the moment is that of the future? The societies that threaten us in our identity are single-mindedly focused on the future and make of it a science – or, I would say, a weapon of domination and control.

Serge Moscovici sees in the West's transformation of time the very essence that makes it *the* worldwide civilization that it is. It is a civilization that irresistibly imposes itself and erases all the others through homogenization:

> If you look at what has happened during the last century, you see that Western civilization is truly the first civilization of time. That is, the first civilization in which time plays a determining role, especially as a measure of things. We measure everything in terms of time: work, distances, history . . . . We temporalize everything . . . . We also temporalize the things that were supposed to vanish in space: the idea of speed, for instance, which is the number-one obsession in our civilization. It is a way of temporalizing space.[5]

The post-industrial Western society obliges all other cultures to fall into line with its rhythm. Through its time-rhythm, which standardizes behavior whatever the place or culture, the West manifests its domination of our era. The era of the colonial army and its parades past the headquarters of the resident general is finished. All that is in the past. In our day domination infiltrates through the familiar presence of a wristwatch. The often bizarre noise of quartz watches, which at all hours interrupts the conversation of two Arabs in the balmy nights of Tripoli or Riyad, illustrates in its very absurdity the sidereal presence of the new form of preoccupation. With this temporalization, which is, among other things, a devaluation of geopolitics, the control of space, which is the basis and essence of the political and economic power of a nation, is today replaced by that of time. Today it is the control of time that is the basis of this power. It is not the oil that lies beneath your soil that makes you rich, but control of the speed of the marketing operations necessary for positioning it on the world market.

Geopolitics was a strategy based on defense of the tangible – territory, frontiers, and the riches found within them. Today that is replaced by the laws of "chronopolitics," a time scenario in which power is achieved through control of the intangible: the flow of signs, the circulation of information, and liquid sums. The multinational corporations are the incarnation of this new form of domination, in which the actors in the political game are no longer bound by spacial considerations. National boundaries have become obsolete, ridiculous. Power and domination use another language: "They are defined in terms of an investment project. The idea of investment is itself a temporal idea; it follows the cycles of production, exchange, etc."[6] The new imperialism that dominates us, the non-Westerners, no longer appears as a physical occupation. The new imperialism is not even economic; it is more insidious – it is a way of reckoning, of calculating, of evaluation. The days of the beloved old nationalist songs that called on us to "throw the enemy out" have ended. The enemy is ingrained in our little calculator. He is in our head, he is our way of calculating, of consuming, of buying. The multinational corporation forces us to make diagnoses, prognostications, and programs according to its models. The vocabulary that we use for our national budget is its language: investment, amortization, debt. America does not have to occupy the Muslim countries in order to bring them to their knees. The new Vietnam smacks of debt and the voices, so far away on the telephone, of the experts of the World Bank and the International Monetary Fund. The West, "drugged with growth," projects its present into the future and forces us to realize that, in order to take up its challenge, we must fight on the grounds that it has chosen: the present.

The arrow of time: that is the challenge of the century. An arrow pointing in the wrong direction, a direction that makes us anxious – the direction of the future. An age being propelled forward, merging with spaceships and interstellar travel. A present that is scarcely distinguishable from the future by which it defines and valorizes itself.

And how do we react to this speeding-up of time, to this propulsion of the present into the future? By sliding, sorrowfully, wounded, and infantilized, back toward our origins, toward an anesthetizing past where we were protected, where we had dominion over the rising and setting of the sun. We glide like tightrope walkers along a taut wire that leads us back toward the celebration of our ancestors – the funeral of our sad present. Appealed to from time to time, our ancestors can be a resource for us, but if they take over, they devour the dawn and the sun and turn our dreams into nightmares.

The Muslims are not the only ones to be terrorized by the misuse of memory. Westerners also suffer from it:

> There is no doubt that for ten years the French, immobilized by the current crisis, have begun to cast tender, longing glances at the supposed harmony of days past. It's all a game of pretend. Leisure activities and hobbies, from nineteenth-century postcards to the outfits of our grandmothers, from amateur genealogy to rural communes, all have a backward-looking appeal.[7]

Remember Marshall McLuhan's anecdote about the man who couldn't recall who he was:

> ". . . and who are you?"
> "I – I hardly know, sir, just at present – at least I know who I was when I got up this morning, but I think I must have been changed several times since then."[8]

The difference between Westerners and us is not so much about attitude toward change as about attitude toward time, anguish about time's arrow draining us as it points toward death. It is true that everyone has to face death in the future, but is it not our role to change the signs, to put death behind us, to dress our ancestors in the robes of death, and then to march with long strides toward a future where creating is possible, where remaking the world justifies living? What characterizes the modern West is its success in masking its fascination with death with a fascination with the future, thus freeing its creative energies. But modern Muslims, under the spell of who knows what deep-seated pain, prefer to die before even living, be it only for a few decades. The difference between the West and us is in the way we consume death, the past. Westerners make it into a last course, and we try to make it the main dish. Westerners consume the past as a hobby, as a pastime, as a rest from the stress of the present. We persist in making it a profession, a vocation, an outlook. By invoking our ancestors at every turn we live the present as an interlude in which we are little involved. At the extreme, the present is a distressing contretemps to us.

Patiently, tactfully, al-Jabiri explains to us that our morbid looking to the past keeps us from understanding it. According to him, we are incapable of understanding that past that we invoke like a magic litany because we are too engrossed in superimposing on it our present obsessions: "The contemporary Arab reader suffers from a poor adjustment to his times, to the times that we are fleeing from. In order to assure ourselves that we exist, we seek escape in magic solutions for our many problems."[9] The fading of the self into the past is one of our main magic formulas. Despite the great works of our tradition, our heritage, and the history of our ancestors, we are incapable of understanding them, of interpreting them. In order to understand the ancient texts, al-Jabiri tells us, you have to be rooted in the present. You have to take up distance from the texts in order to decode them, to give them their meaning. The reader must separate his own time – that of the present – from that of the text. Otherwise, "we project our problems onto the ancestral text, and that projection impedes our understanding it."[10]

It is time to define what I mean when I say "we Muslims."

The expression does not refer to Islam in terms of an individual choice, a personal option. I define being Muslim as belonging to a theocratic state. What the individual thinks is secondary for this definition. Being Marxist or Maoist or atheist does not keep one from obeying the national laws, those of the theocratic state, which define the crimes and set the punishments. Being Muslim is a civil matter, a national identity, a passport, a family code of laws, a code of public rights. The confusion between Islam as a belief, as a personal choice, and Islam as law, as state religion, contributed greatly, I believe, to the failure of Leftist movements, and of the Left in general, in Muslim countries.

If we look again at those who read in the seventh-century texts the necessity to deprive half of the Muslim population – women – of the exercise of their political rights, we have to understand why, according to them, the problem of our times is linked to the problem of democracy, to the exercise by all citizens, whatever their sex, of their public rights. How do the *mal du présent* and the rejection of democracy get combined? How are they then linked to the matter of gender? How do three concepts normally considered independent of each other – the relationship to time, the relationship to power, and the relationship to femaleness – become connected as a discourse on identity? And, above all, how does the identity crisis present in all of us, men and women, as citizens of a culturally invaded area, become transformed by the authors obsessed with the past into a uniquely male problem? If we can answer these questions, perhaps then we can grasp what impels al-Afghani and other scholars to take up their pens and write books about the necessity of excluding women from politics as a condition for safeguarding Muslim identity.

The problem for the Muslim states, after their quasi-disappearance during the colonial period, was that they found themselves almost feminized – veiled, obliterated, nonexistent. After independence, the state had to dramatize its rebirth. Threatened with death, with powerlessness, the Muslim state was forced by colonization to redefine itself, and in so doing it was forced to redefine what its citizen was. But this process of redefinition took place in the river of time, where one never has the chance to bathe twice. The era of the officially totalitarian state, based on oppression by a despot as a founding principle, had become anachronistic. The renascent Muslim states, desirous of recognition by the colonial powers who had cut them adrift, surged onto the international scene. Enthusiastically they thronged into the corridors of the United

Nations to sign the Universal Declaration of Human Rights and to assert their respect for fundamental freedoms as the principle and spirit of their constitutions. In redefining themselves in the eyes of their former colonizers, they were forced to grant their new citizenship to all their new nationals, men and women. But, in doing this, the Muslim state itself, preoccupied with its own renaissance, undermined the sexual hierarchy and destroyed the scale of values that constituted male identity. There were no longer just men as citizens among the Muslims after independence; there were only asexual citizens – at any rate, *vis-à-vis* the state and its laws.

The metamorphosis of the Muslim woman from a veiled, secluded, marginalized object, reduced to inertia, into a subject with constitutional rights, erased the lines that defined the identity hierarchy which organized politics and relations between the sexes. Our traditional identity hardly acknowledged the individual, whom it abhorred as a disturber of the collective harmony. In Islam, the idea of the individual in a state of nature, in the philosophical meaning of the word, is nonexistent.[11] Traditional society produced Muslims who were literally "submissive" to the will of the group. Individuality in such a system is discouraged; any private initiative is *bid'a* (innovation), which necessarily constitutes errant behavior. The traditional society tried to stop the development of individuality at a stage that did not threaten the authority of the leader, creating a ghost of an individual, who would not have autonomy (identified with rebellion). Using the debates in Egypt between the political parties and the new state, Umlil illustrates this point by a skillful analysis of concepts as fundamental for modern democracy as *iradat al-sha'b* (will of the people) and *al-sulta al-tashri'iyya* (legislative power). The fundamentalist movement, from its beginning, challenged and rejected the idea of the people as the origin of political decisions or legislative power, since only Allah makes such decisions. His will is law, and He has revealed it once and for all for everyone.[12] This leads me to conclude that it is not the fundamentalists who are the absurd ones on the contemporary scene; it is the Muslim Left, which believed that it could exist without considering the fundamental secular issue – the transfer of power from the sacred

22

to the human, from a transcendent divine being to an ordinary individual living an everyday life. And the exaggerated lampoons on the political rights of women are a key part of this debate, for they permit people to talk about the issue without naming it. The problem of women allows people to grapple with cosmic changes in power without naming these changes. As an exiled, masked, veiled symbol, woman occupies a central position in the debates on the political scene.

The traditional enthronement of woman – of her who incarnates the very principle of inequality, the basic element of the hierarchy, the *alif*, the beginning of being, who only exists in terms of a relationship of submission to authority – has forced the Muslim in a few decades to face up to what Westerners took centuries to digest (and which they still have difficulty doing): democracy and the equality of the sexes. To call into question social, political, and sexual inequalities all at the same time is enough to make one's head spin.

Imagine the effect of a phrase as inoffensive as "All human beings are born free and equal in dignity and rights" (Article 1 of the Universal Declaration of Human Rights) in societies where inequality of the sexes reproduces, guarantees, and paves the way for political inequality and affirms it as the foundation of cultural existence, as identity! Especially if it is compared to Article 1 of the 1957 Moroccan Code of Personal Status, which states: "Marriage is a legal contract by which a man and a woman are united with the view of a common, lasting conjugal life . . . whose objective is life in fidelity, purity, and desire for procreation by impregnation on a stable basis and *under the direction of the husband* [emphasis added]." The question of the equality of the sexes and the debates that it stirred up as far back as the 1880s with the appearance of Qasim Amin's book, *Woman's Liberation*, must be understood as the tragic cry of individuals who were trying to maintain their balance at a time when citizenship was erasing hierarchies and when technology was erasing national borders. The access of women as citizens to education and paid work can be regarded as one of the most fundamental upheavals experienced by our societies in the twentieth century. By laying siege to the places considered until then the private preserve of men and the privilege of maleness – the school and the workplace – women opened everything up to question, in their personal life as well as in their public role.

The return to the past, the return to tradition that men are demanding, is a means of putting things "back in order." An order that no longer satisfies everybody, especially not the women who have never accepted it. The "return" to the veil invites women who have left "their" place (the "their" refers to the place that was designated for them) to leave their newly conquered territories. And it is implied that this place in which society wants to confine them again is to be marginal, and above all subordinate, in accordance with the ideal Islam, that of Muhammad – the Prophet who, on the contrary, preached in AD 610 a message so revolutionary that the aristocracy forced him into exile.

The journey back in time then is essential, not because the pilgrimage to Mecca is a duty, but because analysis of the past, no longer as myth or sanctuary, becomes necessary and vital.

2

The Prophet and Hadith

How could a very ethnocentric Arab who knew no foreign language, who had traveled very little (just a few excursions northward into Syria as a youth), throw the world into upheaval with a message (the Koran) that gave, and still gives, meaning to life to people belonging to very different cultures – from China (around 20 million in the provinces of Kansu and Yunan) to Senegal; from Russia (valley of the Volga, Siberia, Kazakhstan, Uzbekistan, Turkmenistan, Kirghizistan, Crimea) to India (the Indus valley and the Ganges, Bengal, and Deccan plains)? Is it of more than merely anecdotal significance to say that this man made a success of his life, private as well as public?

The story of Islam is the saga of a happy man who in his youth dreamed of a different world and realized all his dreams in his maturity and vigorous old age, when, filled with success with women and military triumphs, he bent the most recalcitrant of his enemies to his will. The first time that Lalla Faqiha (my teacher in the Koranic school) spoke to us about Christ and Christianity, she ended her lesson mumbling: "What a sad life the Messiah had, yes, very sad. He lost everything, even his life, unlike our Prophet who continued to fight right up to the final triumph."

Muhammad was born in Mecca about AD 570. Mecca, despite its importance as a flourishing commercial center, had no illusions about its power. Compared to the Romans and the Persians, the two giants who dominated the region, the Arabs appeared to be a backward people, reduced to the state of vassal when they were

25

not occupied, or simply ignored in their desert when their tribes did not interfere too much with the interests of the great powers of the age. The Byzantines (the Roman empire) and the Sassanids (the Persian empire), who were continually at war for control of the great international trade routes that crossed Arabia, had each created from among the great Arab tribes vassal states which defended their interests and saw to the propagation of their influence and religion. These Arab tribal kingdoms never hesitated to go to war and to tear each other to pieces if their masters demanded it. In AD 580 (when Muhammad was ten years old) the Ghassanid Arab kingdom, a vassal of the Roman empire, attacked the Lakhmid Arab kingdom, a vassal of the Persians, and burned their capital, Hira, which was located in the Iraqi desert.

Forty-eight years later, in AD 628, at the age of 58, Muhammad – who had been preaching Islam for 20 years, and promising the Arabs who converted to his religion the conquest of the Roman and Persian empires – sent letters to the leaders of those empires: one to Heraclius, the Byzantine emperor, and the other to the Persian emperor, calling on them to become Muslims. The latter, who flaunted his contempt for the Arab tribes, was so outraged, according to Arab sources, that he wrote to his governor in Yemen in the following words: "That Arab who has suddenly appeared in the Hijaz has sent me an unacceptable letter. Send two reliable men to bring him before me in chains so that I can see how best to deal with him. If he refuses to come when ordered, take an army to go find him and bring me his head."[1] Fifteen years later, Iran would be conquered and Islamicized forever.

So, beyond its spiritual dimension, Islam was first and foremost a promise of power, unity, and triumph for a marginalized people, divided and occupied, who wasted their energy in intertribal wars. The Islam that the fundamentalists today lay claim to as the solution to economic problems and military defeats treasures the memory of this scarcely believable life of a young Meccan who declared himself a prophet at the age of 40 and, in 22 years of preaching interspersed with military expeditions, realized before his death the dreams that seemed impossible to his contemporaries: the union of the Arabs through a religious faith (and not through descent from the same ancestor, which is the basis of the tribal system) and their emergence on the international scene as a world power.

Yet the religion of the Meccan prophet was not complicated. The five key duties that Muslims had to, and still have to, carry out directed everyone toward the same idea: submission of the daily behavior of the individual to a strict discipline. Above everything else, Islam is a very earthly religion, rooted in the most banal acts of everyday life (washing, eating, etc.), but also permitting one to constantly situate oneself in the cosmos. The *shahada* is the first duty: it is a profession of faith that consists of recognizing that Allah is the sole God and that Muhammad is his prophet. The *salat*, praying five times a day, is the second. It is an extremely rapid exercise in intense meditation. You must, wherever you are, at home, at work, or in transit, stop what you are doing, face Mecca, and try through the discipline of concentration to transcend your daily problems and put yourself in contact with the divine, and do all this in a very short period of time. The first prayer is said at dawn, the second when the sun is at midpoint, the third when the sun begins its descent, the fourth at sunset, and the fifth when night has fallen. Fasting during the month of Ramadan from sunrise to sunset is the third duty. Giving alms is the fourth. And finally, the pilgrimage to Mecca for those who can make it is the fifth duty.

Mecca was one of the most important towns of Arabia in Muhammad's time. He was a quiet inhabitant who devoted himself to trading, married young, and lived among his people, the Banu Hashim, one of the most esteemed clans of the tribe of Quraysh (literally "little shark"). Mecca had become indispensable for the security of the great international trade routes which flourished in that part of the world, for it was situated at a crossroads linking the two key routes: from west to east (from Africa to Asia) and from south to north (from the Persian Gulf to Europe). Muhammad, as a member of his clan, was destined to become a merchant. He went into business with a businesswoman named Khadija Bint Khuwaylid, a widow who, like him, belonged to the tribe of Quraysh and who had inherited a large fortune from her late husband. Muhammad quickly made such a good impression on the Meccans with his probity and honesty that they nicknamed him al-Amin (The Trustworthy). Upon his return from a journey to Syria, Khadija was so happy with their collaboration and so surprised by his rectitude (which must have been a fairly rare quality) that she proposed marriage to him. He accepted. He was 25 years old and, according to tradition, she was over 40. It was his first marriage. She had already had other husbands, and had borne four daughters and three sons. The sons died at an early age. Although Khadija could not know that 15 years later the man she married would be the prophet of a new religion, she was nevertheless convinced that he was no ordinary husband, and she had complete confidence in him.

Dissatisfied with the customs he found around him, Muhammad went each year, like all the pious men of Mecca, to Mount Hira for meditation and a spiritual retreat. He was held in very high regard among his people: "All the inhabitants of Mecca agreed in recognizing his influence and rectitude . . . . Whoever had money to deposit brought it to him, and all who had disputes among themselves came to him for arbitration."[2] But it was not until later that he received his prophetic mission: "When Muhammad had completed his fortieth year, God sent Gabriel to bring him a vision."[3]

The first revelation that Allah sent him through his angel Gabriel was the first verse of sura 96, "*Iqra*" (Read). So Islam began with an order to read, to inform oneself. That was in the year AD 610. The first revelations were distressing to him, and, terrified by the voice he had heard, he went and described them to Khadija. He was assailed by self-doubt: "O Khadija, I fear I am going mad."[4] She reassured him, convincing him that what had happened was marvelous and unique. He was the chosen prophet, the one who was going to give the Arabs what they lacked: a book revealed by God, which was the foundation of the prestige of Judaism and Christianity, the two religions that had successfully taken root in Arabia despite the strength of polytheism. Khadija celebrated the event by converting to the new religion of her husband; she was Islam's first adherent. The new religion was going to cause great changes in polytheistic Mecca, which housed in its temple, the Ka'ba, not less than 300 idols. The Meccans found absurd the idea of one single God, which Muhammad was now proclaiming publicly, after having preached secretly for the

28

first three years. He had to struggle to make his cult accepted in the only place worthy of it: the sanctuary of the Ka'ba, respected from one end of Arabia to the other and the site of a great yearly pilgrimage that drew travelers from the whole region.

Once he had overcome the surprise of the revelation of the first verses, Muhammad became accustomed to the unexpected, mysterious rhythm of the revelations. Over a period of 22 years he would await those privileged moments when he was touched by divine grace, the moments of *wahy* (inspiration), also called *al-tanzil* (revelation) – the two words referring to the flowing movement of a knowledge that came from Heaven and flooded the earth through the intermediary of *al-rasul*, the Arab messenger. For – and this was the miracle – God spoke to Muhammad in his native tongue, Arabic: *Qu'ran 'arabi* (Koran in the Arabic language). Only the Jews and Christians had had this honor and privilege of direct revelation from God in their native languages. Muhammad would receive his final revelation nine days before his death, June 8, AD 632.[5]

The Prophet received Allah's message orally and transmitted it orally. He controlled neither the time of the revelations nor their length. The suras (chapters) were composed of a number of *ayat* (verses) of varying length: "The rhythm of the revelations varied from two to five verses at a time, sometimes more, sometimes less."[6] He only knew that a chapter was finished when he received the order to say *bismillah al-rahman al-rahim* (In the name of Allah, the Beneficient, the Merciful).[7] The order in which the suras were revealed to the Prophet (*tartib nuzuli*) is different from the order in the text that we have today (*tartib mushafi*). The order of the revelations corresponded to the needs of the moment. The suras revealed at Mecca set forth dogma and the duties of the Muslim. The suras revealed later at Medina related to problems that the Prophet faced and to questions asked of him by the first Muslims. The order given to the revelations in the written text of the Koran, according to the experts, answered a more pedagogic need. The first suras, it is true, were those setting forth the main arrangements of Islam regarding marriage, inheritance, etc.[8] It can be said that it was at Medina that Islam as *shari'a*, social law of divine origin, was born.

The Prophet went into exile at Medina in AD 622, a key date because it constitutes year *one* of the Muslim calendar.[9] The Meccans who migrated with him would be called the Muhajirun (literally "migrants," which is the same word used today to describe the North African migrant workers who go to France and the rest of Europe!). His new adherents, recruited from among the tribes of Medina, would be called the Ansar (auxiliaries, supporters).

In AD 622 the Prophet arrived secretly in Medina. The Meccans were searching for him in order to kill him. He had insulted their gods, and above all their cherished goddesses, al-Uzza, al-Lat, and al-Manat.[10]

Two events brought about the rift between the Prophet and his town: the death of his uncle Abu Talib, and that of his wife Khadija. Abu Talib had a prestigious position in the tribe of the Quraysh as chief of the Banu Hashim clan. For ten years the Meccans tolerated the Prophet's attacks on their religion. But with the death of Abu Talib, about the year AD 619, he lost his chief supporter and the guarantee of tribal protection. That same year Muhammad lost Khadija, his companion and adherent. Saddened and emotionally drained by the loss of his close supporters, Muhammad decided to leave Mecca, which for him had become a hostile place and every day more dangerous. But where was he to go? A person could not travel around in Arabia without first undertaking careful negotiations to insure protection according to the strict code of tribal allegiances. He began by "offering himself to the tribes": "Each year at the time of the pilgrimage the Prophet approached Arabs coming from all directions and propounded his religion to them. He hoped that one of them would believe in him and take him into their tribe and thus rescue him from the people of Mecca."[11] But no one wanted to give asylum to a man who had displeased Mecca.

He took the initiative and went to Ta'if – a city which, like Medina, was not too far from Mecca – in order to negotiate his exile there. The people of Ta'if drove him away.[12] He returned to Mecca and continued to use the time of the pilgrimage to find a city that would give him asylum. It was in these circumstances that he got in contact for the first time with six pilgrims from the city of Medina. He recited some verses from the Koran to them and offered to come and preach in their city.[13] The six Medinese "were well-known people, but of the middle class, neither very illustrious nor of low rank."[14] They explained to him that they were not qualified to make such an important decision; they would have to have the consent of the chiefs of their clans. And they explained to him the tense situation that existed in their community: "We are a community torn by dissension and conflicts . . . . We have to convey your message to the others once we return to Medina."[15] "The following year 12 of them contacted him and pledged allegiance to him . . . . The year after that 72 Medinese met with him during the pilgrimage; this time they represented the principal clans of the Aws and Khazraj tribes."[16] This was the beginning of the great Medinese venture. Medina became the first Muslim community and constituted for generations to come the model to be followed and the experiment to be imitated, for it was led by Muhammad as the political and military chief, the arbiter (*hakam*), and the legislator inspired by God himself. It was Allah who answered, through the medium of *ayat* (verses), the questions of the new converts about the way to be Muslim (*al-ayat jawab li mustakhbir*).[17]

The problem of Hadith came up after the death of the Prophet. During the Medinese period, the community lived out the Muslim ideal, in which God and His Prophet could be consulted at any moment, the former through the intermediary of the latter. It is this decade that is being claimed today as the key moment embodying the principles that should guide the planning of economic and social relationships in modern Muslim societies. But after the death of the Prophet in AD 632, ten years after the Hejira (the flight to Medina), the question of the succession arose. It was necessary to replace the Prophet in both his political and his legislative role. As a solution to the political problem, Muslim experts developed the political theory of the caliphate: what were the qualifications necessary to become caliph, successor to the Prophet in his role as chief of the Muslim state, and how was he to be selected by the community? A whole literature with its experts, its schools, and its theoreticians grew out of this. Islam as political theory has an unparalleled sophistication (you would not think it when you see what goes on in contemporary practice!). To resolve the second problem – that of the *shari'a*, the sacred law, which incarnates, represents, and expresses the divine will – the experts elaborated a body of religious knowledge, the *fiqh*. This consisted of, on the one hand, controlling the interpretation of the Koran, the text revealed by God, and, on the other hand, establishing the Sunna (tradition) of the Prophet by putting into writing Hadith, everything that the Prophet said in order to illuminate the way of Islam.

Choosing the right political leader and making no mistakes about the meaning of the interpretation of the *shari'a*, drawn from the Koran and the Sunna, are the two axes that animate – at least officially – the whole history of Islam. They will justify war and peace. They will be invoked to explain the periods of grandeur and of decadence. And, finally, they constitute the essential points of the aspirations of those contemporary figures who assert the return to Islam as the means for settling the political and economic problems that are tearing modern Muslim society apart. Imam Khomeini took power in Iran in the name of these two eternal motives, that is, to assure social justice by choosing a chief of state who will be inspired by the *shari'a* for leading the people and administering them.

To understand the place of writing, of the sacred text, and of its manipulation on the political chessboard yesterday and today, we have to go back to the events that took place in the days following the death of the Prophet, particularly the naming of his successor and the three who followed him, who are the only ones considered as orthodox. All contemporary demands for a return to Islam refer back to those fateful moments. The political concepts that the Islamic movements propose today as key concepts for the guarantee of democracy refer to the process of the designation of the four orthodox caliphs. How was the first caliph selected?

DEATH OF THE PROPHET

At the time of his death the Prophet did not have a male heir. Ibrahim, his last son, whom he had by his wife Maria, died at a young age (as had those borne by Khadija). However, in his immediate entourage four men played a prominent role. First of all there was 'Ali, his son-in-law and cousin, who had a privileged affectionate relationship with him. Muhammad practically adopted him when 'Ali's father, Abu Talib, was going through a severe financial crisis, and when Muhammad revealed himself as a prophet and received his first revelations, 'Ali became the first man to be converted (the first person was his wife Khadija). 'Ali was not more than ten years old at the time.[18] Later he married Fatima, the Prophet's eldest daughter, followed the Prophet into exile at Medina, and became his right-hand man in the direction of the affairs of the community. After the death of the Prophet, it is through the descendants of 'Ali that his line was to be preserved.

The second closest man to the Prophet was 'Uthman Ibn 'Affan, who was also among the first converts and, like 'Ali, married one of the daughters of the Prophet, Ruqayya. 'Uthman Ibn 'Affan was descended from the clan of the Umayyads, a rival of the Banu Hashim clan, who shared with the former a common ancestor, 'Abd Manaf. The two other men who were extremely close to Muhammad, and who were of the Quraysh tribe like him, were Abu Bakr al-Siddiq and 'Umar Ibn al-Khattab. They only had an in-law relationship with the Prophet, both being his father-in-law. Abu Bakr was the father of his wife 'A'isha, and 'Umar Ibn al-Khattab was the father of his wife Hafsa. (At his death the Prophet left nine wives.) But the privileged place that these two men occupied was the result of a factor considered secondary by the aristocratic tradition of pre-Islamic Arabia: psychological affinity, a great friendship. Abu Bakr, a sensitive, cultured man, took a great interest in history, especially genealogical narratives. 'Umar was a dashing, fiery man, but also proud, fastidious, strict, and rigidly upright.

If, instead of resisting the pressures put on him to name a successor from his clan (it would have been 'Ali), Muhammad had accepted and reproduced the tribal system, Islam would have been identified from the beginning with a tribal "family affair" – in keeping with pre-Islamic tradition.

Muhammad died quietly at home at a respectable old age. He

who had foreseen and planned political campaigns was not able to foresee the problems of his succession. According to all evidence, his preferences were for Abu Bakr and 'Umar, who would become respectively the first and second orthodox caliphs (the first was caliph for two years, 632–4; the second for ten years, 634–44). The assassination of 'Uthman, the third caliph, pitched the community into the first *fitna* (civil war). 'Ali, chosen as the fourth caliph in the middle of the civil war, never really exercised power, the era of turmoil having begun. It was against him that 'A'isha took up arms at the Battle of the Camel in year 36 of the Hejira (AD 658). 'Ali himself was assassinated by political opponents. The traumatizing effect of this first *fitna*, which extended throughout the reign of 'Ali (656 to 661), was to haunt Muslim memory for ever.

In order to protect themselves against political terror and violence, the Muslims plunged into a systematic collection of Hadith: What did the Prophet say about civil war? How is the Muslim to behave in such a case? How, among the various pretenders to the caliphate, is the best qualified one to be chosen? Should one accept an unjust caliph if he can guarantee peace, or should one fight him even if it throws society into civil war? The assassins of President Anwar Sadat of Egypt based many of their arguments and models on the events and Hadith of this period.[19] In a time of crisis, Hadith emerge as a formidable political weapon.

In this sense, one can call a Hadith all the "pertinent" information (with regard to what one wishes to justify) attributed to the Prophet. It is the recording in writing of everything that he is supposed to have said or done. His opinions, his reactions to events, the way in which he justified his decisions had to be put in writing so that they could be drawn upon and referred to later, in order to distinguish what is right from what is wrong, whether it be with regard to the practice of power or something else. How is one to act against an unjust caliph? The answer is to be found in the Koran and in the Hadith establishing the Sunna of the Prophet, his tradition. What are the husband's duties toward his wife or wives? How does one perform the daily ablutions? What is the status of a natural child? The Hadith sayings are in fact a veritable panorama of daily life in the seventh century, a vivid panorama, extremely varied because there are various versions of the same event. Finally, one also finds side by side subjects as different as "how to perform one's ablutions," "how to behave on one's wedding night," and "what is to be done in case of civil war."

The person who took on the task of transcribing the Hadith necessarily had to master the technique that today we call "interview technique," for the word *Hadith* itself comes from the verb *haddatha*, meaning *recount*, or simply *tell*. Each generation of experts had to personally collect the testimony of those who had heard the Hadith directly spoken by the Prophet (those would have been the Companions), or to collect the indirect testimony of those who followed the Companions (*al-tabi'un*, literally "the followers") or of the second generation after the Companions (*tabi'un al-tabi'in*, "the followers of the followers"). The person who recorded the oral Hadith and put it in a written collection had to deal with various methodological problems. Not only did he have to record the Hadith itself as faithfully as possible, but he also had to establish its *isnad*, that is, the chain of people who transmitted it from its source, its source being a Companion of the Prophet who had heard it said or seen it done. A Companion might be a man or a woman, a prominent person or a slave. The important points were that person's proximity to the Prophet, his or her personal qualities, and especially the reputation for having a good memory and for not recounting just anything. This was the reason for the importance attached to the immediate entourage of the Prophet – his wives, his secretaries, his relatives – as sources of Hadith.

The science of establishing the Hadith collection consists not only in putting the content of the Hadith at the disposal of believing readers, but also in furnishing them with information about the informants. The principle of the *isnad* (transmission chain) thus makes it necessary to give the biography of the person transmitting. The believing reader has the right to have all the pertinent information about the source of the Hadith and the chain of its transmitters, so that he or she can continually judge whether they are worthy of credence or not. Islam was, at least during its first centuries, the religion of reasoning, responsible individuals capable of telling what was true from what was false as long as they were well equipped to do so, as long as they possessed the tools of knowledge – specifically, the collections of Hadith. The fact that, over the course of centuries, we have seen believers who criticize and judge replaced by muzzled, censored, obedient, and grateful Muslims in no way detracts from this fundamental dimension of Islam.[20]

One of the reasons for the increase in false, fabricated Hadith, Muhammad Abu Zahra tells us in a chapter entitled "The Increase in Lying Concerning the Prophet and the Schisms and Divisions in the Ranks of the *Fuqaha*," is that after the death of the Prophet the Muslim world was torn by dissension. Beneath the spiritual enthusiasm and fervor, "passions and fierce struggles for earthly power were smoldering, passions which would lead the *umma* [community of believers] into interminable civil wars and finally to schisms that would give to Islam the sects that we know today."[21] The great schism that he refers to is the division of the Muslim world, during the five years of the first *fitna*, into Sunnis (those who follow the Sunna, the tradition) and Shi'ites (schismatics) after the assassination of the fourth orthodox caliph, 'Ali, and the seizure of power by Mu'awiya.

This division, which gave birth to the great Islamic schism, rested on the question, among others, of the proper attitude to have toward an unjust caliph. The Sunnis accepted Mu'awiya as the successor to 'Ali because, according to them, the most important consideration was putting an end to the civil war. The Shi'ites took the contrary position, opposing the successor to 'Ali, at the cost of civil war, on the grounds that his selection was based on a blatantly fraudulent arbitration. According to them, only 'Ali and his descendants were worthy of leading the Muslim community. This schism, which divided Islam into two groups, each developing a different theory of politics and law, then subdivided and gave rise to subgroups, stirring up trouble and confusion:

> The wind of discord was blowing strong, the hatred of some for others was fierce. They [the Muslims] were throwing insults like *kafir* [infidel] and *fasiq* [libertine] at each other

. . . . The *umma* was now divided into Shi'ites [pro-'Ali] and [pro-]Ummayads . . . , the Shi'ites themselves were split into various opposing factions . . . . The result of all this was that many lost interest in religion itself. Religion became weakened. There was such an increase in false Hadith attributed to the Prophet that those in charge among the believers took fright. They sought advice from the experts and tried to palliate this state of affairs by writing down the Hadith that were known, certain, authentic.[22]

To give an idea of the intensity of the struggle for political power engaged in by the first Muslims, we must recall the situation at the time of the burial of the Prophet, who was still uncontestably the representative of the Divine.

The Prophet died on a Monday, and his body was left in a corner of 'A'isha's room. He was not buried until Wednesday night: "The body of the Prophet, covered by a cloak, lay in his house. Everyone was caught up in the election [of the successor]; no one thought about the washing of the body nor of the burial."[23] The struggle for political power in Islam, already begun, would never cease.

A brief look at the process of selection of the first four orthodox caliphs, and their deaths – always violent (with the exception of the first) – allows us both to grasp the events of the past and to understand the debates of the present in their light, and, above all, to familiarize ourselves with the context in which the Hadith, true and false, were elaborated.

POLITICAL DISSENSIONS

Three days after the death of the Prophet in AD 632 at Medina, Abu Bakr was finally selected as the first caliph through a maneuver by 'Umar, as power began to slip away from the Muhajirun (migrants from Mecca) in favor of the Ansar (the Medinese adherents of the Prophet). The competition between the two groups had always been extremely fierce, leading to open conflicts that the Prophet tried to calm. In the course of one expedition (that of the Banu Mustaliq in year 6 of the Hejira, AD 628), Muhammad's army was split in two with the Muhajirun and the Ansar "having recourse to their swords." It was a veritable mutiny in which former tribal divisions took over. 'Abdallah Ibn Ubayy, one of the leaders of those Medinese who had never really accepted the arrival of the strangers (Muhammad and his Meccan Companions), summarized the conflict of interests thus: "We [the Medinese] have been well punished for having enriched the Muhajirun and protected them. This is how they repay us! It is like a dog who has been raised by someone and who, when grown, devours the one who has fed him."[24] The Prophet was extremely grieved by this remark and doubled his vigilance by asserting himself as an arbiter who transcended tribal allegiances. With his death, the Muhajirun/Ansar conflict broke out into the open.

Immediately after the announcement of the death of the Prophet, the Ansar called an urgent meeting of their principal clan chiefs in a *saqifa* (a sort of shed) belonging to one of their clans, the Banu Sa'ida, in order to proceed to the selection from among themselves of a successor to Muhammad.[25] Abu Bakr and 'Umar Ibn al-Khattab, the Companions who were closest to the Prophet and normally the only ones who should have been considered as candidates, were not even notified: "A man entered the mosque and said: 'The Ansar are meeting and administering the oath to Sa'd, the son of 'Ubayda.' Abu Bakr rose and, taking 'Umar by the hand, left with him."[26] This was the reason they were obliged to leave the Prophet's body without carrying out the funeral ritual and to hasten to the *saqifa* of the Banu Sa'ida, where the future of the Muslim community was being decided. The Muhajirun had to engage in intense negotiations with the Ansar, who proposed the election of two leaders: "The merit of you Muhajirun," said the Ansar, "is unquestionable, but we want to name one of our own as leader. So choose one from among yourselves. In this way each of the two parties will be satisfied, and there will be no disputes or claims among us."[27] This would have meant the end of Muhammad's long-term project, which involved the end of tribal allegiances and territorial fiefdoms and their merger into a higher ideal, that of the *umma* –

a community in which the tie uniting the members was spiritual. His two best friends and faithful Companions, Abu Bakr and 'Umar, who wanted to continue the Prophet's tradition, were indeed of the Quraysh, the Meccan tribe of Muhammad, but they did not belong to his clan. And among the Ansar there was no Companion who occupied a position like that of Abu Bakr and 'Umar. How were they to impose their leadership on the Ansar in these difficult conditions? Abu Bakr and 'Umar let the Ansar continue to hold forth, and then at a certain moment 'Umar intervened in such a fast-paced manner that he hypnotized those present:

> 'Umar, fearing that the struggle would be prolonged and become bloody, said to Abu Bakr: "Extend your hand and receive our oath, for you are an esteemed Qurashi and the most worthy." Abu Bakr replied: "No, it is for you to extend your hand and receive my oath." 'Umar seized Abu Bakr's hand and gave his oath to him. When the news spread through Medina, the whole populace ran to the scene, and in the rush Sa'd, the son of 'Ubayda [the candidate of the Ansar], was trampled underfoot and very nearly killed.[28]

And this was the way Islam began after the death of the Prophet: through a process in which only the elite was involved. And they negotiated to preserve what was essential to them – and the essential varied according to the interests of the participants.

On the death of Abu Bakr two years later in AD 634, 'Umar was chosen as his successor. But the process of choosing him was different – less spectacular but even more elitist. Abu Bakr is the only one of the orthodox caliphs who died a natural death in his bed after a brief illness. He had time to plan his succession. He consulted a number of influential persons in private meetings that he demanded to be kept secret. He sought their opinion on the candidature of 'Umar Ibn al-Khattab and asked that they "not repeat to anyone the subject of their interview with him."[29] Then Abu Bakr "presided at a gathering of *ashraf al-nas* [leaders, notables] and asked them: 'Would you accept him whom I will name as my successor?'"[30] He then announced to them that

'Umar was his candidate. "They responded: 'We have heard and we obey.'"[31] Another version says that the people learned indirectly of Abu Bakr's intention to select 'Umar as his successor after his death.[32]

The caliphate of 'Umar lasted ten years. Under his rule the Muslims conquered Iran and Egypt. To him is owed the organization and financial administration of the army. He was stabbed by a foreign slave while in the mosque conducting public prayers. Abu Lu'lu'a, the assassin, was an *'ajami* slave (of non-Arab origin), a Christian, and as such subject to the tax that foreigners had to pay. In fact, 'Umar "had forbidden non-Muslims to stay in Medina."[33] Abu Lu'lu'a, believing that he was paying too much tax, had complained about it to 'Umar, who had decided that he was being justly taxed. 'Umar, wounded, was carried home. On his death bed he took an initiative that ever after would be known as *shura* (consultation): he selected a group of six of the most prominent persons and told them to choose from among themselves a caliph to succeed him.[34] Al-Tabari devotes nine pages to recounting the bargaining that took place and that ended three days after the death of 'Umar with the naming of one of the six as the successor. He was 'Uthman Ibn 'Affan, who became the third orthodox caliph in AD 644. Like the first two caliphs he was a Meccan Muhajir of the Quraysh tribe, but from one of the clans who were rivals of the Prophet's clan – the clan of the Umayyads. The Umayyads and the Banu Hashim (the clan of the Prophet and of 'Ali) were descended from a common ancestor, 'Abd Manaf. In addition, 'Uthman, who had married one of the Prophet's daughters, Ruqayya, had very early on appreciated the exceptional importance of his father-in-law's message and had stood at his side during the conflicts that put him in opposition to the Quraysh tribe. So he was a member of the small group of privileged persons from which were recruited the first caliphs.

But his caliphate ended in tragedy. Eleven years after his selection, at the end of the year 35 of the Hejira (AD 655), a crowd of insurgents, claiming that he was governing the country unjustly, surrounded his house, and he was killed by a group who broke in while he was reading the Koran.[35] With his death began what is called the first *fitna*, a period of instability which, despite the selection of 'Ali as the fourth orthodox caliph, plunged the country into the first civil war.

'Ali was chosen caliph in June AD 656 in a Medina that was in a state of total disarray. Many Muslims took up arms because they challenged his selection. 'A'isha took command of them, and, with an army of insurgents, she went forth to fight 'Ali at Basra a year later at the famous Battle of the Camel.[36] 'Ali inflicted a crushing defeat on her, and it was after this battle that the Hadith declaring defeat for those who let themselves be led by a woman was pronounced. 'Ali, weakened by the Battle of the Camel, nevertheless had to confront another political adversary, militarily more dangerous than 'A'isha: Mu'awiya, governor of Syria, who reproached him, as had 'A'isha, for not having punished the murderers of 'Uthman. Mu'awiya belonged to the same clan as 'Uthman, the clan of the Umayyads who were rivals of the Banu Hashim clan. 'A'isha's army numbered only several thousand, while that of Mu'awiya had not less than 85,000 men. 'Ali arrived from Iraq with 90,000 men.[37]

'Ali and Mu'awiya met at the Battle of Siffin, which was long and bloody, for neither of the two forces could get the upper hand. The dead numbered 70,000 men. It was finally decided by arbitration, which took place in February AD 658 and which designated Mu'awiya as caliph. Nevertheless, there was no unanimity on the result of the arbitration, the outcome of which was rigged. This is what brought about the split of the Muslims into Sunnis (those who accepted the result of the arbitration however rigged it was, the essential point for them being that a strong leader would end the civil war) and Shi'ites, who refused to recognize Mu'awiya. For them, the sole caliph remained 'Ali, Mu'awiya being an impostor. In addition to these two groups, there was a group of extremists, the Kharijites, determined to get rid of both caliphs, resulting in the first act of political terrorism and assassination of a head of state by a splinter group:

In year 40 of the Hejira, a band of Kharijites gathered at Mecca were discussing the dissensions and wars that were overwhelming them when three of them agreed to kill 'Ali,

Mu'awiya, and 'Amr Ibn al-'As [a third person] . . . .
They made a compact among themselves that each would
pursue his chosen victim until he had killed him or perished
in the attempt . . . . The night of the seventeenth or,
according to others, the twenty-first of the month of
Ramadan [January 28, AD 661] was chosen for carrying out
the crime.[38]

The conspirators were partially successful in carrying out their
plot. Although Mu'awiya was only wounded, 'Ali, attacked at
dawn while he was preparing to lead prayers in the mosque, died
from his injuries. At this point the story of the first caliphs ends,
for, with the accession of Mu'awiya to power, no one would any
longer believe in the myth of an "orthodox" choice (today we
would call it "democratic") of the head of the Muslim state.
Mu'awiya would simply name, during his lifetime, his son
Yazid as his heir. Islam, which wanted to avoid the system of
tribal aristocracy, fell back into a similar pattern, but on the scale
of empire – the dynastic pattern. Mu'awiya held power until
AD 680, a long reign which provided time to solidify the bases of
the absolutist state.

BIRTH OF THE HADITH

This summary of the process of choosing the first orthodox
caliphs is intended to familiarize the reader with the historical
events taking place when the Sunna (the tradition, the Hadith) of
the Prophet was being elaborated. And it is particularly intended
to raise an issue which, 15 centuries later, Muslims still do not
seem ready to resolve: How is the principle of the equality of all
believers (whatever their sex and ethnic or social origin) to be
transformed into a practical political system which gives everyone
the right to participate in the choice of the leader of the
community? The "period of orthodoxy," and especially its brutal
end, is both symptom and symbol for an understanding of
modern political violence in Muslim countries. During the first
decade, and before the accession of Mu'awiya to power, political

decisions were made on the basis of consensus among the *ahl al-bay'a* (the people who were qualified to take the oath of allegiance), the *ashraf* (the notables, those who were trusted by the clans and who were their leaders), and the *ahl al-hall wa al-'aqd* (those who could make contracts and annul them, those who could make alliances and break them).

It is easy to imagine how important it was for each interest group to seek legitimacy in and through the sacred text. With the historical events as background, we can now appreciate in their true measure the two contradictory tendencies that were at odds with each other in the elaboration of the Hadith: on one hand, the desire of the male politicians to manipulate the sacred; and on the other hand, the fierce determination of the scholars to oppose them through the elaboration of the *fiqh* (a veritable science of religion) with its concepts and its methods of verification and counterverification.

Al-Bukhari is a good representative of these tensions. As an intellectual he isolated himself from power in order to concentrate on the research necessary for an objective editing of the Hadith, and at the same time he was the object of political pressure which called on him to put his knowledge into the service of politics – which he refused to do. Al-Bukhari was born, as his name indicates, in Bukhara in year 194 of the Hejira (the ninth century of the Christian calendar), and died in year 256 of the Hejira (AD 870). Like all the scholars of his time, he traveled throughout the Islamic lands, seeking better teachers and better universities. After pausing in Syria and Iraq and visiting the Hijaz, he settled for a time in Egypt. The duration of his stay in various places depended on how much he enjoyed the intellectual encounters he had and the quality of the masters. He made the rounds of all the known scholars who were experts in the area in which he was to specialize – the Hadith. Once they were recorded in a collection, the Hadith constituted the Sunna, the teaching of Muhammad. To show believers, through the Hadith (and the commentaries on the Koran, of course), the right way (*al-tariq al-mustaqim*) followed by the Prophet is to map out for them the path that leads to a worthy life on earth and to paradise after death.

Al-Bukhari, methodical, systematic, was able to interview

1,080 persons and collect 600,000 Hadith. His main objective was to be true to Muhammad – that is, to avoid having him say something that he had not said. Once the contents of a Hadith were recorded, the work consisted, above all, of assuring its authenticity. Al–Bukhari's problem was a methodological one. How is the truth or falsity of a Hadith to be verified? For him, writing the history of the Prophet was a serious undertaking: "I wrote only after hearing the testimony of 1,080 persons . . . and I entered no Hadith in the book before having carried out the ritual purification and prayed twice."[39] Al–Bukhari purified himself through prayer, thereby expressing the transcendent dimension of the function that he was performing and the distance that should exist between the scholar and the material he was handling. For the scholars of the first centuries religion was definitely a scientific endeavor. It was necessary to avoid, as much as possible, letting subjectivity intrude, all the while humbly recognizing that it could not be totally mastered. The way to do this was to see that the maximum number of versions was reported, to include repetitions in order not to neglect any point of view, and, above all, to distrust the witnesses and transmitters:

> When his [al–Bukhari's] scientific method had attained its full development, he began to distinguish authentic [*sahih*] Hadith from the others. After having developed a very advanced knowledge of the various kinds of Hadith, he mastered the techniques for uncovering their faults . . . . No one could equal his ability in this matter.[40]

Once his method of verification was perfected, al–Bukhari "retained as authentic only 7,257 Hadith, if the repetitions, which number 4,000, are eliminated."[41]

The great lesson to be drawn from al–Bukhari's experience in coming to grips with the flight of time and failing memory is that one must be true to one's method and honor it, by continuing to mistrust all those who regulate their affairs with the help of Hadith. If at the time of al–Bukhari – that is, less than two centuries after the death of the Prophet – there were already 596,725 false Hadith in circulation (600,000 minus 7,275 plus

4,000), it is easy to imagine how many there are today. The most astonishing thing is that the skepticism that guided the work of the founders of religious scholarship has disappeared today.

Al-Bukhari was not content with verifying what he recorded, but in order to show his veneration of the sacred text, he wrote an important study on the life of the transmitters of Hadith, *Al-tarikh al-kabir* (*The Great History*). The study of the transmitters became a scientific endeavor during the second century of the Hejira, with the triumph of the traditionalists.[42] Al-Bukhari became a celebrity, and the politically powerful were not slow in taking an interest in him: "When al-Bukhari came home to his native city, tents were pitched and the whole population came out to welcome him . . . . He stayed a while [in Bukhara], and then a conflict arose between him and the amir of the city, and he was forced to go into exile."[43] The amir, looking for a highly symbolic act that would show the population that he controlled the *fiqh* (religious knowledge), requested al-Bukhari to come to the palace to read to him in private some excerpts from his *Sahih*. And here is al-Bukhari's response, which earned him exile: " 'Go,' he said to the amir's emissary, 'tell your master that I hold knowledge in high esteem, and I refuse to drag it into the antechambers of sultans.' "[44]

Not all intellectuals had the same pride in their work as al-Bukhari. Many sold themselves for a few dinars to politicians who were trying to pressurize the collectors of religious knowledge to fabricate traditions that benefited them. There were so many liars who tried to put into the mouth of the Prophet words that would benefit them, Abu Zahra tells us, that Qadi Ayad undertook to set up a classification of them. According to him, the first category is those who attribute to the Prophet remarks that he did not make. This category is subdivided into two groups: those who lie for material advantage and those who lie for ideological advantage.[45] The second category is those who did not fabricate the content of the Hadith itself, but simply falsified the chain of transmitters: "For example, they attach onto a weak Hadith a very authentic *isnad*, composed of famous persons."[46] Qadi Ayad added a third category that is no less interesting: "There are those who simply lie. This individual claims to have heard remarks that in fact never reached his ears. He claims to have met people that he never met."[47]

Behind this whole increase in lies about what the Prophet said or did, we must keep in mind the power struggles, the conflicting interests in a Muslim community which, judging by appearances, was growing rich, and in which social mobility, as well as geographic expansion due to conquests, was the order of the day. Claiming to have been close to the Prophet or to have been given some privilege or other by him was used to mask huge economic and political stakes. The source of the invention of Hadith – manipulation *par excellence* of the sacred text – is to be found in the very nature of a political system which never managed to transcend its elitist origins and seek pragmatic ways of mobilizing the whole population to participate in the choice of the head of state. Something so ordinary as the suffrage process – the people filing to the voting booth to express their choice – will be seen in our day, despite the principle of the equality of all, as a foreign idea imported from the West. The greater the number of people affected and excluded, the more violent were the dissensions within the governing elites and the more pressing the need to manipulate the sacred.

Time was the great challenge for the founders of Islam in making it a scientific body of knowledge. They had to establish the rules for verification of the authenticity of the Hadith. The rules went from affirmation of principles and methodological axioms to simple techniques for the detection of lies. For example, if one discovered that for transmitter X to have been able to transmit Hadith x to transmitter Y he would have had to be 250 years old, one deduced from that that transmitter Y had lied. But al-Bukhari was neither the first one nor the only one to develop this method of authentication. All those who dealt with the sacred text – *'alim* (scholar), *faqih* (expert in religious knowledge), *qadi* (judge of Muslim law), *imam* – emerged as leaders of public opinion and participants in all the negotiations where power and wealth were at stake. Caliphs and princes, conscious of the importance not only of those who study the sacred text but also of those who manipulate memory – like genealogists, poets, storytellers – tried to control them or, if they failed to do so, to get rid of them. Taha Husayn, in his study of pre-Islamic poetry, describes the popular dimension of this phenomenon:

> The storytellers came to recite tales to crowds in provincial mosques. They recounted to them the old stories of the Arabs and the non-Arabs; they spoke to them of the prophets and used this material to slip in explications of the Koran, the Hadith, and the biography of the Prophet. Military expeditions and conquests were also touched on. These storytellers led the crowd through these subjects, carried along by imagination, knowing nothing of the limits imposed by scientific discipline and the rigor of authentication. The crowds, fascinated by the storytellers, gulped down all the stories they were told. The caliphs and princes, quickly realizing the political and religious importance of this new means of communication, encouraged and controlled it. They used and exploited it for their own purposes.[48]

Al-Isbahani, a writer of the fourth century of the Hejira (eleventh century AD), tells us about the case of a deal between a powerful man and a poet whom he asked to fabricate for 4,000 dirhams (not to be confused with today's Moroccan dirham) a poem that he would date back to the time of the Prophet. The poem was intended to enhance the image of his clan, the Umayyads, the rival clan to the Prophet's. The Umayyad said: "After writing your verses, say that you heard Ibn Thabit [the Prophet's official poet] declaim them in the presence of the Prophet, may the prayer of Allah and His peace be upon him." The poet replied: "I am too afraid of Allah to create lies concerning the Prophet. On the other hand, if you wish, I can say that I heard 'A'isha recite the verses."[49]

The Umayyad, not finding 'A'isha important enough, declined the poet's offer, insisting: "I want you to say that you heard Hasan Ibn Thabit declaim them before the Prophet while he was seated."[50]

The powerful men, having huge assets at their disposal, tried to buy not only the work of poets but also genealogies, which were the equivalent of our identity cards. Buying a genealogy is like, in our day, trying to falsify one's papers. Ibn al-Kalbi, author of one of the rare books on the pre-Islamic religions and a great expert on the subject of genealogy, confessed to having sold one: "The first lie that I told was when Khalid Ibn 'Abdallah al-Qasri asked me to tell him about his grandmother." Instead of revealing that his grandmother was a prostitute, Ibn al-Kalbi fabricated a splendid genealogy, and obviously, he added, "Khalid was extremely happy and rewarded me for it."[51]

Taha Husayn, in the study quoted above, which had the effect of a bombshell when it appeared, called into question the authenticity of one of the pillars of Arab knowledge – pre-Islamic poetry, widely used as a reference for grammar and vocabulary by commentators on the Koran, biographers of the Prophet, and historians. He advanced the revolutionary theory that this poetry, key to our understanding of the sacred literature, especially the Koran, was a fabrication pure and simple. Calling into question a large part of the poetry contained in a text as fundamental as the *Sira* (biography of the Prophet) of Ibn Hisham, he reminded us that the original text of that biography was initially written by Ibn Ishaq, who apologized profusely for not knowing many poems. So, asked Taha Husayn, where did those long poetic passages that are part of the text that we have in our hands come from? Are they not additions designed to enliven the text?[52] He adds that if poetry and genealogies were the object of business deals, it is easy to imagine what conflicts there were over interpretation of the power-texts – the Koran and the Hadith. The body of the 'ulama (scholars) was very heterogeneous, riddled with conflicting interests of all kinds, with ethnic conflict not being the least. There were not only experts of Arab origin. Many specialists on the interpretation and elaboration of religious literature were foreigners, belonging to other cultures (al-Tabari was from Tabaristan, al-Bukhari from Bukhara, etc.). Other conflicts were internal to the profession, like the rivalries that we know so well today between experts belonging to different disciplines.

This panorama gives us an idea of the magnitude of the political and economic stakes that presided over, and still preside over, the manipulation of the sacred text, since that Monday of the year AD 632 when the Prophet, who had succeeded in creating a community that was both democratic and powerful, lay forgotten and unburied.

3
A Tradition of Misogyny (1)

According to al-Bukhari, it is supposed to have been Abu Bakra who heard the Prophet say: "Those who entrust their affairs to a woman will never know prosperity."[1] Since this Hadith is included in the *Sahih* – those thousands of authentic Hadith accepted by the meticulous al-Bukhari – it is *a priori* considered true and therefore unassailable without proof to the contrary, since we are here in scientific terrain. So nothing bans me, as a Muslim woman, from making a double investigation – historical and methodological – of this Hadith and its author, and especially of the conditions in which it was first put to use. Who uttered this Hadith, where, when, why, and to whom?

Abu Bakra was a Companion who had known the Prophet during his lifetime and who spent enough time in his company to be able to report the Hadith that he is supposed to have spoken. According to him, the Prophet pronounced this Hadith when he learned that the Persians had named a woman to rule them: "When Kisra died, the Prophet, intrigued by the news, asked: 'And who has replaced him in command?' The answer was: 'They have entrusted power to his daughter.'"[2] It was at that moment, according to Abu Bakra, that the Prophet is supposed to have made the observation about women.

In AD 628, at the time of those interminable wars between the Romans and the Persians, Heraclius, the Roman emperor, had invaded the Persian realm, occupied Ctesiphon, which was situated very near the Sassanid capital, and Khusraw Pavis, the

Persian king, had been assassinated. Perhaps it was this event that Abu Bakra alluded to. Actually, after the death of the son of Khusraw, there was a period of instability between AD 629 and 632, and various claimants to the throne of the Sassanid empire emerged, including two women.[3] Could this be the incident that led the Prophet to pronounce the Hadith against women? Al-Bukhari does not go that far; he just reports the words of Abu Bakra – that is, the content of the Hadith itself – and the reference to a woman having taken power among the Persians. To find out more about Abu Bakra, we must turn to the huge work of Ibn Hajar al-'Asqalani.

In the 17 volumes of the *Fath al-bari*, al-'Asqalani does a line-by-line commentary on al-Bukhari. For each Hadith of the *Sahih*, al-'Asqalani gives us the historical clarification: the political events that served as background, a description of the battles, the identity of the conflicting parties, the identity of the transmitters and their opinions, and finally the debates concerning their reliability – everything needed to satisfy the curiosity of the researcher.

On what occasion did Abu Bakra recall these words of the Prophet, and why did he feel the need to recount them? Abu Bakra must have had a fabulous memory, because he recalled them a quarter of a century after the death of the Prophet, at the time that the caliph 'Ali retook Basra after having defeated 'A'isha at the Battle of the Camel.[4]

Before occupying Basra, 'A'isha went on pilgrimage to Mecca, where she learned the news of the assassination of 'Uthman at Medina and the naming of 'Ali as the fourth caliph. It was while she was in Mecca that she decided to take command of the army that was challenging the choice of 'Ali. Days and days of indecision then followed. Should she go to Kufa or Basra? She needed to have an important city with enough malcontents to aid her cause and let her set up her headquarters. After numerous contacts, negotiations, and discussions, she chose Basra. Abu Bakra was one of the notables of that city and, like all of them, in a difficult position. Should he take up arms against 'Ali, the cousin of the Prophet and the caliph, challenged maybe but legitimate, or should he take up arms against 'A'isha, the "lover of the

Beloved of God" and the "wife of the Prophet on earth and in paradise"?[5] If one realizes, moreover, that he had become a notable in that Iraqi city, which was not his native city, one can better understand the extent of his unease.

It can be said that Islam brought him good fortune. Before being converted, Abu Bakra had the hard, humiliating life of a slave in the city of Ta'if, where only the aristocracy had the right to high office. In year 8 of the Hejira (AD 630) the Prophet decided that it was time for him to undertake the conquest of Ta'if. He had just conquered Mecca, making a triumphal entry into that city, and now felt himself strong enough to subdue the inhabitants of Ta'if, who were still resisting Islam. But they put up a strong defense. The Prophet camped outside the city and besieged the citadel for 18 days. In vain. The chief tribe that controlled the city, the Banu Tamim, and their allies were entrenched in the fort and used bows and arrows against the attackers, causing casualties among Muhammad's army. Twelve of his men were killed, causing him distress, as he had hoped to win without losses. Each soldier was a Companion; he knew their families; this was not an anonymous army. He decided to lift the siege and depart. But before doing so, he sent messengers to proclaim around the fort and the besieged city that all slaves who left the citadel and joined his ranks would be freed.[6] A dozen slaves answered his call, and Abu Bakra was one of them. The Prophet declared them free men, despite the protests of their masters, and after their conversion to Islam they became the brothers and equals of all.[7] In this way, Abu Bakra found both Islam and freedom.

And then we see him a few years later, a notable in an Iraqi city, the incarnation of Muhammad's dream – that all the poor, the humiliated of the world, could accede to power and wealth. The rapid rise of this one Companion summarizes very well what Islam meant for a man like Abu Bakra, who would never have been able to imagine leaving his native city as a free man and especially changing his social status so quickly: "You, the Arabs, were in an unspeakable state of degradation, powerlessness, and profligacy. The Islam of Allah and Muhammad saved you and led you to where you are now."[8] In fact, since his conversion Abu Bakra had scaled the social ladder at a dizzying pace: "Abu Bakra was very pious and remained so throughout his life. His children were among the notables of Basra as a result of their fortune and their erudition."[9]

When the task of establishing for posterity the biographies of the Companions was begun, some experts were put in an awkward position because the paternity of Abu Bakra was not at all certain. Imam Ibn Hanbal, who did research on the genealogies of the Companions, admitted to "having passed rapidly over the case of Abu Bakra without going into details, because he was advised not to delve too deeply."[10] Abu Bakra is one of those persons so numerous at the end of the pre-Islamic era whose paternity is difficult to trace. Not having an illustrious genealogy meant scarcely existing socially in tribal and aristocratic Arabia. It is true that in Muslim society the status of natural children is not at all high, but the reasons for looking down on them are entirely different. In the pre-Islamic period, being able to trace one's paternal line to the most distant ancestor was the mark and privilege of the aristocrat. Slaves and all other classes could not trace theirs with the required assurance because of constant uprooting and moving about. In Islam the natural child is looked down on because its mother has failed to obey Muslim law, which permits the sex act for free women only within the framework of marriage. This was not the case in the period of the *jahiliyya*, the time of ignorance according to Muslim terminology, the time when people did not have criteria for distinguishing the permitted from the forbidden, the licit from the illicit. It was this that Islam brought to them, and in terms of paternity this was an innovation.

One of the revolutionary practices (revolutionary in the sense of a break with the past) that Islam institutionalized was the *'idda*, the waiting period that required a Muslim woman, separated from her husband for one reason or another (divorce or death), to not remarry before the passing of several menstrual cycles. The objective of the *'idda* is to ascertain, in case the woman is pregnant, the natural father of the child in order to link the child to him. In the pre-Islamic period the linking of the child to the father was either unimportant (for the tribes still practicing matriarchy) or inadequate (for women prisoners of war living with their captors or for slaves passing from one master to another) or impossible, and apparently not very important, in cases of temporary marriage, *mut'a*.[11] In the latter case, which continues to the present day to stir debate between Sunnis (who condemn it) and Shi'ites (who tolerate it), a man and a woman can decide to live together as husband and wife for a few days, a few weeks, or a few months. All that is necessary is that the date of breakup be fixed at the beginning and that the marriage in fact end at the date agreed upon by the two partners. This kind of marriage, practiced by nomads or traders who went on long journeys, was forbidden by the Sunnis, who regarded it as in flagrant contradiction with the principles of the Muslim family and particularly the rule of paternity that linked a child to its natural father.

Abu Bakra's case, then, was not an isolated one. On the contrary, it was the fate of that whole population of "uprooted" people who suffered from the doubts hanging over their paternity, and whose lives reflected their resulting subordinate status. Many of the biographies of the Companions begin with one or two sentences by the authors about the difficulty they have had in tracing the paternity of their subjects. Abu Bakra, then, was a man to whom Islam had given not only fortune and prestige, but, still more important, an identity: "I am your brother in religion," he loved to repeat to those around him.[12] With such a background, it is easy to imagine that he was the enemy of any civil war that could undermine the establishing of Muslim society.

So why was he led to dig into his memory and make the prodigious effort of recalling the words that the Prophet was supposed to have uttered 25 years before? The first detail to be noted – and it is far from being negligible – is that Abu Bakra recalled his Hadith after the Battle of the Camel. At that time, 'A'isha's situation was scarcely enviable. She was politically wiped out: 13,000 of her supporters had fallen on the field of battle.[13] 'Ali had retaken the city of Basra, and all those who had not chosen to join 'Ali's clan had to justify their action. This can explain why a man like Abu Bakra needed to recall opportune traditions, his record being far from satisfactory, as he had refused to take part in the civil war. Not only did he refrain from taking part, but, like many of the Companions who had opted for nonparticipation, he had made his position known officially. 'A'isha, who often used to accompany the Prophet on military expeditions, knew the procedure for the negotiations that took place before the military occupation of a city and had conducted matters correctly. Before besieging the city, she had sent messengers with letters to all the notables of the city, explaining to them the reasons that had impelled her to rebel against 'Ali, her intentions, and the objectives that she wanted to attain, and finally inviting them to support her.[14] It was a true campaign of information and persuasion, a preliminary military tactic in which the Prophet excelled. And 'A'isha was going to use the mosque as the meeting place for a public discussion to inform the population before occupying the city. Abu Bakra was thus contacted from the beginning in his capacity as a notable of the city.[15]

'A'isha did not take this course of action only because of faithfulness to Muhammad's methods. There was a more important reason. This was the first time since the death of the Prophet that the Muslims found themselves on opposite sides in a conflict. This was the situation that Muhammad had described as the worst possible for Islam: *fitna*, civil war, which turned the weapons of the Muslims inward instead of directing them, as Allah wished, outward, in order to conquer and dominate the world. So 'A'isha had to explain her uprising against 'Ali. She reproached him for not having brought the murderers of 'Uthman, the assassinated third caliph, to justice. Some of those who had besieged 'Uthman and whose identity was known were in 'Ali's army as military leaders. Many Muslims must have thought like 'A'isha, because a large part of the city of Basra welcomed her, giving her men and weapons. After driving out the governor who represented 'Ali, 'A'isha set up her headquarters in Basra, and with her two allies, Talha and al-Zubair, members of the Quraysh tribe like herself, she continued her campaign of information, negotiation, and persuasion through individual interviews and speeches in the mosques, pressing the crowds to support her against the "unjust" caliph. It was year 36 of the Hejira (AD 656), and public opinion was divided: should one obey an "unjust" caliph (who did not punish the killers of 'Uthman), or should one rebel against him and support 'A'isha, even if that rebellion led to civil disorder?

For those who held the first opinion, the gravest danger that the Muslim nation could face was not that of being ruled by an unjust leader, but rather of falling into civil war. Let us not forget that the word *Islam* means *submission*. If the leader was challenged, the fundamental principle of Islam as order was in danger. The others thought that the lack of justice in the Muslim chief of state was more serious than civil war. A Muslim must not turn his back when he sees his leader commit injustices and reprehensible acts (*al-munkar*): "The Prophet said: 'If people see *al-munkar* and they do not try to remedy it, they incur divine punishment.'" Another version of this Hadith is: "Let him who sees a situation in which *al-munkar* is being perpetrated endeavor to change it."[16] This was the argument of the group who assassinated Anwar Sadat of Egypt, and is representative of the very prolific literature of the Muslim extremists of today.[17]

At Basra in year 36 the dilemma that confronted a Muslim — whether to obey an unjust caliph or to take up arms against him — was not just being posed in the circles of the ruling elite. The mosques were veritable plenary assemblies where the leaders came to discuss with the people they governed the decisions to be taken in the conflict between 'A'isha and 'Ali, and it must be pointed out (after reading the minutes of those meetings) that the people spoke up and demanded to be informed about what was going on. The ordinary people did not even know what the quarrel was about; for those citizens the important problem was the absence of democracy. It seemed mad to them to get involved without knowing the motives that were driving the leaders and the conflicts that divided them. They gave as the reason for their refusal to get involved on either side the lack of democracy in the selection of the caliph. In one of the debates that took place at the Basra mosque when 'A'isha's partners were invited by the people to explain their motives, a young man who did not belong to the elite made a speech that illuminated a whole area that was not very clear in the dynamics of Islam at the beginning and is often "forgotten" today — the nondemocratic dimension of Islam, which was noted and felt as such by the ordinary people. This young man took the floor in the Basra mosque, an act that would cost him his life, and addressing the allies and representatives of 'A'isha who were pushing him toward subversion, said to them:

It is true that you Muhajirun [the original migrants from Mecca] were the first to respond to the Prophet's call. You had the privilege of becoming Muslims before all the others. But everyone had that privilege later and everyone converted to Islam. Then, after the death of the Prophet, you selected a man from among you without consulting us [the common people, who were not part of the elite]. After his death, you got together and you named another [caliph], still without asking our advice . . . . You chose 'Uthman, you swore your allegiance to him, still without consulting us. You became displeased with his behavior, and you decided to declare war without consulting us. You decided, still without consulting us, to select 'Ali and swear allegiance to him. So what are you blaming him for now? Why have you decided to fight him? Has he committed an illegal act? Has he done something reprehensible? Explain to us what is going on. We must be convinced if we are to decide to take part in this war. So what is going on? Why are you fighting?[18]

Thus the decision not to participate in this civil war was not an exceptional one, limited to a few members of the elite. The mosques were full of people who found it absurd to follow leaders who wanted to lead the community into tearing each other to pieces. Abu Bakra was not in any way an exception.

When he was contacted by 'A'isha, Abu Bakra made known his response to her: he was against *fitna*. He is supposed to have said to her (according to the way he told it *after the battle*):

It is true that you are our *umm* [mother, alluding to her title of "Mother of Believers," which the Prophet bestowed on his wives during his last years]; it is true that as such you have rights over us. But I heard the Prophet say: "Those

56

who entrust power [*mulk*] to a woman will never know prosperity."[19]

Although, as we have just seen, many of the Companions and inhabitants of Basra chose neutrality in the conflict, only Abu Bakra justified it by the fact that one of the parties was a woman.

According to al-Tabari's account, Basra, after 'A'isha's defeat, lived through many days of understandable anxiety. Was 'Ali going to take revenge on those who had not supported him, one of whom was Abu Bakra? "In the end 'Ali proclaimed a general amnesty . . . . All those who threw down their arms, he announced on the day of the battle, and those who returned to their homes would be spared."[20] "'Ali spent some days on the battlefield; he buried the dead of both sides and said a common funeral prayer for them before returning to the city."[21]

Nevertheless, everything was not quite so simple, if we take the example of Abu Musa al-Ash'ari, another Muslim pacifist who had refused to get involved in a civil war that he regarded as senseless. Abu Musa al-Ash'ari lost both position and fortune. However, it is true that the situations of Abu Musa and Abu Bakra are not comparable, except for their refusal to get involved. Abu Bakra's support was solicited by 'A'isha, the losing party, while that of Abu Musa was sought by 'Ali, the victor. Abu Musa was none other than a governor in 'Ali's service, his representative, and the symbol of the Muslim state as the head of the Iraqi town of Kufa. 'Ali, before proceeding to Basra, then occupied by 'A'isha, sent emissaries to Abu Musa demanding that he mobilize the people and urgently send him troops and weapons. Not only did Abu Musa personally choose not to obey his caliph, but he also thought himself obligated to "consult with" the population he governed. He decided to involve the people, whom he called together in the mosque for information and discussion, and to enlighten them about the position of the Prophet on the subject of civil war. Abu Musa recited to them the Hadith condemning *fitna*, and ordered them to disobey the caliph and not answer his call to enlist. For him, the duty of a Muslim in the case of *fitna* was absolute opposition to any participation. He recited many Hadith at the Kufa mosque, all of them against *fitna* –

against civil war plain and simple. It was not a question of the sex of the leader![22] Al-Bukhari assembled all Hadith on the subject of civil war in a chapter entitled "*Al-Fitna*"; among them was Abu Bakra's Hadith – the only one to give as a reason for neutrality the gender of one of the opponents.[23]

What is surprising to the modern reader who leafs through the chronicles of that famous Battle of the Camel is the respect that the people, whatever their position toward the war, showed to 'A'isha. Very rare were the occasions on which she was insulted – and even then it was never by one of the political leaders, but by some of the ordinary people.[24] The historians recall that only the Shi'ite chroniclers (the pro-'Ali ones) find fault with 'A'isha. Why, then, did Abu Bakra distinguish himself by a completely unprecedented misogynistic attitude?

Abu Musa al-Ash'ari was dismissed from his post and banished from Kufa by 'Ali. He was replaced by a governor who was less of a pacifist, and above all more tractable.[25] If this happened to Abu Musa, the situation of other "pacifists" who were less highly placed was very delicate indeed. It would seem providential to also remember having heard a Hadith that intimated an order not to participate in a war if a woman was at the head of the army.

Abu Bakra also remembered other Hadith just as providential at critical moments. After the assassination of 'Ali, Mu'awiya the Umayyad could only legitimately claim the caliphate if Hasan, the son of 'Ali and thus his successor, declared in writing that he renounced his rights. And this he did under pressure and bargaining that were more or less acknowledged.[26] It was at this moment that Abu Bakra recalled a Hadith that could not have been more pertinent, under political circumstances that had unforeseen repercussions. He is supposed to have heard the Prophet say that "Hasan [the son of 'Ali] will be the man of reconciliation."[27] Hasan would have been a very small baby when the Prophet, his grandfather (through his daughter Fatima), would have said that! Abu Bakra had a truly astonishing memory for politically opportune Hadith which curiously – and most effectively – fitted into the stream of history.

Once the historical context of a Hadith was clarified, it was time to go on to its critical evaluation by applying to it one of the methodological rules that the *fuqaha* (religious scholars) had defined as principles of the process of verification.[28]

The first of these rules was to consider "this religion as a science," in the tradition of Imam Malik Ibn Anas (born in year 93 of the Hejira, the eighth century AD), who was considered, with Shafi'i and Abu Hanifa, one of "the three most famous imams in Islam because of their contribution to the elaboration of the knowledge that enables the believer to distinguish the permitted from the forbidden."[29] Malik Ibn Anas never ceased saying:

> This religion is a science, so pay attention to those from whom you learn it. I had the good fortune to be born [in Medina] at a time when 70 persons [Companions] who could recite Hadith were still alive. They used to go to the mosque and start speaking: The Prophet said so and so. I did not collect any of the Hadith that they recounted, not because these people were not trustworthy, but because I saw that they were dealing in matters for which they were not qualified.[30]

According to him, it was not enough just to have lived at the time of the Prophet in order to become a source of Hadith. It was also necessary to have a certain background that qualified you to speak: "Ignorant persons must be disregarded." How could they be considered sources of knowledge when they did not have the necessary intellectual capacity? But ignorance and intellectual capacity were not the only criteria for evaluating the narrators of Hadith. The most important criteria were moral.

According to Malik, some persons could not under any circumstances transmit a Hadith:

> Knowledge [al-'ilm] cannot be received from a *safih* [mentally deficient person] nor from someone who is in the grip of passion and who might incite *bid'a* [innovation] nor from a liar who recounts anything at all to people . . . . And finally one should not receive knowledge from a shaykh, even a respected and very pious one, if he has not mastered the learning that he is supposed to transmit.[31]

Malik directs suspicion at the transmitters, emphasizes the necessity for Muslims to be on their guard, and even advises us to take the daily behavior of sources into consideration as a criterion for their reliability:

> There are some people whom I rejected as narrators of Hadith, not because they lied in their role as men of science by recounting false Hadith that the Prophet did not say, but just simply because I saw them lying in their relations with people, in their daily relationships that had nothing to do with religion.[32]

If we apply this rule to Abu Bakra, he would have to be immediately eliminated, since one of the biographies of him tells us that he was convicted of and flogged for false testimony by the caliph 'Umar Ibn al-Khattab.[33] This happened during a very serious case that 'Umar punished by execution – a case involving *zina* (fornication), an illicit sex act. In order to end the sexual licentiousness and promiscuity that existed in pre-Islamic Arabia and in an effort to control paternity, Islam condemned all sexual relations outside marriage or ownership as *zina*, encouraging women and men to marry and labeling celibacy as the open door to temptations of all kinds. It gave men the right to have several wives and to divorce them easily and replace them by others, provided that it was all within the framework of Muslim marriage.

'Umar, the second caliph of a new community still under the influence of pre-Islamic customs, had to act rapidly and severely to see that a key idea of Islam, the patriarchal family, became rooted in the minds of believers. Capital punishment for *zina* would only be applied if four witnesses testified to having seen the adultery with their own eyes and at the same time. These were conditions so difficult to prove that it made this punishment more a deterrent than a realistic threat. It was necessary, moreover, to avoid having enmities and slanders lead to the condemnation of innocent persons. If there were only three witnesses who saw the accused *in flagrante delicto*, their testimony was not valid. In addition, any witness who slandered someone by accusing him of the crime of *zina* would incur the punishment for *qadhf* (slander) – he would be flogged for false testimony.[34]

Now this was what happened in the case of Abu Bakra. He was one of the four witnesses who came before 'Umar to officially make the accusation of *zina* against a well-known person, a Companion and a prominent political man, al-Mughira Ibn Shu'ba. The four witnesses testified before 'Umar that they had seen al-Mughira Ibn Shu'ba in the act of fornication. 'Umar began his investigation, and one of the four witnesses then admitted that he was not really sure of having seen everything. The doubt on the part of one of the witnesses made the others subject to punishment by flogging for slander (*qadhf*), and Abu Bakra was flogged.

If one follows the principles of Malik for *fiqh*, Abu Bakra must be rejected as a source of Hadith by every good, well-informed Malikite Muslim.

To close this investigation, let us take a brief look at the attitude of the *fuqaha* of the first centuries toward that misogynistic Hadith that is presented to us today as sacred, unassailable truth. Even though it was collected as *sahih* (authentic) by al-Bukhari and others, that Hadith was hotly contested and debated by many. The *fuqaha* did not agree on the weight to give that Hadith on women and politics. Assuredly there were some who used it as an argument for excluding women from decision making. But there were others who found that argument unfounded and unconvincing. Al-Tabari was one of those religious authorities who took a position against it, not finding it a sufficient basis for depriving women of their power of decision making and for justifying their exclusion from politics.[35]

After having tried to set straight the historical record – the line of transmitters and witnesses who gave their account of a troubled historical epoch – I can only advise redoubled vigilance when, taking the sacred as an argument, someone hurls at the believer as basic truth a political axiom so terrible and with such grave historical consequences as the one we have been investigating. Nevertheless, we will see that this "misogynistic" Hadith, although it is exemplary, is not a unique case.

4

A Tradition of Misogyny (2)

Throughout my childhood I had a very ambivalent relationship with the Koran. It was taught to us in a Koranic school in a particularly ferocious manner. But to my childish mind only the highly fanciful Islam of my illiterate grandmother, Lalla Yasmina, opened the door for me to a poetic religion.

She suffered from what we now call insomnia, but in that time such ideas, which revealed too much preoccupation with oneself, did not exist. At least, not in our house. She took advantage of her insomnia to say the dawn prayer, and thus transformed her sleep problem into an ethic and an art of using the first hours of the day. A little later she would wake us up with the tempting odors of *mahrash* (a pancake made with semolina, eaten by peasants) and mint tea. While we – my brother, sister, cousins, and I – ate our breakfast, she dreamily told us a tale of a fabulous journey: the pilgrimage to Mecca. She chanted to us odds and ends of information about a classic era which she pieced together in her own way, and in which kept recurring the two words that ever since have inspired in me the desire to fly far away – *al-Madina al-munawwara*, Medina the radiant, Medina the city of light, which was the destination of her journey. When we interrupted to remind her that the destination of the journey was Mecca, she reassured us with the sly confidence of illiterate Moroccans: "Don't worry. I am just going to make a little stop, for the most important thing is the tomb of The Beloved [the Prophet]. I hope that in your school they haven't moved it, because he was buried in Medina. At least that is what I learned on my own." There was a war going on between her and the men of learning – a war that I could not understand at the time. She chanted to us the various stages of the *hajj* (the pilgrimage to Mecca) while she made her bread. The journey that she recounted was not the same as the one they taught us so forcefully at the Koranic school. Sometimes she would forget 'Arafa (one stage of the ritual journey of the *hajj*); sometimes it was the stage of Mina that disappeared from her story because she was in such a hurry to get to her ideal destination – Medina, the eternal city of light, where a gentle and welcoming Prophet would receive us. "No mint tea there, children. You must expect something else. I have forgotten what it is, but I know it is something different," she concluded in her realistic but adventurous way. Her Islam was an occasion to journey to strange countries, to spread one's wings, and to discover love and enlightenment there.

After these early-morning epics, it was hard for me to settle into the cramped and harsh world of school. While with Lalla Yasmina we could freely play with words, at the Koranic school the least fault in pronunciation was marked down and punishment followed: "The Koran must be read as it descended from Heaven." Wednesday was the day for recitation. Every mistake in pronunciation was punished, depending on its nature or seriousness, with a certain number of whacks administered by the *muhadriya*, the oldest students. They were rarely the most brilliant, and we could "buy them off" with cherries or peaches or pomegranates, depending on what was in season. Lalla Faqiha (the teacher) was so obsessed with pronunciation that she barely explained to us what the words meant. For Lalla Faqiha, to read and write an incomprehensible text was a way of celebrating the Koran as a mystery. On Monday we wrote on our *luhat* (tablets) the verses to be learned. Sitting cross-legged, we intoned them until Wednesday. We were allowed to rock back and forth when we became carried away by the rhythm: "*Al-qur'an nagham*" (the Koran is music), she told us, while holding her long stick over our heads. "If you don't feel the harmony of it, you should go serve the Christians and Jews." To my misfortune, I only really retained the verses in which the words fluttered around like threads of Chinese silk:

Wa al-tur
Wa kitabin mastur
Fi riqqin manshur
Wa al-bait al-ma'mur

By the Mount,
And a Scripture inscribed,
On fine parchment unrolled,
And the House frequented.

Verses like these (from sura 52), of which I only remember the rhythm, allowed me to escape the stern eye of Lalla Faqiha for hours at a time as I rocked back and forth. I left school far behind and hastened to Medina, the city of light where one drank wondrous concoctions.

This dual attitude that I had toward the sacred text was going to remain with me. Depending on how it is used, the sacred text can be a threshold for escape or an insurmountable barrier. It can be that rare music that leads to dreaming or simply a dispiriting routine. It all depends on the person who invokes it. However, for me, the older I grew, the fainter the music became. In secondary school the history of religion course was studded with traditions. Many of them from appropriate pages of al-Bukhari, which the teacher recited to us, made me feel extremely ill at ease: "The Prophet said that the dog, the ass, and woman interrupt prayer if they pass in front of the believer, interposing themselves between him and the *qibla*."[1]

I was very shocked by such a Hadith. I hardly ever repeated it, in the hope that by dint of silence it would be erased from my memory. I, who found myself intelligent, creative, good, passionate, enthusiastic, as only a 16-year-old can, used to say to myself: "Why would the Prophet have said a Hadith like that, which does me harm? Especially since this kind of saying doesn't correspond at all with what they tell us elsewhere about the life of Muhammad." How could Muhammad, "The Beloved," so hurt a young girl who, in the bloom of youth, had transformed him into a pillar of her romantic dreams? Muhammad was not just a chief of state. He was also the lover of 'A'isha: "'Amr Ibn al-'As [a Companion] asked the Prophet: 'Who is the person you love most in the world?' "A'isha,' he responded."[2] Surprised to hear that it was not a man who held first place in his leader's heart, 'Amr Ibn al-'As, a Companion whose military zeal was known to all, was taken aback. How was it that it was not military men who took precedence? And returning to the charge, he asked, "And among men, who is the one you love the most?" And the Prophet avowed that the man he loved most was Abu Bakr, the father of 'A'isha, his beloved.[3] Abu Bakr was a man known for his sensitivity, which bordered on sentimentality. He could not read the Koran without weeping!

In an Arabia where power predominated, where the saber was king, this prophet, who publicly stated that he preferred women to men, was preaching a very unusual message. Apparently Abu Hurayra, that Companion who put woman in the same category as the ass and the dog as disturbances for the believer, did not at all understand his *risala* (message), since he made woman an element that interrupted worship by "interposing herself between him and the *qibla*." To understand the danger of such a Hadith, we must describe what the *qibla* is.

The *qibla* is an orientation, the orientation toward the place of the Ka'ba, the age-old sanctuary taken over by Islam in year 8 of the Hejira (AD 630), when Muhammad reconquered his native city. The *qibla* gives to Muslim prayer – in addition to its spiritual objective (meditation) and its pragmatic objective (discipline) – its cosmic dimension. It puts the Muslims into their orbit, makes it possible for them to situate themselves in the world and to connect themselves to the universe, including Heaven. The Ka'ba did not always represent the sacred orientation for Muslims. For some months, encouraged by their Prophet, they turned toward a foreign holy place, Jerusalem. During Muhammad's childhood, the Ka'ba was the center of idolatrous cults. But from the time that he was visited by Gabriel and received the first revelations, it was naturally toward the Ka'ba that he turned with his wife Khadija to offer for the first time his strange prayer. When Mecca proved hostile, scorning his message and persisting in its idolatry, Muhammad dreamed of seeking the divine elsewhere, and he turned toward Jerusalem:

> When the Prophet arrived in Medina, for a period of 16 months he said his prayers turned toward Jerusalem. Then, one day a man who had previously said his prayers with the Prophet among a group of Ansaris said: "I testify that I saw the Prophet say his prayers with his face turned toward the Ka'ba, so change your direction."[4]

Why this about-face? Behind this change in direction lies the genius of Islam as the most clever expression of Arab nationalism, one that was going to challenge world dynamics forever. When you think of it, Islam as a monotheistic initiative in seventh-century Arabia was almost condemned, given the georeligious structure of the region, to being nothing more than a subvariant of Judaism or Christianity, with, of course, a sprinkling of the ingredients of local idolatrous cults. What direction could Muhammad, who wanted to create something new, something specifically Arab, choose? He did not have many options, did he? The Ka'ba was the direction of the idolators. In AD 622 they had just chased him out of Mecca. Turn towards Jerusalem? That would be doing obeisance to the Jews and Christians. But at first glance the hostility of the Meccans made the Jews and Christians, "people of the Book" (*ahl al-kitab*), seem to him to be more logical allies, more ideologically harmonious. While Christianity had the magnanimous face, understanding but distant, of the legendary Negus of Ethiopia, who sheltered the first persecuted Meccans, the Jews, on the other hand, very numerous and influential in Medina, were dead set against him.[5]

The Jewish community used all its influence to undercut the Prophet by accusing him of being an impostor, by hindering him from claiming the Judeo-Christian heritage as the basis of his mission. There is an extensive literature, scattered in the Arab sources, about this struggle over knowledge between the Jews of Medina and Muhammad, who was convinced at the beginning that he would obtain their support against their common enemy, polytheism. He only renounced Jerusalem in favor of the Ka'ba when he had despaired of the Jews:

> When the Prophet came to Medina, where the dominant cults were those of the Christians and Jews, whose faith was directed toward Jerusalem, God ordered him also to turn in that direction for prayer, in order to avoid provoking them and to make them favorable to him . . . . Nevertheless, deep within himself, he wanted the direction of prayer to be toward the Ka'ba, the sanctuary which had also been the *qibla* of Abraham and Ishmael. He prayed every day to God to grant this wish.[6]

The orientalists all make a close study of this question, generally seeing it in terms of the international context in which Muhammad began his mission, and especially the opposing forces that faced each other in the struggle over religion and knowledge. We can see in the attitude of those who accused Muhammad of being a false prophet – an epileptic according to some, an hysteric according to others – the reflection of the Jews of Medina toward an Arab who had the audacity to appropriate for himself Judeo-Christian knowledge.[7]

If Muhammad seemed a more substantial threat to the Jews than to the Christians, it is partly a result of geographical proximity and thus to a conflict of interests. In Medina, power was shared between the two polytheistic tribes (the Aws and the Khazraj) who invited Muhammad to come to Medina and the Jewish community. One of the bases of the power of that community was the control of Judeo-Christian knowledge. So Muhammad, who was laying the groundwork for an Arab nationalist ideology, could only assert himself in one of two ways – either with the support of the Jewish community or by combatting it if it discredited and denigrated him. The remainder, especially the expulsion of the Jews and sometimes their physical liquidation, was the result of the implacable logic imposed by the war for knowledge, the only total war, as is shown today in the conflict between the West, which dominates the production of technological knowledge, and the Third World countries, who only consume it.

What the Prophet did was to "nationalize," to "Arabicize" the Judeo-Christian heritage, as if in our day there should emerge an Arab prophet who would claim Einstein, Marx, and Freud not only as ancestors of modern Arab Muslims, but as the heritage that only a Muslim society is capable of making bear fruit, the only one able to develop their scientific message.

The Jews saw the Prophet as an impostor who stole their prophets and "indigenized" them to his own advantage. It was in their interest to get rid of the Prophet for two reasons. Not only was he sapping the source of their prestige – access to the sacred, to Heaven, to the book revealed by God, to the prophets – but he was also using their own prophets, their own legends, their own knowledge, to constitute himself as a force that would dominate the world. The Prophet was naïve enough to believe that the Jewish community would see in him only an ally. It was only during the critical years – 5 to 8 of the Hejira, those years of military insecurity and economic crisis – that he decided to declare total war on them. What might Islam have become if the Jews had given their support to Muhammad? It is possible that it would never have seen the light of day, that it might have become a somewhat deviant Judaism, a rather specialized sect in the vast Mediterranean area which has already seen so many.

Nevertheless, we should remember that if the Prophet succeeded in his mission, it was because the Arab terrain was ripe for an ideological bouleversement. Arabia was experiencing a very serious ideological crisis which reflected a deep economic and social crisis, and which explained the foothold held by the Christians and Jews in the area. The Arabs admired them as communities that had obtained what they lacked: a sense of identity, a feeling of belonging to a superior civilization, the feeling of being a chosen people with whom God carried on a dialogue. This is the reason that in the Koran there is so much emphasis on the fact that the book revealed by God is Arab. The Arab world was in such a state of crisis that its people did not believe themselves worthy of having a prophet of their own lineage nor a God who would speak Arabic to them. Al-Tabari's commentary on verse 3 of sura 41, which states that the Koran is "a Lecture in Arabic for people who have knowledge," expresses very well Islam's role as a response to a nationalist crisis, a crisis of self-confidence.[8] The old tribal solidarities, which had functioned well up until now, were threatened by new economic ties, by commercial alliances. The breakdown in the economic and social structures was seen by many, just like today, as an intellectual malaise, a religious crisis, a quest for a God who would make it possible for the Arab tribes, who were in a state of complete disintegration, to make themselves a force in the world.

This was the situation that made Muhammad change his decision about the *qibla* – to turn away from Jerusalem and instead to pray in the direction of Mecca. Jerusalem had to be abandoned as a symbol; it represented a greater danger than Mecca. And this choice of the Ka'ba as the direction that organizes the sacred and structures space made Islam what it has become: both a religion that is embedded in the Judeo-Christian monotheistic tradition and a separate religion which poses itself as a rival power and contends for universal domination, while nevertheless distancing itself from the elitist Jewish message. Islam addresses itself to all. For Muhammad's mosque, unlike in other religions, is not a building, a construction, but a perspective. The mosque is everywhere. "The whole earth became my mosque."[9] All a believer has to do to pray is to face the direction of Mecca (for North Africans it is east, the direction of the rising sun; for Indonesians and Chinese it is the opposite), and place in front of himself an object that symbolically represents the sacred shrine. The *qibla* makes the universe turn, with an Arab city as its center. Excluding women from the *qibla*, then, is excluding them from everything – from the sacred dimension of life, as from the nationalist dimension, which defines space as the field of Arab and Muslim ethnocentrism.

In Islamic space one can pray anywhere – in the street, in a passageway, in a garden, or on the battlefield. The Prophet, for example, used to plant his saber in front of himself and thus create his *qibla*. He could even, when traveling or on a military expedition, go through the motions of prayer.[10] However, once a person has set up a symbolic *qibla*, he must avoid letting anything get in the way of him and that *qibla*, so as not to be distracted. Since the whole earth is a mosque, aligning woman with dogs and asses, as does the Hadith of Abu Hurayra, and labeling her a disturbance, amounts to saying that there is a fundamental contradiction between her essence and that of the divine. By lumping her in with two familiar animals the author of the Hadith inevitably makes her a being who belongs to the animal kingdom. It is enough for a woman to appear in the field of vision for contact with the *qibla* – that is, the divine – to be disturbed. Like the dog and the ass, she destroys the symbolic relation with the divine by her presence. One has to interrupt one's prayer and begin again.

Arab civilization being a civilization of the written word, the only point of view we have on this question is that of Abu Hurayra. According to Ibn Marzuq, when someone invoked in front of 'A'isha the Hadith that said that the three causes of interruption of prayer were dogs, asses, and women, she answered them: "You compare us now to asses and dogs. In the name of God, I have seen the Prophet saying his prayers while I was there, lying on the bed between him and the *qibla*. And in order not to disturb him, I didn't move."[11] The believers used to come to 'A'isha for verification of what they had heard, confident of her judgement, not only because of her closeness to the Prophet, but because of her own abilities:

> I have seen groups of the most eminent companions of the Prophet ask her questions concerning the *fara'id* [the daily duties of the Muslim, the rituals, etc.], and Ibn 'Ata said: "'A'isha was, among all the people, the one who had the most knowledge of *fiqh*, the one who was the most educated and, compared to those who surrounded her, the one whose judgement was the best."[12]

Despite her words of caution, the influence of Abu Hurayra has nevertheless infiltrated the most prestigious religious texts, among them the *Sahih* of al-Bukhari, who apparently did not always feel obliged to insert the corrections provided by 'A'isha. The subject of many of these Hadith is the "polluting" essence of femaleness.

To understand the importance for Islam of that aspect of femaleness, evoking disturbance and sullying, we would do well to look at the personality of Abu Hurayra, who, as it were, gave it legal force. Without wanting to play the role of psychoanalytical detective, I can say that the fate of Abu Hurayra and his ambivalence toward women are wrapped up in the story of his name. Abu Hurayra, meaning literally "Father of the Little Female Cat," had previously been called "Servant of the Sun" ('Abd al-Shams).[13] The Prophet decided to change that name, which had a very strong sense of idolatry about it. "Servant of the Sun" was originally from Yemen, that part of Arabia where not only the sun, a female star in Arabic, was worshipped, but where women also ruled in public and private life. Yemen was the land of the Queen of Sheba, Balqis, that queen who fascinated King Solomon, who ruled over a happy kingdom, and who put her mark on Arab memory, since she appears in the Koran:

22. . . .[the hoopoe] said: I have found (a thing) that thou apprehendest not, and I come unto thee from Sheba with sure tidings.
23. Lo! I found a woman ruling over them, and she hath been given (abundance) of all things, and hers is a mighty throne.
24. I found her and her people worshipping the sun instead of Allah . . . .[14]

Abu Hurayra came from the Yemeni tribe of the Daws.[15] At the age of 30 the man named Servant of the Sun was converted to Islam. The Prophet gave him the name 'Abd Allah (Servant of Allah) and nicknamed him Abu Hurayra (Father of the Little Female Cat) because he used to walk around with a little female cat that he adored.[16] But Abu Hurayra was not happy with this nickname, for he did not like the trace of femininity in it: "Abu Hurayra said: 'Don't call me Abu Hurayra. The Prophet nicknamed me Abu Hirr [Father of the Male Cat], and the male is better than the female.'"[17] He had another reason to feel sensitive about this subject of femininity – he did not have a very masculine job. In a Medina that was in a state of full-blown economic development, where the Medinese, especially the Jews, made an art of agriculture, and the immigrant Meccans continued their commercial activities and managed to combine them with military expeditions, Abu Hurayra preferred, according to his own comments, to be in the company of the Prophet. He served him and sometimes "helped out in the women's apartments."[18] This fact might clear up the mystery about his hatred of women, and also of female cats, the two seeming to be strangely linked in his mind.

He had such a fixation about female cats and women that he recalled that the Prophet had pronounced a Hadith concerning the two creatures – and in which the female cat comes off much better than the woman. But 'A'isha contradicted him, a Companion recounted:

> We were with 'A'isha, and Abu Hurayra was with us. 'A'isha said to him:
> "Father of the Little Cat, is it you who said that you heard the Prophet declare that a woman went to hell because she starved a little female cat and didn't give it anything to drink?"
> "I did hear the Prophet say that," responded Father of the Little Cat.
> "A believer is too valuable in the eyes of God," retorted 'A'isha, "for Him to torture that person because of a cat . . . . Father of the Little Cat, the next time you undertake to repeat the words of the Prophet, watch out what you recount."[19]

It is not surprising that Abu Hurayra attacked 'A'isha in return for that. She might be "The Mother of the Believers" and "The Lover of the Lover of God," but she contradicted him too often. One day he lost patience and defended himself against an attack by 'A'isha. When she said to him, "Abu Hurayra, you relate Hadith that you never heard," he replied sharply, "O Mother, all I did was collect Hadith, while you were too busy with kohl and your mirror."[20]

One of the constant themes of conflict in Islam from the very beginning is what to do about menstrual periods and the sex act. Are periods the source of sullying? 'A'isha and the other wives of the Prophet never lost any opportunity to insist that the Prophet did not have the phobic attitude of pre-Islamic Arabia on that subject. Did the Prophet purify himself after making love during the holy month of Ramadan? "I heard Abu Hurayra recount that he whom the dawn finds sullied [*janaban*, referring to sullying by the sex act] may not fast."[21] Upon hearing this new law decreed by Abu Hurayra, the Companions hastened to the wives of the Prophet to reassure themselves about it: "They posed the question to Umm Salama and 'A'isha . . . . They responded: 'The Prophet used to spend the night *janaban* without making any ritual of purification, and in the morning he fasted.' "[22] The Companions, greatly perplexed, returned to Abu Hurayra:

> "Ah, so. They said that?" he responded.
> "Yes, they said that," repeated the Companions, feeling more and more troubled, because Ramadan is one of the five pillars of Islam. Abu Hurayra then confessed, under pressure, that he had not heard it directly from the Prophet, but from someone else. He reconsidered what he had said, and later it was learned that just before his death he completely retracted his words.[23]

Abu Hurayra was not the only one to report Hadith about the purification ritual, and this was a real bone of contention between 'A'isha and the Companions. "Ibn 'Umar ordered women who were doing the purification ritual to undo their braids [before touching their hair with wet hands]." 'A'isha is supposed to have responded when someone reported to her the teaching that he was propounding: "That's strange . . . . Why, when he was about it, didn't he order them to shave their heads? When I used to wash myself with the Prophet, we purified ourselves with the same bucket of water. I passed my wet hand over my braids three times, and I never undid them!"[24] 'A'isha insisted on these corrections because she was conscious of the implications of what was being said. Pre-Islamic Arabia regarded sexuality, and the menstruating woman in particular, as a source of pollution, as a pole of negative forces. This theory about pollution expressed a vision of femaleness that was conveyed through a whole system of superstitions and beliefs that Muhammad wanted to condemn. He saw it as, on the one hand, the essence of the *jahiliyya* (the era of ignorance) and, on the other hand, the essence of the beliefs of the Jewish community of Medina.

The *fuqaha* who took part in the debate on the subject of pollution, recorded at length in the religious literature, came down on the side of 'A'isha. Their argument was that her version of the Hadith seemed to agree more with the attitude of the Prophet, who tried by all means to "struggle against superstition in all its forms."[25]

This was not a matter that interested only the imams. The caliphs were also greatly concerned about it: "Mu'awiya Ibn Abi Sufyan asked Umm Habiba, the wife of the Prophet, if the Prophet – may God pray for him – had ever prayed in the garments in which he had made love. She said yes, he had, because he saw nothing bad in it."[26] Imam al-Nasa'i explains to us why he laid such stress on the subject of menstruation in his chapter on the purification ritual. The Prophet, he said, wanted to react against the phobic behavior of the Jewish population of Medina, who declared a woman who was having her period unclean: "He ordered them [the male believers who had asked him questions on this subject] to eat with their wives, drink with them, share their bed, and do everything with them that they wanted except copulate."[27]

The books of *fiqh* devote whole chapters to the purification rituals that every Muslim must carry out five times a day before praying. It is undeniable that Islam has an attitude bordering on anxiety about bodily cleanliness, which induces in many people an almost neurotic strictness. Our religious education begins with attention focused on the body, its secretions, its fluids, its orifices, which the child must learn to constantly observe and control. The sex act imposes a more elaborate ritual for the grown man and woman, and after menstruating the woman must wash her entire body according to a precise ritual. Islam stresses the fact that sex and menstruation are really extraordinary (in the literal meaning of the word) events, but they do not make the woman a negative pole that "annihilates" in some way the presence of the divine and upsets its order. But apparently the Prophet's message,

15 centuries later, has still not been absorbed into customs throughout the Muslim world, if I judge by the occasions when I was refused admittance at the doors of mosques in Penang, Malaysia, in Baghdad, and in Kairwan.

According to the meticulous al-Nasa'i, Maymuna, one of the wives of the Prophet (he had nine at the time that concerns us here, the last years of his life in Medina), said: "It happened that the Prophet recited the Koran with his head on the knee of one of us while she was having her period. It also happened that one of us brought his prayer rug to the mosque and laid it down while she was having her period."[28] Already at the time that Imam al-Nasa'i was writing (he was born in year 214 or 215 of the Hejira, the ninth century AD), the scholars suspected that there was a message there that was disturbing the misogyny ingrained in the peoples of the Arab Mediterranean area, before and after the Prophet, and they made great efforts not to betray that very disturbing aspect of the Prophet's message. These *fuqaha*, who saw in misogyny the danger of betrayal of the Prophet, doubled their precautions and did a thorough investigation of the sex life of the Prophet by listening to the reports of his wives, the only credible sources on this subject. They accumulated details about his life at home as well as in the mosque. Ibn Sa'd devoted a chapter of his book to the layout of the Prophet's house. This chapter, as we shall soon see, is extremely important for the clarification of a key dimension of Islam: the total revolution it represented *vis-à-vis* the Judeo-Christian tradition and the pre-Islamic period with regard to women. However, very quickly the misogynistic trend reasserted itself among the *fuqaha* and gained the upper hand. We will see the resurgence in many Hadith of that superstitious fear of femaleness that the Prophet wanted to eradicate.

One can read among al-Bukhari's "authentic" Hadith the following one: "Three things bring bad luck: house, woman, and horse."[29] Al-Bukhari did not include other versions of this Hadith, although the rule was to give one or more contradictory versions in order to show readers conflicting points of view, and thus to permit them to be sufficiently well informed to decide for themselves about practices that were the subject of dispute.

However, there is no trace in al-Bukhari of 'A'isha's refutation of this Hadith:

> They told 'A'isha that Abu Hurayra was asserting that the Messenger of God said: "Three things bring bad luck: house, woman, and horse." 'A'isha responded: "Abu Hurayra learned his lessons very badly. He came into our house when the Prophet was in the middle of a sentence. He only heard the end of it. What the Prophet said was: 'May Allah refute the Jews; they say three things bring bad luck: house, woman, and horse.' "[30]

Not only did al-Bukhari not include this correction, but he treated the Hadith as if there was no question about it. He cited it three times, each time with a different transmission chain. This procedure generally strengthens a Hadith and gives the impression of consensus concerning it. No mention was made of the dispute between 'A'isha and Abu Hurayra on this subject. Worse yet, al-Bukhari followed this misogynistic Hadith with another along the same lines which reflected the same vision of femaleness as a pole of destruction and ill luck: "The Prophet said: 'I do not leave after me any cause of trouble more fatal to man than women.' "[31] The source of this Hadith is 'Abdallah Ibn 'Umar (the son of 'Umar Ibn al-Khattab, the second caliph), who was known for his rare asceticism and for nights interrupted by prayers and purifications.[32] 'Abdallah was a source very highly valued by Bukhari. He was the author of another famous Hadith, in which he throws women into hell: " 'Abdallah Ibn 'Umar said: 'The Prophet said: "I took a look at paradise, and I noted that the majority of the people there were poor people. I took a look at hell, and I noted that there women were the majority." ' "[33]

What conclusion must one draw from this? That even the authentic Hadith must be vigilantly examined with a magnifying glass? That is our right, Malik Ibn Anas tells us. Al-Bukhari, like all the *fuqaha*, began his work of collecting by asking for Allah's help and acknowledging that only He is infallible. It is our tradition to question everything and everybody, especially the *fuqaha* and imams. And it is more than ever necessary for us to disinter our true tradition from the centuries of oblivion that have managed to obscure it. But we must also guard against falling into generalizations and saying that all the imams were and are misogynistic. That is not true today and was not true yesterday. The example of this is Imam Zarkashi, who, luckily for us, recorded in writing all of 'A'isha's objections.

Imam Zarkashi was of Turkish origin, but born in Egypt in the middle of the fourteenth century (actually in year 745 of the Hejira). Like all the scholars of his time, he traveled throughout the Muslim world in search of knowledge. He specialized in religious knowledge and left behind no less than 30 compendiums. Many of these are lost to modern researchers, and we know only their titles. Among those that have come down to us is a book devoted to 'A'isha's contribution to Islam, her contribution as a source of religious knowledge. The book begins as follows:

> 'A'isha is the Mother of the Believers . . . . She is the lover of the Messenger of God . . . . She lived with him for eight years and five months; she was 18 years old at the time of the death of the Prophet . . . . She lived to be 65 years old . . . . We are indebted to her for 1,210 Hadith.[34]

And he explains:

> This book is devoted to her particular contribution in this field, especially the points on which she disagreed with others, the points to which she supplied added information, the points on which she was in complete disagreement with the religious scholars of her time . . . . I have entitled this book *Collection of 'A'isha's Corrections to the Statements of the Companions (Al-'irada fi ma istadrakathu 'A'isha 'ala al-sahaba)*.[35]

This book remained in manuscript form until 1939. Al-Afghani discovered it while doing research for his biography of 'A'isha in the Al-Dahiriya Library of Damascus. Why did Imam Zarkashi, one of the greatest scholars of the Shafi'i school of his time, undertake his work on 'A'isha? A work that, by all accounts, he must have considered extremely important, since he dedicated his book to the Judge of Judges (*qadi al-qudat*) – the equivalent of the Minister of Justice today, the supreme authority in religious matters in a Muslim city. Because, he says, "the Prophet recognized 'A'isha's importance to such an extent that he said: 'Draw a part of your religion from little *al-humayra.*' "[36] One of the Prophet's favorite pet names for 'A'isha was *al-humayra*, referring to her very white skin made radiant by a light sunburn, something rather rare in the Hijaz, the northern part of Arabia.[37]

'A'isha disputed many of Abu Hurayra's Hadith and declared to whoever wanted to hear it: "He is not a good listener, and when he is asked a question, he gives wrong answers."[38] 'A'isha could take the liberty of criticizing him because she had an excellent memory: "I never saw anyone who had so much knowledge about religion, poetry, and medicine as 'A'isha."[39] Abu Hurayra knew how to rile her. "But who has heard about that from Abu al-Qasim [the Prophet's surname]?" she exclaimed when someone recounted to her another of Abu Hurayra's traditions, this time describing what the Prophet did after making love.[40]

It is not wasted effort to us to tarry over the personality of Abu Hurayra, the author of Hadith that saturate the daily life of every modern Muslim woman. He has been the source of an enormous amount of commentary in the religious literature. But he was and still is the object of controversy, and there is far from being unanimity on him as a reliable source. The most recent book about him, jointly published by a Lebanese and an Iraqi firm, is a tribute written by one of his admirers who devotes not less than 500 pages to defending him. 'Abd al-Mun'im Salih al-'Ali gave his book a rather eloquent title: *In Defense of Abu Hurayra.*[41] It was obviously a success since a new edition was published in 1983. The author begins by asserting that "the Zionists and their allies and supporters have found another weapon against Islam; it is to introduce doubt about the narrators of traditions . . . and especially about those who were the source of many Hadith."[42] This gives an idea of the intensity of the controversy surrounding

Abu Hurayra. What is certain is that Abu Hurayra, long before Zionism, was attacked by Companions of his own generation. He had a very dubious reputation from the beginning, and al-Bukhari was aware of it, since he reports that "people said that Abu Hurayra recounts too many Hadith."[43] Abd al-Mun'im, to his credit, cites all the incidents in which he was strongly challenged, including by those other than 'A'isha. He assures us that 'Umar Ibn al-Khattab, the second orthodox caliph, did not say that "the worst liar among the *muhaddithun* [narrators of Hadith] is Abu Hurayra."[44] He disputes the claim that 'Umar threatened to exile him, to send him back to his native Yemen, if he continued to recount Hadith.[45]

'Umar, who enjoyed an unparalleled influence on the Prophet and the Muslim community of yesterday (and still does today) because of his prestige as a man of politics, his boldness in military matters, his strong personality, and his horror of lying, avoided recounting Hadith. He was terrified at the idea of not being accurate. For that reason, 'Umar was one of those Companions who preferred to rely on their own judgment rather than trust their memory, which they considered dangerously fallible.[46] He was very irritated by the facile manner in which Abu Hurayra reeled off Hadith: "'Umar al-Khattab," we can read in al-'Asqalani's biography of him, "is supposed to have remarked as follows about Abu Hurayra: 'We have many things to say, but we are afraid to say them, and that man there has no restraint.'"[47]

For the pious Companion the fallibility of memory was an occasion for meditating on the fragility of existence in the face of the flowing river of time, which steals not only youth, but especially memory. 'Umar Ibn Hasin, another Companion who was conscious of the treacherousness of memory, said:

> If I wanted to, I could recite traditions about the Prophet for two days without stopping. What keeps me from doing it is that I have seen some of the Companions of the Messenger of God who heard exactly what I myself heard, who saw what I saw, and those men recounted Hadith. Those traditions are not exactly what we heard. And I am afraid of hallucinating, as they hallucinate.[48]

The Arabic word is *yushbah*, literally "to hallucinate," that is, to see a reality that does not exist but that has the appearance of reality.

Abu Hurayra, on the contrary, for the three years that he spent in the company of the Prophet, would accomplish the *tour de force* of recalling 5,300 Hadith.[49] Al-Bukhari listed 800 experts who cited him as their source.[50] Here is how Abu Hurayra explains his excellent memory: "I said to the Prophet: 'I listen attentively, I take in many of your ideas, but I forget many.'"[51] Then the Prophet is supposed to have told him to spread out his cloak while he was speaking to him, and afterwards to pick it up at the end of the session. "And this is the reason that I no longer forgot anything."[52] Telling the story of the cloak was not the best way to be convincing in a religion like Islam, which has a horror of mysteries of all sorts, where Muhammad resisted the pressure of his contemporaries to perform miracles and magical acts, and where the *fuqaha* became well versed from very early on in an exaggerated pragmatism.

Abu Hurayra also gave another explanation that was a bit more realistic than the first. The other Companions, he said, put their energy into business matters and spent their time in the bazaars drawing up contracts and increasing their fortunes, while he had nothing else to do but follow the Prophet everywhere.[53] 'Umar Ibn al-Khattab, who was well known for his physical vigor and who awoke the city every day to say the dawn prayer, disliked lazy people who loafed around without any definite occupation. He summoned Abu Hurayra on one occasion to offer him a job. To his great surprise, Abu Hurayra declined the offer. 'Umar, who did not consider such things a joking matter, said to him:

> "You refuse to work? Better people than you have begged for work."
> "Who are those people who are better than me?" inquired Abu Hurayra.
> "Joseph, the son of Jacob, for example," said 'Umar to put an end to a conversation that was getting out of hand.
> "He," said Abu Hurayra flippantly, "was a prophet, the son

of a prophet, and I am Abu Hurayra, son of Umayma [his mother]."[54]

With this anecdote we come back to our point of departure, the relationship of "Father of the Little Female Cat" to femaleness, and to the very mysterious and dangerous link between the sacred and women. All the monotheistic religions are shot through by the conflict between the divine and the feminine, but none more so than Islam, which has opted for the occultation of the feminine, at least symbolically, by trying to veil it, to hide it, to mask it. Islam as sexual practice unfolds with a very special theatricality since it is acted out in a scene where the *hijab* (veil) occupies a central position. This almost phobic attitude toward women is all the more surprising since we have seen that the Prophet has encouraged his adherents to renounce it as representative of the *jahiliyya* and its superstitions. This leads me to ask: Is it possible that Islam's message had only a limited and superficial effect on deeply superstitious seventh-century Arabs who failed to integrate its novel approaches to the world and to women? Is it possible that the *hijab*, the attempt to veil women, that is claimed today to be basic to Muslim identity, is nothing but the expression of the persistence of the pre-Islamic mentality, the *jahiliyya* mentality that Islam was supposed to annihilate?

What does the *hijab* really represent in the early Muslim context? What does the word signify? What are its logic and justification? When was it inaugurated, for whom, and why?

PART II

Medina in Revolution:
The Three Fateful Years

5

The Hijab, *the Veil*

The *hijab* – literally "curtain" – "descended," not to put a barrier between a man and a woman, but between two men. The descent of the *hijab* is an event dating back to verse 53 of sura 33, which was revealed during year 5 of the Hejira (AD 627):[1]

> O ye who believe! Enter not the dwellings of the Prophet for a meal without waiting for the proper time, unless permission be granted you. But if ye are invited, enter, and, when your meal is ended, then disperse. Linger not for conversation. Lo! that would cause annoyance to the Prophet, and he would be shy of (asking) you (to go); but Allah is not shy of the truth. And when ye ask of them (the wives of the Prophet) anything, ask it of them from behind a curtain. That is purer for your hearts and for their hearts.[2]

The *fuqaha* speak of "the descent of the *hijab*." This expression in fact covers two simultaneous events that take place in completely different realms: on the one hand, God's revelation to the Prophet, which is in the intellectual realm; and on the other hand, the descent of a cloth *hijab*, a material object, a curtain that the Prophet draws between himself and the man who was at the entrance of his nuptial chamber.

The verse of the *hijab* "descended" in the bedroom of the wedded pair to protect their intimacy and exclude a third person – in this case, Anas Ibn Malik, one of the Prophet's Companions.

Anas was excluded by the *hijab* as a witness and the symbol of a community that had become too invasive, and it was this witness himself who reported the event. When one realizes the repercussions that this act/event was to have on the life of Muslim women, the account given by Anas becomes important. The Prophet had just got married and was impatient to be alone with his new wife, his cousin Zaynab. He was not able to get rid of a small group of tactless guests who remained lost in conversation. The veil was to be God's answer to a community with boorish manners whose lack of delicacy offended a Prophet whose politeness bordered on timidity. This at least is the interpretation of al-Tabari, who reports Anas Ibn Malik as saying:

> The Prophet had wed Zaynab Bint Jahsh. I was charged with inviting people to the wedding supper. I carried out this charge. Many people came. They arrived in groups, one after the other. They ate and then they departed. I said to the Prophet:
>
> "Messenger of God, I invited so many people that I can't find anyone else to invite."
>
> At a certain moment, the Prophet said: "End the meal." Zaynab was seated in a corner of the room. She was a woman of great beauty. All the guests departed except for three who seemed oblivious of their surroundings. They were still there in the room, chatting away. Annoyed, the Prophet left the room. He went to 'A'isha's apartment. Upon seeing her, he greeted her, saying:
>
> "Peace be unto you, member of the household."
>
> "And peace be unto you, Prophet of Allah," responded 'A'isha to him. "How do you like your new Companion?"
>
> He thus made the round of the apartments of his wives, who greeted him in the same manner as 'A'isha. Finally, he retraced his steps and came again to Zaynab's room. He saw that the three guests had still not departed. They were still there continuing to chat. The Prophet was an extremely polite and reserved man. He quickly left again and returned to 'A'isha's apartment. I don't remember any more whether it was I or someone else who went to tell him that

the three individuals had finally decided to leave. In any case, he came back to the nuptial chamber. He put one foot in the room and kept the other outside. It was in this position that he let fall a *sitr* [curtain] between himself and me, and the verse of the *hijab* descended at that moment.[3]

In this version al-Tabari uses two concepts that tend to become merged: *hijab* and *sitr*, the latter meaning literally "curtain." Let us go back over the most salient facts in this account:

1 While drawing the curtain, Anas tells us, the Prophet pronounced what was to become in the Koran verse 53 of sura 33, which for the experts is "the verse of the *hijab*." They are the words that Anas heard murmured by the Prophet when he drew the *sitr* (curtain) between them – words that were the message inspired by God in His Prophet in response to a situation in which Muhammad apparently did not know what to do nor how to act. We should remember that the Koran is a book rooted in the daily life of the Prophet and his community; it is often a response to a given situation.

2 The second fact to take note of is that the Prophet was celebrating his marriage to Zaynab Bint Jahsh.

3 He invited to this event nearly the whole Muslim community of Medina.

4 All partook of the wedding supper and departed, with the exception of three impolite men who continued to chat without concern for the Prophet's impatience and his desire to be alone with his new wife.

5 The Prophet, irritated, went out into the courtyard, walked up and down, returned to the room, and left again to wait for the visitors to leave.

6 Upon their departure, Allah revealed the verse on the *hijab* to the Prophet.

7 The Prophet drew a *sitr* between himself and Anas, while reciting verse 53 of sura 33.

In describing the "descent of the *hijab*," al-Tabari does not try to give us the reasons for the irritation of the Prophet, who was known for his composure and infinite patience. This irritation was to precipitate the revelation of such a grave decision as the establishment of the *hijab*. Already we have seen, in the circumstances that led to the revelation of the *hijab*, the exceptional rapidity of the sequence of events: the Prophet's irritation and the divine reaction that took place at once. We will have occasion to study various verses and their *asbab al-nuzul* (causes of their revelation). Often between the moment when the problem is brought to the Prophet's attention and the moment when the solution is revealed, there is a period of gestation, as it were, a time of waiting. However, in the case of the *hijab*, the rather unusual rapidity of the revelation does not tally with the normal psychological rhythm of revelations, and especially with what we know of the character of the Prophet.

The Prophet was renowned for his incredible capacity for self-control. He was never one for rash impulses, but used to take whole days to reflect when he was confronted with a problem, and people were accustomed to not having immediate answers. The habit of taking note of a problem and reflecting long and hard about it before making a decision, even when the answer was not expected from God in the form of a revelation, was the character trait that made it possible for him to survive and communicate with a society with very violent customs. The dominant impression that emerges from the "official" picture of him, as it is portrayed in the history books, is of a mild and timid man:

> [The Prophet] was of medium height, neither very tall nor very short. He was fair-skinned with a ruddy complexion; his eyes were black, his hair thick, glossy, and beautiful. His beard bordered his whole face and was very bushy. His hair was long and hung to his shoulders and was black. His neck was pale . . . . His face had such a sweet expression that one hated to leave his presence . . . . No one who had seen him admitted ever having seen, either before or after, a man who spoke so winningly.[4]

Paradoxically, in a society in which, according to al-Tabari, people turned very quickly to the sword to settle problems,

The Hijab, *the Veil*

Muhammad was renowned for his ability to absorb tension and remain calm. The Prophet was a public man, experienced in the art of dealing with people, of charming them, of convincing individuals and groups with different opinions. He was accustomed to tolerating crude, boorish men. Without extraordinary self-control, one could not assert oneself as an authority in Arab society of that period. It was this that earned the Prophet from a very early age a reputation as a *hakam*, an arbiter in cases of conflict. How then can we explain that such a minor irritation so rapidly precipitated a draconian decision like that of the *hijab*, which split Muslim space in two?

The historical context can help us to begin to clear up this mystery. Year 5 of the Hejira (AD 625) was not a year like the others. It was the Prophet's most disastrous year as military leader of a monotheistic sect that was trying to assert itself in an Arabia that was polytheistic and happy to be so.

Let us go back to the moment when Muhammad, persecuted in his native city, decided to leave Mecca to find asylum with the tribes of Medina. A city like Medina of townspeople and peasants would not have decided to give refuge to a troublemaker who was declaring war on the whole of Arabia and its gods, including formidable, powerful Mecca, if it was not hoping to gain something thereby.

It was necessary to look at things realistically. Muhammad and the success of his enterprise only won as a result of constant attention to reality and its tensions. In fleeing Mecca after having failed to conquer its sanctuary, Muhammad knew that he could only triumph by returning there, and the Meccans equally knew it and were determined to prevent him. So whoever gave the Prophet refuge risked war with one of the most powerful tribes in Arabia, the Quraysh, and their allies. The Quraysh was in fact the Prophet's tribe, but he threatened their interests.

The Prophet knew that the Medinese expected him to be militarily successful in the region. Winning victories on the field of battle was essential in order to give the Muhajirun (the Meccan migrants) confidence in themselves and to show the Medinese that they had made a good choice by opting for Islam. Year 5 was the year of stagnation and despondency after the military defeat at

Uhud, which took place in year 3 of the Hejira. It was a year made all the more difficult by Muhammad's troops having tasted success in the Battle of Badr in year 2.

At Badr the number of Muslims was ridiculously small compared to that of their adversaries. There were no more than 314 of them – 83 Meccans and 231 Ansar (their Medinese allies), of whom 61 were from the Aws tribe and 170 from the Khazraj tribe.[5] The Meccans numbered "950; 100 of them were on horseback and the others were mounted on camels."[6]

When the battle began around the hill of Badr:

> the Prophet, with Abu Bakr, entered the hut, knelt down once again, wept, and implored: "O Lord, if this band that is with me perishes, there will be no one after me to worship You; all the believers will abandon the true religion." He raised his hands toward Heaven as he prayed.[7]

God then sent an army of 5,000 invisible angels to reinforce him.[8] But the Prophet did not depend just on prayer. He used all available military tactics: intelligence about the enemy, reconnaissance of the area (resulting in the occupation of a strategic well), heart-to-heart talks with his men, prophetic dreams, and various other tactics to turn a handful of individuals into the beginning of a conquering army.

> The Prophet prayed for a long time. Then he emerged from the hut, and the Muslims formed up in battle order. The Prophet, with cudgel in hand, passed in front of the troops to inspect the alignment. One of the Ansar, named Sawad, son of Ghaziya, stepped a little out of rank. The Prophet struck him on the belly with the cudgel.[9]

The enemy suffered severe losses: 72 Meccans killed and an equal number of prisoners captured against only 14 Muslims killed.[10] As most of the prisoners were aristocrats, their relatives had to ransom them (in order to save them from slavery), which brought the Muslims a handsome booty.

Alas, the miracle of Badr was not duplicated when the Muslims

had to confront an enormous army of Meccans at the Battle of
Uhud 13 months later. Uhud was a disaster:

> [The Meccan force] numbered three thousand fully armed
> men, partly Meccans and partly bedouin Arabs. Two
> hundred were mounted on horses and the others on camels.
> Seven hundred wore breastplates. They marched on Medina.
> Arrived at the gates of the city, they stopped near a mile-high
> mountain.[11]

The Prophet hastened to meet them to keep them from taking
Medina. He went out at the head of 1,000 men. There was only
one horse in addition to the Prophet's. Knowing that the number
of men with armor and with mounts guaranteed who the victor
would be, one understands how the Meccans gained a quick
victory: "The Prophet, on foot, saw the Muslims fleeing toward
Medina. He regrouped with his companions on a sand hill and
cried out: 'My friends, I am here, I, the Prophet of God!' But they,
although hearing his voice, did not return."[12] Many, many pages
of the history books are filled with descriptions of this battle and
especially the reasons for the defeat, including the fact that some
Muslims were more interested in plunder than in holy war.[13] The
return to Medina was the hardest part. The Muslim losses totaled
70 men: "There was not a single house in Medina that was not in
mourning. When the Prophet reentered the city, he heard
lamentations at the door of the mosque. He asked the meaning of
it. They told him it was the wives of the Ansar who were weeping
for the dead of Uhud".[14]

Year 5 of the Hejira – the year of the descent of the *hijab* – was,
then, a particularly disastrous year. Since Uhud, the Prophet had
ceaselessly organized expeditions to keep alive the desire for
victory and the memory of Badr. But he was unsuccessful in
realizing his dream of conquering the Meccans in order to become
militarily credible in the eyes of his Companions, the Medinese,
and eventually all the other Arabs. Worse still was the fact that
the other Arabs, under the command of the Meccans, came that
year to besiege Medina itself. The verse of the *hijab* is part of
sura 33, *Al-Ahzab* ("The Clans"). This sura describes among other

things the siege of Medina, known as the Battle of the Khandaq, the Battle of the Trench, for Muhammad ordered his forces to dig a trench around the city to protect it.

Islam went through a time of severe military crisis, which it did not surmount until the spring of year 8 (AD 630), when the Prophet won a decisive victory over the Meccans, after which he conquered Mecca and then all of Arabia. The incident that took place during the night of the Prophet's wedding to Zaynab must be resituated in its context – an epoch of doubts and military defeats that undermined the morale of the inhabitants of Medina.

Verse 53 of sura 33 is regarded by the founders of religious knowledge as the basis of the institution of the *hijab*. The books of *fiqh* always devote a chapter to "the descent of the *hijab*." This verse is not the only one on this event, but it was the first of a series which in effect led to a splitting of Muslim space. A careful rereading of this verse reveals to us that Allah's concerns in this verse are about tact. He wanted to intimate to the Companions certain niceties that they seemed to lack, like not entering a dwelling without asking permission.

In addition to the rules of etiquette, the last part of the verse touches on another subject, Allah's decision to forbid Muslims to marry the Prophet's wives after his death. The verse of the *hijab* ends with these words: "And it is not for you to cause annoyance to the messenger of Allah, nor that ye should ever marry his wives after him. Lo! that in Allah's sight would be an enormity."

Al-Tabari, who comments on the Koran sentence by sentence, deals with this last part separately. The Prophet was threatened by men who stated during his lifetime their desire to marry his wives after his death. How could this be? The crisis in society must have been deep indeed for such an attack on him to be made – only verbal it is true, but symbolically dangerous. In addition to the incident about the lack of politeness of the guests at the wedding, it seems that the *hijab* came to give order to a very confused and complex situation. The *hijab* was to be the solution to a whole web of conflicts and tensions. However, a rapid reading of the Koranic text, like Anas's testimony reproduced by al-Tabari, gives the opposite impression. This leaves us with the following methodological impression: Are we obliged to limit our investigation of that verse to the wedding night of Zaynab or, on the contrary, are we entitled to seek the causes elsewhere – in the historical context, for example? Apparently the scholarly tradition inaugurated by the *fuqaha* encourages us to push the investigation as far as possible. Al-Suyuti, for example, the author of a book entitled *Asbab al-nuzul* (*The Causes of the Revelations*), tells us: "It is impossible to understand a verse without knowing the *qissa* [the story] and the causes that led to its revelation."[15] He adds that "it often happens that the *mufassirun* [commentators who explain the Koran] advance many causes [*asbab*] of the same verse."[16] Despite the proliferation of commentaries and interpretations of the Koranic text, it is not possible to find anywhere (to my knowledge) a synthesis that integrates all the causes relating to a given verse in chronological order and with an analysis of its psychological and social impact. Both al-Suyuti, who aims at identifying the causes of the revelation, and al-Tabari, who is bent on explicating the verse and so claims to be doing a more encompassing work, are satisfied just with chronicling the events that took place. Al-Suyuti's book on the causes is a summary of some hundreds of pages of al-Tabari's enormous *Tafsir*, which comprises 30 volumes, and which adds to the circumstances of the revelation the linguistic analysis of each word, the nuances and debates outlined by the experts concerning the interpretation, and finally the conclusion of al-Tabari himself. But as for synthesis – nothing. However, without synthesis we today cannot understand all the complexities of the event. And this makes it necessary for us to examine all the information we have at our disposal, especially the linguistic dimensions of the word *hijab*.

The concept of the word *hijab* is three-dimensional, and the three dimensions often blend into one another. The first dimension is a visual one: to hide something from sight. The root of the verb *hajaba* means "to hide." The second dimension is spatial: to separate, to mark a border, to establish a threshold. And finally, the third dimension is ethical: it belongs to the realm of the forbidden. So we have not just tangible categories that exist in the reality of the senses – the visual, the spatial – but also an abstract reality in the realm of ideas. A space hidden by a *hijab* is a forbidden space. The *Lisan al-'Arab* dictionary (*Language of the*

Arabs) does not help us much. It tells us that *hajaba* means "hide with a *sitr*." And *sitr* in Arabic means literally "curtain." So we have an act that divides space in two parts and hides one part from view. The dictionary adds that some synonyms of the verb *hide* are formed from the two words *sitr* and *hijab. Satara* and *hajaba* both mean "hide." If you have the patience to follow the author of this dictionary through the examples that he carefully mentions, you gradually succeed in clarifying and enriching your understanding of this fundamental idea.

The keeper of the key of the Ka'ba, the sacred shrine, is entitled to the privilege of the *hijaba*: "Banu Qusayy," the dictionary explains, "said that they had the *hijaba* of the Ka'ba, that is, that they were in charge of protecting it and they had the keys to it." It also cites the *Hijab al-Amir, Hijab* of the Prince: the most powerful man of the Muslim community has recourse to the veil to escape the gaze of his entourage – a tradition that would cause an uproar if applied by Arab chiefs of state today. The *hijab* is among other things the curtain behind which the caliphs and kings sat to avoid the gaze of members of their court, the *Encyclopedia of Islam* tells us:

> This custom, which appears to have been unknown to the early inhabitants of the Hidjaz, seems to have been introduced into Islam by the Umayyads, probably under the influence of the Sassanid civilization. The partition is also known as *sitara* or *sitr*, but the custom is the same, and it finally developed into an institution.[17]

This custom, which seems strange to us today, was first practiced at the time of Mu'awiya, the fifth caliph.[18] Later it was introduced into Andalusia, North Africa, and Egypt, where the Fatimid dynasty (909–1171) developed it into a veritable ceremonial. With the Fatimids the sacred dimension of the caliph acquired a special significance:

> The caliph, considered as the hypostasis of the Active Intelligence of the world, was almost the object of worship. Because of this, he was expected to hide himself as far as

possible from the eyes of his faithful followers, who were thus protected from the radiance of his countenance.[19]

We cannot fully explore the meaning of the word *hijab* without mentioning the use made of it by the Muslim Sufis, which has nothing to do with a curtain. With them, a person has access to boundless spiritual horizons, which the Muslim must aspire to. In this context the *hijab* is an essentially negative phenomenon, a disturbance, a disability: "In Sufism, one calls *mahjub* (veiled) the person whose consciousness is determined by sensual or mental passion and who as a result does not perceive the divine light in his soul. In this usage it is man who is covered by a veil, or a curtain, and not God."[20] In Sufi terminology, the *mahjub* is the one who is trapped in earthly reality, unable to experiment with elevated states of consciousness. The person who is not initiated into Sufi discipline does not know how to explore his extraordinary capacities for multiple perceptions which, through training and discipline, can be raised out of the realm of the physical and directed toward on high, toward Heaven, toward the divine.

For the Sufi master al-Hallaj, it is the constant seeking of God that allows one to go beyond the *hijab* that imprisons our consciousness: "Men lose their way in a dark night while searching for You and perceive nothing but hints."[21] For mystics, the opposite of the *hijab* is the *kashf*, the discovery.[22]

So we see that the concept of the *hijab* is a key concept in Muslim civilization, just as sin is in the Christian context, or credit is in American capitalist society. Reducing or assimilating this concept to a scrap of cloth that men have imposed on women to veil them when they go into the street is truly to impoverish this term, not to say to drain it of its meaning, especially when one knows that the *hijab*, according to the Koranic verse and al-Tabari's explanation, "descended" from Heaven to separate the space between two men.

We now see that the *hijab* can express a spatial dimension, marking a threshold between two distinct areas, and that it can hide something from view, as in the case of the *hijab al-amir* (the *hijab* of the prince). But it can also express the opposite idea, as in the case of the Sufi *hijab*, which blocks knowledge of the divine. In this latter example, it is the limited individual who is veiled. So although the *hijab* that separates you from the prince is to be respected, the one that separates you from God should be destroyed.

To complete the analysis it is necessary to point out the anatomical use of the word *hijab*, which designates both a boundary and a protection. The eyebrow, the *Lisan al-'Arab* tells us, is an example that combines both ideas: "*Al-hajiban* [eyebrows] are the two bones above the eye with their muscles and their hairs . . . . They are so named because they protect the eye from the sun's rays." Anything that separates and protects is a *hijab*. This explains its current usage in anatomy – the diaphragm is *hijab al-jawf* (*hijab* of the stomach), and the hymen is *hijab al-bukuriyya* (*hijab* of virginity).

When we leave the field of linguistics and return to the Koranic text, we discover a negative *hijab*, similar to the Sufi idea, an obstacle that prevents one from seeing God:

> . . . the Kur'an, though it [*hijab*] is found there only seven times, provides valuable information on the basic and metaphorical meaning of the term, as it does to a certain extent on its evolution. In general *hidjab* in the Kur'an means a separation: it is the veil or the curtain behind which Mary isolated herself from her people (XIX, 17); it is also the separate establishment (later, the gynaeceum) which was imposed at first only on the wives of the Prophet (XXXIII, 53; cf. XXXIII, 32), apparently on the advice of 'Umar. On the Day of Judgement, the saved will be separated from the damned by a *hidjab* (VII, 46), which is glossed as wall (*sur*) by the commentators, who deduce this interpretation from Kur'an LVI, 13. "It belongs not to any mortal that Allah should speak to him, except by revelation, or from behind a veil" (XLII, 51), a veil apparently meant to protect the elect from the brilliance of the divine countenance.[23]

Sometimes in the Koran this latter meaning of the *hijab*, a veil that hides God from men, takes on an eminently negative significance, when it describes the inability of certain individuals to perceive

God. This is the case in verse 5 of sura 41, where, according to al-Tabari, the veil expresses the difficulties that the Quraysh, traditionally polytheistic, had in understanding the monotheistic message of Muhammad: "And they [the polytheists] say: Our hearts are protected from that unto which thou (O Muhammad) callest us, and in our ears there is a deafness, and between us and thee there is a veil [hijab]." In this verse, the *hijab* is something that diminishes human intelligence. Moreover, the translation of the title of this sura (*Fusilat*) is "They [the verses] Are Expounded."[24] Al-Tabari says that *hijab* in this verse signifies "a difference of religion that produces conflict,"[25] for the Quraysh, who were in conflict with the Prophet, were worshippers of idols, while the Prophet was inviting them to worship one sole God: "The *hijab* that they [the polytheists] claimed existed between them and the Prophet of Allah was in fact their divergent choice in religious matters."[26] The one who is most blinded by the *hijab* is the polytheist. For some theologians the *hijab* is a punishment. This is the case with al-Nisaburi: "Among the invocations recited by al-Siriy al-Siqti, we can point out the following: 'God, if Thou must torture me with something, don't torture me with the humiliation of the *hijab*.'"[27]

So it is strange indeed to observe the modern course of this concept, which from the beginning had such a strongly negative connotation in the Koran. The very sign of the person who is damned, excluded from the privileges and spiritual grace to which the Muslim has access, is claimed in our day as a symbol of Muslim identity, manna for the Muslim woman.

Many new editions of books on women, Islam, and the veil have recently been published by religious authorities who are "concerned for the future of Islam," books that explain in their introductions that their aim is to "save Muslim society from the danger represented by change." This is happening at a time when Arab publishing is experiencing a severe crisis, as a result, among other things, of the war in Lebanon (traditionally the prime center of book publishing), and when prices are soaring from one month to the next. So it is indeed surprising to find that these new editions are often issued in luxurious (gilded!) bindings and are circulating at astonishingly low prices. For the equivalent of about six dollars you can buy the new 1981 edition of the *Kitab ahkam al-nisa'* (*Statutory Provisions Concerning Women*) by Ibn al-Jawzi,[28] a very conservative author of the thirteenth century (died in year 589 of the Hejira). With Ibn al-Jawzi the imprisoning dimension of the *hijab* goes beyond all bounds. A quick reading of some of his chapter titles gives the picture: Chapter 26, "Advise Women Against Going Out"; Chapter 27, "The Benefits for the Woman Who Opts for the Household"; Chapter 31, "Evidence Proving that It Is Better for a Woman Not to See Men." Obviously the participation of women in public prayer becomes a clandestine act. He cites a strange Hadith in which the Prophet's wives sneaked into the mosque in the middle of the night, said their prayers totally covered in their veils, and left in haste before dawn.[29] As for the right to make the *hajj*, the pilgrimage to Mecca, Ibn al-Jawzi begins that chapter by giving the conditions required of a woman to enable her to undertake such a journey. She must be free (the woman slave is thus automatically deprived of making the *hajj*); she must be past the age of puberty; she must be capable of reasoning. She must also be rather wealthy (in order to pay for the journey), and finally, she must be accompanied by a man who is forbidden to her as a husband. He adds that in any case a woman cannot make a journey of more than three days if she is not accompanied by her father, husband, or son.[30] Spokesman of the *Madhhab*, the most conservative, most ascetic, and most rigid of the four schools of Sunni Islam, Ibn al-Jawzi details the physical mutilations that are imposed on women, such as excision, which have absolutely nothing to do with Islam and which were completely unknown in the seventh-century Arabia of Muhammad. Chapter 6 is entitled "Circumcision of Women,"[31] and Chapter 67 gives the husband "the right to hit his wife."[32]

The republication of Ibn al-Jawzi's book is not an isolated case. It is part of a veritable media campaign. Since 1983 a first edition has been published, coming from Cairo this time, of the *Fatwas Concerning Women* by Shaykh Ibn Taymiyya (a fourteenth-century writer), extracted from his monumental *Majmu' al-fatawa al-kubra* (*Collection of the Great* Fatwas; *fatwas* are judgements by great religious authorities on a given subject). The publishers of this book have culled all the items concerning women from the 35 volumes of *fatwa*s, juridico-religious decisions on problems of all sorts. Their objective is to help us Muslim women by putting all the *fatwa*s at our disposal in a single easy-to-handle volume, so that we can "do battle with those who speak today about women's liberation."[33] Hiding the female body seems to be an obsession in this book. One chapter details "the necessity to veil the face and the hands during prayer"; another asks, "Is a woman's prayer worthless when her hair is not covered?" Finally, still another chapter poses an economic dilemma that seems to have tormented our shaykh: "Should a woman who possesses 1,000 dirhams use it to make the pilgrimage to Mecca or to buy a trousseau for her daughter?" Of course, we find a chapter on "The Circumcision of Women," which, as already stated, has nothing to do either with Islam or with Arab culture!

But first prize among the current crop of "women's books" goes to the new edition (1980) of the work by the Indian writer, Muhammad Siddiq Hasan Khan al-Qannuji, *Husn al-uswa*, which surpasses all the others in its misogyny.[34] For the equivalent of about eight dollars, you can read everything you want to know about "women's great sexual appetite" (p. 52) and about the fact that women "don't tend to go to the mosque or to Friday prayer" (p. 345). You can read in detail "everything that was reported to us about women's inability to reason, their lack of ability in all matters concerning religion" (p. 365). And, of course, he teaches us everything he knows about "the number of women among the population of hell" (p. 331).

This look back into history, this necessity for us to investigate the *hijab* from its beginnings through its interpretation in the centuries that followed, will help us to understand its resurgence at the end of the twentieth century, when Muslims in search of identity put the accent on the confinement of women as a solution for a pressing crisis. Protecting women from change by veiling them and shutting them out of the world has echoes of closing the community to protect it from the West. Only by keeping in mind this double perspective – women's body as symbolic representation of community – can we understand what the *hijab* signified in year 5 of the Hejira, what stakes it represented, and what stakes it brings into play in today's explosive, passionate, and sometimes violent debates.

The "descent of the *hijab*" had a double perspective from the beginning. There was a concrete aspect: the Prophet drew a tangible curtain between himself and Anas Ibn Malik. There was also an abstract aspect: the descent of the verse, from Heaven to earth, from God to the Prophet, who recited it. The Prophet drew a real curtain between himself and the only man in his house who was still there after the departure of the other guests, and at the same time he recited the verse which was inspired in him on the spot by God.

In one of al-Bukhari's versions, Anas tells us: "When the people were gone, the Prophet returned to the room [of the bride], entered, and let down a curtain." And he adds an important detail: "And I was still with him in the room when he began to recite: 'O ye who believe! Enter not the dwellings of the Prophet for a meal without waiting for the proper time, unless permission be granted you.' "[35] In this description by al-Bukhari, as in the one by al-Tabari, the *hijab* is a division of the space into two areas, isolating each of the two men present, the Prophet on the one hand, and Anas, the witness who describes the event, on the other. This dimension of the *hijab* as a delimitation of areas is strongly affirmed in some versions, where it is said that "the Prophet banged a *sitr* down between himself and Anas, and the *hijab* descended,"[36] the *sitr* (curtain) referring to a physical curtain, and the *hijab* to the Koranic verse.

A relatively minor incident – after an evening meal some guests delay their departure longer than they should – provokes a response so fundamental as the splitting of Muslim space into two universes – the interior universe (the household) and the exterior universe (public space). One can only be astonished at the disproportion between the incident and the response, since the Prophet could have simply asked people to no longer come uninvited to his dwelling. He was loved and respected so much that he would have been obeyed. The verse, like the explanations of it given to us, allows us to suppose that people used to visit the Prophet without any formality. It also allows us to suppose that the Prophet's house was easily accessible to the community, and in addition that there was no separation between his private life and his public life, between private space (the Prophet's house, the apartments of his wives) and public space (the mosque, which was the place of prayer and the gathering site for the community).

If we look again at the facts scattered throughout this chapter, it comes down to saying that the Prophet, during a troubled period at the beginning of Islam, pronounced a verse that was so exceptional and determining for the Muslim religion that it introduced a breach in space that can be understood to be a separation of the public from the private, or indeed the profane from the sacred, but which was to turn into a segregation of the sexes. The veil that descended from Heaven was going to cover up women, separate them from men, from the Prophet, and so from God. Having clarified this aspect of the subject – the linguistic, social, historical, and religious reality of the *hijab* – should we not ask ourselves how the Prophet, who felt such an absolute and radical need to protect his privacy, lived? What were his relations with his Companions, his wives, and his fellow citizens, and in what kind of spaces did these relations unfold?

6

The Prophet and Space

During the whole period of his prophetic mission, whether in Mecca (AD 610 to 622) or in Medina (AD 622 to 632), Muhammad gave a major place to women in his public life. He was 40 years old (some versions say 43) when he received his first revelation in AD 610, and it was in the arms of his first wife Khadija that he sought comfort and support. There are many descriptions of the anguish suffered by the Prophet during those first revelations, and all of them depict him drawing from his marriage the strength that he needed. He did not turn to a man to pour out his fears:

> Muhammad descended from the mountain. He was stricken with trembling and returned to his house . . . . His whole body trembled from the fear and terror that Gabriel had inspired in him . . . . He bent his head and said: "Cover me! Cover me!" Khadija covered him with a cloak and he slept. Khadija, who had read the ancient writings and knew the history of the prophets, had learned to recognize the name of Gabriel.[1]

One of the reasons the Prophet suffered such anguish was that he did not want to be like the poets and visionaries, who were moved by invisible forces that dictated words they did not control, but that simply poured forth.[2] That was what terrified him. Khadija, who had an uncle, Waraqa Ibn Nawfal, who was a

Christian convert, convinced him that he was neither mad nor a poet, but well and truly the prophet of a new religion. Khadija was his first adherent:

> "Whom shall I appeal to? Who will believe in me?" Muhammad asked her one day during one of the long conversations they had each time Gabriel appeared to him. Happy to see that he no longer doubted his new mission, Khadija exclaimed, "At least you can call on me before all others. For I believe in you!" The Prophet was very happy. He recited the profession of faith to Khadija and Khadija believed.[3]

The profession of faith referred to is the *shahada*: "There is no God but Allah, and Muhammad is His Prophet."

This is the way Islam began, in the arms of a loving woman. After the death of Khadija, the Prophet sought love with other women. He remarried; he became polygynous and came to know about the lot of polygynous husbands: disputes, jealousy, but also the pleasure of being the center of attention of beautiful, intelligent women. On the eve of the Hejira, the migration to Medina, he married a woman of his own age, Sawda. The great love of his life would be 'A'isha, though, the daughter of one of his Companions and friends, Abu Bakr. He became engaged to her just before the departure for Medina. With her he came to know the laughter of the child-wife, watching her keen intelligence blossom, admiring her excellent memory for the genealogies that she learned from her father, Abu Bakr. Nevertheless, he married other women, and she was sometimes jealous enough of them to plot against them. For example, she plotted against Maria the Copt, a curly haired beauty who gave him a son, Ibrahim. The Prophet was 'A'isha's first husband (which was not the case with some of the other wives – Umm Salama, for example), which explains the young woman's attitude. Some of his marriages were dictated by military considerations, to strengthen alliances with newly converted tribes. He married Juwayriyya Bint al-Harith after the defeat of her tribe during the expedition against the Banu Mustaliq tribe in year 6 of the Hejira. But in other cases, the physical beauty of the women was the prime factor. Zaynab Bint Jahsh (it was during her wedding night that the verse of the *hijab* was revealed) was his own cousin, and there was no military advantage to justify that marriage.[4] In addition, she was married to his adopted son Zayd when the Prophet fell in love with her.

Al-Tabari, like all the historians, describes that famous case of love at first sight. Zaynab was "the most beautiful woman of her time," he tells us: "One day the Prophet went to look for Zayd at his house. He put his hand on the door and opened it. Seeing Zaynab seated in her apartment with her head uncovered, he asked her, as he turned his face away, the whereabouts of Zayd. She replied that he had gone out."[5] He had often before had occasion to see Zaynab. But, according to al-Tabari, it was the fact that he had surprised her in her intimate surroundings that had such a great effect on him: "She made a great impression on him, and not wanting to look at her a second time, he closed his eyes and said: 'God be praised, God is great, God who commands hearts and eyes!' And then he went out."[6] It was, in effect, love at first sight. He married her after her divorce.

At the time of his death, the Prophet had nine wives, but he only engaged in sexual relations with those for whom he felt the strongest physical attraction from the beginning. Was that the only reason? They were also the ones, like 'A'isha and Umm Salama, with whom he had a strong intellectual relationship. War did not separate him from his wives. Whether it was on hit-and-run raids or for very long sieges, he was accompanied by one or two of them, chosen by lot to avoid jealousy and rancor.

Muhammad was a chief of state who publicly acknowledged the importance of affection and sex in life. And, during expeditions, his wives were not just background figures, but shared with him his strategic concerns. He listened to their advice, which was sometimes the deciding factor in thorny negotiations. During the negotiation of the treaty of Hudaybiyya with the Meccans in AD 628, which was opposed by some of the Companions as being militarily humiliating, the Prophet was at a loss as to what to do, and he confided in the wife who was accompanying him:

After the conclusion of the treaty, the Prophet ordered the Muslims to shave their heads and put themselves in a state of penitence. None of them responded to his call, which he repeated three times. Very distressed, the Prophet went back to the tent of his wife, Umm Salama, whom he had brought with him. When she asked him the cause of his distress, he told her: "I ordered them three times to shave their heads; no one obeyed." Umm Salama said: "Do not worry at all, Apostle of God, but you yourself shave your head and carry out the sacrifice."

The Prophet stood up, cut the throat of the camel destined for the sacrifice that he himself was to make, and shaved his head. His Companions, seeing him do this, spoke of it to each other, and all shaved their heads and sacrificed their animals.[7]

The first Muslim community was not led by an asexual man completely consumed by the quest for power. He is supposed to have led 26 expeditions himself (other versions say 27), and in addition "to have had his troops carry out 35 expeditions in which he did not personally take part."[8] His military and religious activities did not, however, ever cause him to devalue his private life or to relegate it to the background. His marital problems occupied him to such an extent that he used to speak about them to his closest Companions, especially his fathers-in-law, Abu Bakr and 'Umar. It was precisely his insistence on putting his private life and his public life on the same footing that was used against him by a Medina that had become, during the crisis years of 4, 5, and 6, as hostile and venemous as Mecca had been before.

It was through his wives that the *munafiqun*, the Hypocrites, those Medinese who saw in him a threat to their interests and the security of their city, attacked him and undermined his emotional ties. In a Medina mourning the defeat at Uhud (in year 3) and bloodied by the Battle of the Trench (in year 5), the political opposition took on the hideous face of those whom the Prophet called *munafiqun*, because they rarely attacked directly but preferred to use slander, rumor, and other even more insidious tactics, such as following the Prophet's wives in the street and harassing them. Demoralized by his military difficulties, the Prophet was defenseless against such tactics, which led him to doubt his wives and to accept the famous *hijab*.

In AD 622, when the Prophet arrived at Medina, he first lodged with an Ansari family, in the house of a man called Kulthum. But he organized his meetings with the notables of the city at the home of a bachelor named Sa'd Ibn Khaythama: "When he left the house of Kulthum to go meet people," explains Ibn Hisham, "he did it at Sa'd's house, because Sa'd was a bachelor; he had no family. His was the house where the bachelors among the Muhajirun met."[9] From the time of those first contacts, the differences in customs between the Muhajirun (the Meccan migrants) and the Ansar (the Medinese), particularly the customs regarding man/woman relations, was evident. For the Ansar the separation of the sexes seemed to be a minor issue. Thus 'Ali Ibn Abi Talib, who had joined the Prophet three nights after his arrival, was lodging in the home of a woman "who had no husband."[10] In the days to come, these small details were to take on unexpected proportions and become one of the most worrisome subjects of tension and conflict between the two communities. There were also other problems. Much sought after by the Ansar, the Prophet was faced with a delicate problem: how was he to take into consideration the various political susceptibilities and rivalries in choosing a place to stay? All the Ansar wanted to welcome the Prophet into their home, but he knew that accepting one or the other of these offers would open the door to accusations of preference and privilege, which he certainly wished to avoid. He found a solution that would be seen very often later on – a solution based on a concern for rigorous equality. He asked people not to block the street in front of his camel. He would choose a place to live wherever it stopped: "Let it go where it wants . . . . Let it pass, it has a mission to accomplish," he said.[11]

The camel stopped in front of a house with a *mirbad*, a place for drying dates. It was the house of an Ansari called Abu Ayyub.[12] Muhammad dismounted, asked who owned the land and what its price was. He decided to live there and build a mosque, which would be a gathering place for his adherents for prayer and discussion of the problems of the community. (It is interesting to note that today the Muslim state is opposed to the mosque again becoming a political arena where social and economic problems are debated!) He compensated the owners for the land and had the work begun,[13] living on the site during the period of the construction of the mosque and his apartments. He did not only supervise the building: "In order to spur the Muslims on to take part in the construction, he himself worked on it."[14] One believer improvised a poem in which he noted that it was practically impossible to "stay seated while the Prophet was toiling away on the construction site."[15]

When the building was finished, there was not only a mosque but nine new apartments for the personal use of the Prophet. Five were constructed of *jarid* (palm leaves) covered with earth, the four others were of stone.[16] As they arrived on the scene, the wives of the Prophet would occupy the rooms that the historians sometimes called *buyut* (rooms), sometimes *hujurat* (apartments); the word referring to them as a whole was *manazil* (dwellings). "The *manazil* of the Prophet's wives," explains Ibn Sa'd, "were on the left side [of the mosque], when you rise for prayer, facing the imam standing at the *minbar* [pulpit]."[17] Special mention is made of 'A'isha's apartment, which the Prophet arranged with direct access to the mosque: "The Prophet constructed 'A'isha's apartment, and he opened a door in the wall of the mosque that faced 'A'isha's apartment. He used that door when he went to pray in the mosque."[18] The mosque and 'A'isha's room were so close together that sometimes for the purification ritual the Prophet had 'A'isha wash his hair without his having to leave the mosque: "The Prophet had only to lean his head from the mosque to 'A'isha's doorstep, and she then washed his head while she was having her period."[19] Ibn Sa'd cites this detail to throw light on the problem of sullying that we have already discussed.

In fact, the arrangement of space was such that the mosque and the apartments of the Prophet and his intimates and Companions formed a single unit. When a new migrant arrived, he or she tried first of all to find lodging in the vicinity of the mosque, which was becoming not only a religious and political center, but also the favored residential area for the community – for the Ansar as well as for the migrants from Mecca. When Fatima, the daughter of the Prophet and the wife of 'Ali, arrived a little later on, she could only find lodgings far from the mosque. The Prophet wanted her to be closer. Among all his daughters, she was the one whom he particularly cherished. One of the reasons was that she, being married to 'Ali, his cousin and a Hashimite like himself, and the mother of 'Ali's two sons, Hasan and Husayn, guaranteed the continuance of the Prophet's line. Right up until today, all *sharifs* – that is, those who claim to be descended from the Prophet – trace their genealogy back to Hasan or Husayn. This is true, for example, of the current king of Jordan. For the Shi'ites, Fatima is without question the first lady of Islam and its most edifying model of womanhood. But during the lifetime of the Prophet her affection for him was so excessive that she had extremely strained relations with 'A'isha, whom she saw as a rival. As 'A'isha had no children, the Prophet treated Hasan and Husayn as his own. This was the reason Fatima insisted on living as close as possible to her father. But although Muhammad wanted as much as she did that she should find lodgings near him, he hesitated to intervene with a house owner who "had houses next to the mosque and nearby."[20] Fatima insisted and urged the Prophet to act, but he said, "He has already given us so many lodgings that I am embarrassed to ask for one more."[21] In the end, the house owner got wind of the matter and voluntarily came forward to suggest an exchange of houses.[22]

But why all these details, you may ask. They are intended to give an idea of the socio-spatial context in which the first years of Islam were lived. The relationship of a political leader with his entourage is totally different if he lives in a palace far from the people, on a mountain, or in an inaccessible valley, than if he chooses a home among the people he "governs," lives in the same conditions as they do, and is linked to them by neighborly relations and constant contact. This closeness between governor and governed should help us to understand the Prophet's extreme sensitiveness to rumors, gossip, and everything that was going on in the city. Because of the compactness of the living space he had arranged, he was immersed in the daily preoccupations of the people and could feel the tensions, pressures, and opposition that surrounded him.

Among the Companions, who were also his neighbors, there were not only good Muslims but also those who, giving purely verbal allegiance, are known to history as the *munafiqun*, the Hypocrites. The 70 notables who had concluded the agreement with the Prophet, inviting him to settle in Medina, were supposed to represent the whole population. That population was estimated at 10,000 inhabitants, if not more.[23] As we know that the negotiations were mostly concerned with tribal protection, the negotiating team's makeup probably owed more to patronage than to democratic principles. The *munafiqun* then were individuals who apparently did not feel strongly bound by their leaders' oath of allegiance to the Prophet. Medina was an ancient population center located 300 kilometers northeast of Mecca. The inhabitants led a settled life, devoting themselves to agriculture and the cultivation of fruit trees. It was not so much a city as a "collection of hamlets, farms, and strongholds scattered over an oasis, or tract of fertile country, of perhaps some 20 square miles, which was in turn surrounded by hills, rocks, and stony ground – all uncultivable."[24]

Among those who had not invited the Prophet to come to Medina nor given their agreement to that decision was the Jewish community:

> Medina was occupied by two tribes: the Aws and the Khazraj, who were the most numerous. Some of the Medinese villages, like Khaybar, Qurayza [*sic*], Wadi al-Qura, and Yanbu' were inhabited by Jews or Arab descendants of Banu Isra'il who had come from Syria and Jerusalem . . . . The Aws and the Khazraj wanted to take possession of those villages, but they had not succeeded because the Jews had large, strong forts.[25]

Medina then was a place where the interests of the various communities diverged and where major conflicts between Jews and non-Jews existed side by side with interclan conflicts, and of course intraclan conflicts and conflicts within families.

It can be argued that the term *munafiqun* designates those among the inhabitants of Medina who, not being Jews, owed allegiance to the chiefs of the Aws and Khazraj tribes, but who did not approve of the installation of a foreign leader in the city. They were those whose convictions varied according to circumstances – that is, according to their political and economic interests. The term *munafiqun* is applied to opportunists of every type, from political opponents of Muhammad to those who criticized his private life. You cannot understand the influence that these *munafiqun* had if you do not take account of the role played by public opinion and rumor in the life of the city, as a result both of the density of the living arrangements of the migrant community and of the intense relationships among its members. Ibn Saʿd reports that Nuʿman Ibn Harith, who owned land near the mosque, yielded it "to the Prophet each time a relation of his arrived in Medina," to the point where in the end "all of Ibn Harith's houses passed into the hands of the Prophet or his wives."[26] Intermarriage between families of migrants, which was a common practice, reinforced the intensity of relationships and also the spread of rumors.

The more intense the life of a community is, the less common individual initiative is. Those who have lived in the medinas of old cities or in small hamlets know this well. But this intensity, which the inhabitants of the anonymous suburbs of the great European cities dream of, has its disadvantages – the weight of social control that hangs over individuals and prevents their being different, being innovative, changing things around them. And it is the weight of that social control, because of the liveliness of the personal interchanges in that first Muslim community, that would come to function as an unparalleled resistance to change. To better understand that spatial proximity that existed in the early days of Islam, we need to read Ibn Saʿd. He tells us that with the triumph of Islam, it became important to enlarge the mosque. And the most obvious thing done was the integration of the women's apartments into it: "I saw the apartments of the Prophet's wives when ʿUmar Ibn ʿAbd al-ʿAziz was governor of Medina in the caliphate of al-Walid Ibn ʿAbd al-Malik [AD 705–15]. He had decided to destroy them to enlarge the mosque." The author adds that the Medinese wept when this decision was taken because they wished "that people would not spend too much money on the new construction and that people could see with their own eyes where the Prophet, that man who had the keys of the universe in his hand, used to live."[27] His apartments were very modest, and their shabbiness must have embarrassed the caliphs who, a few decades later, were already living in palaces. The caliphs of the Abbasid dynasty have given us the expression so meaningful today, "the palace of the Thousand and One Nights." A youthful witness shows us what a great difference there was between those scenes of pomp and Muhammad's humble dwelling: "I was still an adolescent when I went into the Prophet's house; I could easily touch the ceiling with my hand."[28]

The simplicity of the lodgings, their closeness to each other, and their closeness to the mosque gave a democratic dimension to the Islamic community that makes us all dream – dream about that lack of distance between the leader and "his people." Thanks to the ease of exchange among the Muhajirun and the presence of the mosque, the integration of the Ansar and all the other new converts proceeded with rapidity. To accelerate the amalgamation of Medinese and Meccans, Muhammad had recourse to some rituals that created fraternal links: each Ansari was to accept a Muhajir as "brother," for whom he was to be, as it were, responsible for "helping him to conquer the feeling of uprootedness."[29]

But everywhere where there was love, admiration, and enthusiasm, there was also inhibition and resistance. That spatial intimacy between the mosque and the dwelling and the almost tribal love with which the migrant families surrounded the Prophet gave him the strength and enthusiasm that he needed, but it also often constituted a brake on his projects, especially the most revolutionary ones. All changes in attitudes to the libido, even the most minimal ones, become, as we know so well today, a threat to the inner being and awaken violent resistance. The Prophet's simple manner of living was a threat to those around him, for he cared nothing for the virtues of the public/private division of space, and male supremacy can only exist and be consolidated if the public/private division is maintained as an almost sacred matter.

To help us understand that everyday Islam, Islam as a practice that embraced space and through it dramatized its desires for limitless horizons, where architecture equaled fluidity, I will focus on the critical time of the final illness and death of Muhammad. The Prophet began to feel unwell at the end of Safar, the second month of the year AD 633. He was forced to take to his bed on the first day of the third month, and he died on the thirteenth day of that month.[30] During his illness he worried about the future of Islam as well as his ability to lead the prayer ritual that symbolized it. At the beginning, he led the prayers from ‘A’isha’s apartment, where he lay in bed, since it opened directly onto the mosque. When he became too weak to do it any longer, he asked Abu Bakr to lead the prayers in place of him:

> One day the Prophet, feeling a bit better, came to the mosque to attend morning prayer. Abu Bakr, standing before the people, was leading the prayer. When the Prophet entered the mosque, supported by ‘Ali, . . . there was a stir among the people. Abu Bakr, without interrupting the prayer, stepped back. But the Prophet kept him in his place at the *mihrab* [prayer niche] by pressing his hand on his back and stood to his right. Then, not able to remain standing, he sat down and finished his prayer thus. Afterward the Prophet returned to his house and went back to bed.[31]

The day of his death he made an appearance on the doorstep of ‘A’isha’s room:

> One morning the people were saying the morning prayer when the Prophet lifted the *sitr* [curtain], opened the door, and stood on ‘A’isha’s doorstep. The Muslims were so happy to see him and so excited by his presence that the prayer service almost turned disorderly. He made a sign to them to continue and smiled when he saw their discipline as they prayed.[32]

During his illness Ansar and Muhajirun came to visit him in ‘A’isha’s apartment. There was a continuous coming and going of men and women, both those close to his family and those who were acquaintances.[33] There were such good acoustics between the two areas that Muhammad could follow everything that was taking place in the mosque, as the following episode tells us. When he realized that he no longer had the strength to lead the prayer ritual, he ordered that Abu Bakr be called upon to do it. 'A'isha took the initiative of failing to obey him, regarding the chosen person as inadequate. Although Abu Bakr was her own father and such an action could be seen as the Prophet's designation of his political successor, 'A'isha called upon another Companion, 'Umar. Later she explained that she dreaded the moment when Abu Bakr would be called upon to succeed the Prophet. She would have preferred that he stand aside, for she was aware of the conflicts that were sure to follow. When the Prophet, still confined to bed in 'A'isha's room, heard 'Umar's voice in the mosque, he cried out in surprise and annoyance, "But where is Abu Bakr?"[34] 'A'isha explained to him that she had summoned 'Umar instead of her father, because her father had a weak voice and was so sensitive that he wept when he recited the Koran. 'Umar, she explained, had a voice that carried far.[35] It was at this point that the Prophet, angry at being disobeyed, made the remark, aimed at 'A'isha, that in every woman there sleeps a traitor like the lover of Joseph (*sawahib Yusuf*).[36] This offhand observation, which even at its worst seems tinged with tenderness, came to assume through centuries of misogynistic practice the harshness of a veritable condemnation of the female sex. My professor of literature at the lycée repeated it to us every time one of us misquoted a poem or mixed up some dates.

In conclusion, we can say that the Prophet's architecture created a space in which the distance between private life and public life was nullified, where physical thresholds did not constitute obstacles. It was an architecture in which the living quarters opened easily onto the mosque, and which thus played a decisive role in the lives of women and their relationship to politics. This spatial osmosis between living quarters and mosque had two consequences that official modern Islam did not see fit to retain or did not envisage. The first is that this equation between public and private facilitated the formulation by women of political demands, especially the challenge of male privileges concerning inheritance and the right to bear arms. The second, which was a consequence of the first, is that the *hijab*, which is presented to us as emanating from the Prophet's will, was insisted upon by 'Umar Ibn al-Khattab, the spokesman of male resistance to women's demands. Muhammad only yielded on this point when the community was in the middle of a military disaster and when economic and political crises were tearing Medina apart and delivering it, in a state of fragility and uncertainty, to the fierce struggles of the *ahzab*, which in Western languages is translated as "factions" or "clans," but which in Arabic really means "political divisions." The concept evolved to mean political parties in today's modern Arabic.

7

The Prophet and Women

The Muslim God is the only monotheistic God whose sacred place, the mosque, opens on to the bedroom, the only one to have chosen a Prophet who does not keep silent about his concerns as a man, but who, on the contrary, voices his thoughts about sexuality and desire.

Clearly, the imams were able to take advantage of our ignorance of the sacred texts to weave a *hijab* – a screen – to hide the mosque/dwelling. But everyone knows that, as the Koran tells us, "of use is the reminder,"[1] and all we have to do is pore over the yellowed pages of our history to bring to life 'A'isha's laughter, Umm Salama's fiery challenges, and to be present to hear their political demands in a fabulous Muslim city – Medina open to the heavens.

THE WIVES OF THE PROPHET: THE HAPPY YEARS

When the Prophet asked for the hand of Umm Salama in year 4 of the Hejira (AD 626), 'A'isha was very jealous because she had heard about Umm Salama's beauty. When she saw her for the first time, she caught her breath: "She is more beautiful than they led me to believe!"[2] The author of *Al-Isaba* describes Umm Salama as "a woman of uncommon beauty, very sound judgment, rapid powers of reasoning, and unparalleled ability to formulate correct opinions."[3]

Umm Salama, like Muhammad, belonged to the Quraysh aristocracy. She had four children by her first marriage when the Prophet asked for her hand. At first she refused, for, she said, "I already have children, and I am very jealous."[4] To persuade her, the Prophet told her that he was going to ask God to rid her of her jealousy, and as for the question of age, in any case he was much older than she was.[5] It was Umm Salama's son who gave her in marriage to the Prophet. The bride was nursing her last-born, Zaynab, when she joined the Prophet's household, and he used to greet her when he came to her apartment by saying, "Where is Zunab?", the affectionate nickname of Zaynab.[6]

Umm Salama was one of those women of the Quraysh aristocracy in whom physical beauty and intelligence assured them as they grew older a special ascendancy over their entourage, and the privilege of being consulted on matters of vital concern to the community.[7] The Prophet's first wife, Khadija, was also typical of such women, full of initiative in public life as well as private life. Khadija had had two husbands before the Prophet and had borne a child by each. It was she who "asked for the hand of the Prophet," because she found that he had the qualities she most appreciated in a man. She was also, as we have seen, the heiress of a large fortune left to her by her previous husband, a fortune that she augmented by investing it in wide-ranging trading operations. Tradition stresses the difference in age at the time of marriage between Muhammad (25) and Khadija (40), but one may question whether she really was that old, since in 15 years of marriage together she bore seven children to the Prophet.

A typical example of the dynamic, influential, enterprising woman in public as well as private life is Hind Bint 'Utba, who played such a central role in the Meccan opposition to Muhammad that, when he conquered Mecca, her name was on the list of the few Meccans condemned to death by the Prophet. He never forgave her the songs and dances she performed among the dead Muslims on the battlefield of Uhud: "The women, coming down from the mountain, stood behind the army, beating their tambourines to spur on the soldiers. Hind, the wife of Abu Sufyan, skipped and danced as she sang this verse:

We are daughters of the morning star.
We trample cushions underfoot.
Our necks are adorned with pearls.
Our hair is perfumed with musk.
If you battle us, we will crush you in our arms.
If you retreat, we will let you go.
Farewell to love."[8]

One of women's roles in pre-Islamic Arabia was to spur men on during war to fight to the end, to not flinch, to brave death on the battlefield. This role obviously has nothing to do with the image of the nurturing woman who bandages wounds and comforts the dying. Hind and her war song express, on the contrary, an image of woman as exhorter to death. In addition, Hind is described as a cannibal, because she is supposed to have eaten the liver of Hamza, the Prophet's uncle, whom she particularly detested.[9] Al-'Asqalani justifies Hind's excessive behavior on the battlefield of Uhud by recalling that she had a grudge against the Prophet's uncle because he had killed *her* uncle, Shayba, and taken part in the intrigues that led to the death of her father, 'Utba.[10] Her hatred of Islam was not just simply acknowledged, but considered justified because Islam had decimated her clan.

So it is understandable that the Prophet demanded her head upon his triumphal entry into Mecca in year 8 of the Hejira (AD 630). But she was the wife of Abu Sufyan, the chief of the city, who pleaded mercy for her from Muhammad. Once it was granted, she had to appear before Muhammad with a delegation of the female population of Mecca to swear the oath of allegiance, after, of course, having recited the declaration of faith. Hind's oath of allegiance, which has been transcribed word for word by the historians, is a masterpiece of humor and political insolence by a woman forced to submit, but in no way renouncing her right to self-expression. When the Prophet commanded her to swear to "not commit adultery," Hind replied: "A free woman never commits adultery." The Prophet is supposed to have thrown an amused glance at 'Umar, "because he was aware of Hind's love affairs and her relations with 'Umar before his conversion to

Islam."[11] The historians have been so fascinated by Hind's personality that they have devoted pages and pages to her.[12] How do they speak about Hind, that woman who accepted Islam with so much reluctance? As strange as it may seem today, and to the great honor of the Muslim historians, Hind's personality emerges in all its complexity, with her excessive hate and her cannibalism on the one hand, but also with her undeniable gifts on the other: "Hind became Muslim the day of the conquest of Mecca. She was one of the women most gifted in judgment."[13]

The Prophet then was not surprised to hear a woman like Umm Salama, in contrast to the still adolescent 'A'isha, raise very political questions that only mature women were in a position to do: " 'Why,' she asked the Prophet one day, 'are men mentioned in the Koran and why are we not?' "[14] Once her question was asked, she awaited the reply from Heaven.

One day when she was calmly combing her hair, worried about her question still not having been answered (in those days God used to respond when a woman or a man asked a question about his or her status and position in the new community), she heard the Prophet recite in the mosque the latest verse that had been revealed to him and that concerned her:

> I had asked the Prophet why the Koran did not speak of us as it did of men. And what was my surprise one afternoon, when I was combing my hair, to hear his voice from the *minbar*. I hastily did up my hair and ran to one of the apartments from where I could hear better. I pressed my ear to the wall, and here is what the Prophet said:
>
> "O people! Allah has said in his book: 'Men who surrender unto Allah, and women who surrender, and men who believe and women who believe,'" etc. And he continued in this vein until he came to the end of the passage where it is said: "Allah hath prepared for them forgiveness and a vast reward."[15]

The answer of the Muslim God to Umm Salama was very clear: Allah spoke of the two sexes in terms of total equality as believers, that is, as members of the community. God identifies those who are part of his kingdom, those who have a right to his "vast reward." And it is not sex that determines who earns his grace; it is faith and the desire to serve and obey him. The verse that Umm Salama heard is revolutionary, and reading it leaves no doubt about it:

> Lo! men who surrender unto Allah, and women who surrender, and men who believe and women who believe, and men who obey and women who obey, and men who speak the truth and women who speak the truth, and men who persevere (in righteousness) and women who persevere, and men who are humble and women who are humble, and men who give alms and women who give alms, and men who fast and women who fast, and men who guard their modesty and women who guard (their modesty), and men who remember Allah much and women who remember – Allah hath prepared for them forgiveness and a vast reward.[16]

Was Umm Salama's concern shared by other women, or was it just a purely individual initiative, an eccentricity on the part of an ambitious and arrogant aristocrat? Did it reflect a whim on the part of Umm Salama or was it the general viewpoint among the women of Medina?

Many signs lead us to believe that it represented a veritable protest movement by the women. Umm Salama's question was the result of political agitation and not the capriciousness of an adored wife. First of all, some versions tell us that the initiative came from the women of the community: "Some women came to the wives of the Prophet and said to them: 'Allah has spoken of you [the Prophet's wives] by name in the Koran, but he has said nothing about us. Is there then nothing about us that merits mention?' "[17]

Not only did the women share Umm Salama's concern, but they also took that answer from Heaven for what it was: a break with pre-Islamic practices, the calling into question of the customs that ruled relations between the sexes. Whatever those traditions were, the women apparently hoped to see things change with the new God. They were so successful that a sura bears their name, sura 4, *An-Nisa* ("Women"), containing the new laws on inheritance, which deprived men of their privileges. Not only would a woman no longer be "inherited" like camels and palm trees, but she would herself inherit. She would enter into competition with men for the sharing of fortunes: "Unto the men (of a family) belongeth a share of that which parents and near kindred leave, and unto the women a share of that which parents and near kindred leave, whether it be little or much – a legal share."[18] This little verse had the effect of a bombshell among the male population of Medina, who found themselves for the first time in direct, personal conflict with the Muslim God. Before this verse, only men were assured the right of inheritance in Arabia, and women were usually part of the inherited goods: "When a man died, his eldest son inherited his widow. He could, if she was not his own mother, either marry her or pass his rights over her to his brother or his nephew, if he so desired. They could then marry her in his place."[19]

As far as men were concerned, the new regulations on inheritance tampered with matters in which Islam should not intervene – their relations with women. According to many of the Companions, Islam ought to change everything except their privileges with regard to women. They were doubly affected: their inherited goods were reduced, since women, who constituted a good part of it, were no longer included; in addition, they had to share with women the little that remained to be inherited.

In pre-Islamic tradition women had no assured right to inheritance, which in any case was a matter between men, the men of the husband's clan or her own relations:

Before Islam, when a man lost his father, brother, or son, and that person left a widow, the heir, taking advantage of the privileges of the dowry paid by the dead man, hastened to the widow, covered her with his cloak, and thus arrogated to himself the exclusive right to marry her. When he married her, he deprived her of her right to the part of the inheritance constituted by the dowry. But if the widow succeeded in getting to her own clan before the arrival of the heir, he lost his rights over her in favor of her own clan.[20]

A wife, at a time of inheritance, seemed to be nothing but an object to be claimed by male heirs, whether they belonged to the clan of the dead man or to her own clan.

The new laws threw all this into question. Islam affirmed the idea of the individual as a subject, a free will always present in the world, a sovereign consciousness that cannot disappear as long as the person lives. The men opposed these laws, understanding that if they let them come into effect, Muhammad and his God would soon support other demands by women, especially the right to make war and the right to booty.

In war, women were passive, outside of the conflict. In the case of defeat, they were reduced to the status of *sabaya* (prisoners of war), while men were killed. Arabia was a slave society, where individuals belonged to one of two categories: free persons (*ahrar*) or slaves (*'abid*). And this was true for both sexes. However, while the sovereign will of a free man could not easily be suspended – if he were captured, he was usually killed – that of a woman disappeared in the case of inheritance or of military defeat. Free women could be "inherited" or reduced to the status of captives if they were not ransomed. And the status of captive was very similar to that of slave.[21]

"Of use is the reminder," the Koran tells us (sura 87, verse 9). In the light of the past, the present takes on a disturbing clarity. The way in which the Prophet's Companions reacted to these laws is very well known. They began first of all by rejecting these new laws, wishing to continue to apply the customs of the *jahiliyya* despite their conversion to Islam. Then they complained to the Prophet and tried to put pressure on him to change the laws. Finally, in desperation, they took to interpreting the text as a means of escaping it. All this was done during the Prophet's lifetime. But the women did not take this passively. They hastened to the Prophet when the men persisting in applying the pre-Islamic practices.

Umm Kajja was a case in point. She was an Ansari woman who

complained to the Prophet: "My husband is dead, and they are preventing me from inheriting." Her husband's brother had told her, by way of justifying his decision to hold to tradition and ignore the new laws: "Women don't mount horses and don't go into battle,"[22] and therefore could not inherit since inheritance is a compensation for the danger of engaging in war. Umm Kajja had five daughters who were completely debarred from inheritance by the men of the clan. At that time, "only men inherited. The male child and the woman were excluded from succession."[23] They were regarded as second-class citizens, because they did not take part in war. And in a society of scarcity, war was an activity that gave the tribe the opportunity for booty, which, along with trading and inheritance, was one of the most common ways of acquiring wealth.

But Umm Kajja was not the only complainant. The Prophet faced a constant parade of women who came to demand the application of the new law. The case of Kubaysha Bint Ma'an had important repercussions, because a revelation came to solve the problem. Kubaysha's son-in-law wanted to inherit her in the traditional way. "Prophet of Allah," she said, "I have neither inherited from my husband nor retained the freedom to remarry whom I wish."[24] Her son-in-law, Abu Qays Ibn al-Salt, refused to apply the new law and persisted in trying to inherit the wife of his father – the former apparently having other ideas in mind. The conflict that stirred men up against women was once more tearing the community apart. However, once again the women triumphed, because Allah answered their appeal, and verse 19 of sura 4, "Women," fell like a knife to cut the knot. Qays lost the prerogatives of manhood that gave him the right to mount horses and wield the sword and bow: "O ye who believe! It is not lawful for you forcibly to inherit the women (of your deceased kinsmen), nor (that) ye should put constraint upon them that ye may take away a part of that which ye have given them, unless they be guilty of flagrant lewdness."[25]

The male population of Medina, especially the Ansar, were particularly distressed by this verse. Kubaysha was quite simply demanding the end of the customs of that city:

Inheritance among the people of Yathrib [the ancient name of Medina] ran thus: When a man died, his son inherited his stepmother. She could not oppose this appropriation. He could marry her if he so desired, and then he could have with her the same relations that his father had had before him; or he could separate from her if he no longer wanted her. When the son and heir was too young, the stepmother was prevented from remarrying, and she was obliged to wait until he became old enough to be able to make a decision regarding her.[26]

The clan and the male heirs were less interested in the physical charms of the stepmother than in her right to the inheritance. In principle, the heir had to return his stepmother's share in the inheritance to the men of her clan if he did not marry her, the crassness of the material interest being masked by the ceremony of marriage.

The Meccans, who were considerably less refined with their women than the Medinese, did not even bother with the formalities used by the Ansari men. In Mecca, for example, they employed the 'adl, a true form of arrest. They resorted to virtual blackmail, written into a contract, which could even take place when inheritance was not involved:

The 'adl existed among the Quraysh in Mecca. A man married a noblewoman [sharifa]. If he did not like her, he separated from her after making an agreement with her that she could only remarry with his permission. The husband summoned some witnesses and in their presence put the terms of the agreement into a written contract. If a suitor asked for the hand of that woman, she could not make any agreement without the permission of her former husband. And in order to get his permission, she had to pay a sum of money sufficient to compensate and satisfy him. Otherwise he would oppose it.[27]

The practice of 'adl and that of a wife being inherited by her husband's heir were the subject of many verses, all of which condemned the practices as immoral. Married women were not the only ones to fall victim to constraint and blackmail. In the case of the death of the head of the family, a young girl was also vulnerable. Her situation was in fact worse. It is to these young girls that we owe the string of verses dedicated to fatherless children – for example, in sura 4 ("Women") verses 2, 3, 6, 10, 36, 127, in sura 2 ("The Cow") verses 177, 215, etc. Many Arabs found these verses incomprehensible. To them, it was the height of absurdity that a young girl should claim her share of an inheritance. Verse 2 of sura 4, for example, gives the following order to men regarding young heirs and heiresses: "Give unto orphans their wealth. Exchange not the good for the bad (in your management thereof) nor absorb their wealth into your own wealth. Lo! that would be a great sin."[28]

Not only were young girls deprived of their inheritance according to pre-Islamic customs, but they were also the object of sexual abuse and mistreatment of all sorts. The guardian sometimes forced the prettiest ones to marry him, thus controlling their share of an inheritance and at the same time avoiding paying a dowry for them. If a fatherless girl had the misfortune not to be pretty enough to please her guardian, he could invoke her ugliness to justify opposing a marriage for her. In this way he did not have to pay her share of the inheritance: "If a fatherless girl was ugly, he did not pay her her share. He kept her from marrying, and he waited for her to die so that he could take over her inheritance."[29] The idea of accepting children of both sexes as having inheritance rights encountered such strong resistance that God decided to list among the seven mortal sins the act of not giving fatherless children their due.[30]

The idea that an ugly fatherless girl – ugly in the opinion of the chief of the clan – could inherit was a shocking thought to many. Jabir Ibn 'Abdallah had a blind girl cousin who was ugly and who had inherited a large fortune from her father. Jabir had no intention of marrying her, but he opposed letting her marry anyone else, not wishing her husband to get his hands on her fortune. He consulted the Prophet on the question, and he was not the only one to do so. Many men like Jabir, who were responsible for fatherless girls, did not see why Muhammad wanted to change the old order of things.

"Does an ugly young girl who is blind have the right to inherit?" he exclaimed in front of the Prophet. The Prophet replied: "Yes, absolutely." And then he went on to recite: "They ask of you a decision on the subject of women. Say: God has informed you of a decision. It has been told to you in the part of the book concerning fatherless girls to whom you have not handed over what is prescribed."[31] The verse referred to made it clear to men that Muhammad and his God were not always acting with their interests in mind, and that the new religion represented not just the promise of conquests, but also an ethical system that imposed some sacrifices. The conflict between God and the Muslim Companions was coming into the open:

> "How," say men, "can one give the right of inheritance to women and children, who do not work and do not earn their living? Are they now going to inherit just like men who have worked to earn that money?" They waited for a rectification from Heaven. Then they said to themselves: "We must go ask for clarification." And they went to the Prophet and asked him some questions on this subject.[32]

The Prophet was not intimidated by them. He maintained his position: God had informed them of His decision on this subject. They had only to comply. However, confronted with laws they did not like, they tried to distort them through the device of interpretation. They tried to manipulate the texts in such a way as to maintain their privileges.

WOMEN AND *AL-SUFAHA* (THE FOOLISH)

In the face of the resistance to the new laws on inheritance, verses kept coming down from Heaven hammering out the same messages. The sura on women devoted many of its verses to minutely detailing the share of an inheritance that goes to each person in all conceivable situations. A woman as a mother would have the right to so much; as a wife her share would be such and such; as a sole daughter or a daughter with brothers, such and such an amount. The amount for each situation was fixed in precise detail in order to avoid any ambiguity: "And unto you belongeth a half of that which your wives leave, if they have no child; but if they have a child then unto you the fourth of that which they leave."[33]

Despite all those precautions and clarifications, men continued to try to suppress the egalitarian dimension of Islam. These men, who came to Islam to enrich themselves and have a better life, were caught by surprise by this dimension of the new religion. They suddenly found themselves stripped of their most personal privileges. And, unlike slavery that affected only the wealthy, the change in the status of women affected them all. No man was spared, whatever his class or means. However, a verse that uses a somewhat ambiguous word, *al-sufaha* (the foolish), was going to serve them as a springboard for nullifying the new laws.

This verse says: "Give not unto the foolish (what is in) your (keeping of their) wealth, which Allah hath given you to maintain."[34] This was the verse they were waiting for: since the foolish are excluded, then women are the foolish – it was very simple. "The *sufaha* are women and children, some people say, and both of them must be excluded from inheritance."[35] Obviously this was a throwback to the pre-Islamic customs of the *jahiliyya*, the era of ignorance when the criteria of good and evil had not yet been revealed. If they insisted strongly enough that the concept of *sufaha* included women, then all males would be happy, and the Muslim God and his Prophet could keep their harebrained laws about inheritance. Men came to a happy understanding among themselves.

The most conservative men were jubilant. According to them, the word *sufaha* designated "women and young children," but what is clear is that "the most foolish of the foolish are certainly women" (*al-nisa asfaha al-sufaha*).[36] How did al-Tabari, in his role as guardian of the sacred text, react some centuries later to this conflict between the Muslim God and male believers?

Al-Tabari does his work adroitly. He transmits to us 29 testimonials with diverse interpretations of this verse, while reminding us that he had already given copious commentaries on the word *sufaha*, which had previously occurred several times in the Koran.[37] If we study all the other occurrences of the word *sufaha*, we are no better off than before. In one instance, *sufaha* refers to ignorant persons, in another to children, and sometimes it designates Jews and sometimes polytheists.[38] Finally, *sufaha* can designate persons who lack discernment, that is, who are incapable of distinguishing good from evil.[39] So it remains to us as believers to find the best way to understand the word *sufaha*.

There are two possible interpretations: (1) that the word *sufaha* has nothing to do with sex but relates to lack of discernment and squandering of money on trifles;[40] and (2) that the word includes women among the foolish, making their right to inheritance null and void. Al-Tabari, who undertook the compilation of his *Tafsir* (*Explication*) precisely in order to clarify for future generations the "true" meaning of the Koranic text, found himself confronting a problem of some consequence, since this verse was controversial even in the Prophet's lifetime. It was a fundamental problem in the religious literature (*fiqh*), and is an illustration of the ease with which the sacred can be manipulated because of the absence of synthesis and an excess of empiricism. The Muslim scholar of religion tries not to interpose himself between the sacred text and its reader. As he wants to be as objective as possible, he merely presents us with a multiplicity of opinions and then adds his own. Fearing the intrusion of any subjectivity, he disallows himself any initiative in the way of synthesis. What one finds, then, is a succession of cases, a variety of opinions, but no attempt to extract from this empirical material any principles, laws, or axioms that would allow the reader to distinguish the structural from the circumstantial.

Al-Tabari simply adds his opinion after having cited all the others. He does not try to sift out from all this a principle about the relationship between the sexes – namely a principle of equality:

> According to us, the correct way of interpreting Allah's words – "Give not unto the foolish [*sufaha*] (what is in) your (keeping of their) wealth" – is that God has used the word *sufaha* in its general meaning; he did not limit it to one precise

category of foolish people. This verse then means that one should not hand over to a foolish person his or her fortune, whatever that person's age or sex. *Sufaha* here means persons incapable of managing their fortune, who might squander their assets. That person must be put under guardianship with the guardian controlling the usage of the assets.[41]

Never at any time does al-Tabari take a stand on a principle. So what argument does he put forward to get to the bottom of this debate? Sticking to the text, he resorts to grammar for his decisive argument, insisting on the fact that the word is general: *sufaha* only excludes those who have not achieved maturity in the sense of discernment, and, he adds, excluding women from inheritance is to introduce a specification by sex that does not exist in the Koranic text. "Those who say that in this verse *sufaha* specifically designates women are simply distorting the language. The Arabs only use the plural form exemplified by *sufaha* for the masculine plural or for the masculine/feminine plural." And he concludes by giving an explanation about plural forms in the Arabic language. According to him, if Allah meant that women were foolish, he could have used the appropriate plural form.[42]

There are no theoretical schemas that define the principles of Islam as a philosophy, as a vision of civilization. Because of their wish to master their subjectivity, the *fuqaha* (religious scholars) were reduced to simply accumulating various cases and opinions concerning them. Since they gave to each person the right to have an opinion, the end result is a literature of juxtapositions of opinions. The religious literature wanted to be scientific, and it was. But it was an empirical science, in which each author limited himself to a work of collation without drawing any syntheses that would aid us in "distinguishing" the essential from the secondary. The imam humbly effaces himself before the facts. And in doing this, he opens the way to manipulation through interpretations, as the debate around the word *sufaha* clearly shows. When it is a controversial verse that is at stake, everyone is going to choose and support the opinion that suits him best among the multiplicity of those that the *fiqh* accumulates.

We can imagine, or dream, that an elaboration of a system of fundamental principles would probably have allowed Islam as a civilization of the written word, to come logically to a sort of declaration of human rights, similar to the grand principles of the Universal Declaration of Human Rights, a universal declaration that still today is challenged as being alien to our culture and imported from the West. The position of modern Islam as a society on the questions of women and slavery is a good illustration of that utter neglect of principles, that inability of political Islam as a practice (as opposed to an ideal) to enforce equality in daily social life as an endogenous highly valued characteristic. The paradoxical result is that, despite Islam's opposition to slavery in principle, it only disappeared from the Muslim countries under pressure from and intervention by the colonial powers.

It is in order to evaluate the depth of the contemporary Muslims' amnesia, which sees equality of the sexes as an alien phenomenon, that we must return to Medina, to its narrow streets where the debate on equality of the sexes raged and where the men were obliged to discuss it, but refused to accept it although Allah and His Prophet demanded it. As today, the men professed Islam, but openly rejected it when it supported equality between the sexes.

WOMEN AND BOOTY

After Umm Salama's success and the verses affirming women's equality and especially their right to inheritance, a critical period followed. Other verses came, which temporized on the principle of equality of the sexes and reaffirmed male supremacy, without, however, nullifying the dispositions in favor of women. This created an ambiguity in the Koran that would be exploited by governing elites right up until the present day. In fact, women's triumph was of very short duration. Not only did Heaven no longer respond to their pleas, but every time they formulated a new demand, revelations did not, as before, come to their rescue.

Encouraged by the fact that Allah considered them to be believers just like men, women were emboldened to claim the right to go to war in order to gain booty and the right to have a say with regard to the sex act. These claims were surely going to be perceived by men for what they were: a challenge to the very foundations of male supremacy. The heads of family, realizing that what women were demanding was eminently political, mobilized a veritable opposition movement with an elite leader: 'Umar Ibn al-Khattab, a military chief without peer. His courage had always galvanized the Muslim troops, and the Prophet himself recognized that "the conversion of 'Umar to Islam was a conquest and a triumph in itself."[43] 'Umar had boundless admiration for the Prophet and his projects for change, for the creation of an Arab society. He was prepared to go far with the Prophet, to follow him in his desire to change society in general. But the point at which he was no longer prepared to follow him came when it was a question of relations between the sexes. 'Umar could not imagine an Islam that overturned the traditional – that is, pre-Islamic – relations between men and women. Women's demands to bear arms and to participate actively in military operations instead of passively waiting to be taken prisoner, as the *jahiliyya* tradition required, seemed absurd to him. He was ready to destroy the gods of polytheistic Mecca that his ancestors had worshipped and thus to upset the equilibrium of the heavens. But to envisage that the Arab woman could claim a different status on earth seemed an intolerable change to him.

This was happening at the moment when the women, in a triumphant mood, were taking action. The most virulent of them became openly provocative by declaring that the Koranic verse that said that "a man's share is double that of a woman" did not apply only to inheritance, but also to sin. At the last judgment, they said, every man would have the surprise of seeing the number of his sins multiplied by two: "Since they have two shares of inheritance, let them have the same for sins!"[44] The situation was heating up!

To the great surprise of women, Heaven intervened this time on the side of men and affirmed their privileges. Verse 32 of the sura on women is divided into two arguments and responds to two requests that must be carefully distinguished: women's desire to have the same privileges as men, and their declaration that real equality is achieved in terms of wealth. So, for them to be really the equals of men, Allah had to give them the right to go to war and thus to gain booty. Allah answered in terms of the obvious: since the rights of each are proportional to what they earn, women, who are exempted from going to war, cannot claim to be treated equally: "Unto men a fortune from that which they have earned, and unto women a fortune from that which they have earned."[45] This part of the verse, al-Tabari tells us, is an answer to women's demand to bear arms. They then pushed the reasoning about equality to its logical limit. Since the share of each person is equal to what he or she acquires, and since men only grow rich through war, they demanded the right to this privilege.

To understand women's insistence on this point, we have to have some appreciation of the mechanisms of war and booty and their importance to Medina's economy. *Al-ghazawa*, according to the *Lisan al-'Arab* dictionary, were "raids on an enemy to strip him of his possessions." The dictionary says that a "failed raid is one in which no booty is seized." *Al-ghazawa* were one of the most common means of "creating" wealth. They were intertribal forays, extremely ritualized, whose primary aim was to capture "the wealth of the other," camels most of the time, while avoiding bloodshed. Causing bloodshed was a very serious act which was to be avoided at all costs, because the *ghazi* (attacker) would then be exposed to revenge by the tribe of the person killed. Bloodshed unleashed a chain of reprisals with interminable vendettas governed by the law of an eye for an eye. Nevertheless, two kinds of *ghazawa* coexisted, one that we have just discussed for possessions, and the other for war, in which no quarter was given. War with access to booty, along with the trading of the Meccans and the agriculture of the Medinese, was one of the possible and important sources of revenue. Muhammad himself engaged in it, while using it, however, for an objective that went beyond the traditional *ghazawa*. If he had done otherwise, he would have become just one of the many small tribal chieftains of Arabia whom history would have forgotten or noted only briefly. However, the Prophet quickly discovered the limits and contradictions of such an activity. The laws of *ghazawa* were implacable and left to the victor only a choice between two equally inhumane alternatives with regard to the defeated: kill the men and reduce the women (occasionally the men too) to slavery, or, if the men and women were of aristocratic origin, exchange them for a large ransom. But the question Muslims had to face was: What should be done with prisoners who declare themselves converts to Islam? Although one gains a believer, one also loses booty, which was the original aim of the enterprise.

The women took advantage of the new questions that arose to slip in their own demands. "During the pre-Islamic period, men excluded women and children from inheriting, because, they said, they did not go on raids and did not share in booty."[46] Umm Salama, in her usual clear and concise way, formulated in a petition the essential point of women's new claim: "Messenger of God, men make war, and we do not have the right to do it although we have the right to inheritance!" In another version Umm Salama is supposd to have said: "Messenger of God, why do men make war and we do not?"[47]

This was a demand that brought into question the very foundation of the law of *ghazawa*. That law gave to the victor the right to kill men (or to exchange them for ransom if they were aristocrats), and to reduce the women and children of the loser to the state of *sabaya*, prisoners of war. A woman prisoner could be sold by her captor as part of the booty. Her captor could also subject her to a conjugal relationship, either as the mother of his children or as a concubine, or he could just use her as labor.[48] Female slavery was a source of sexual gratification, of domestic labor, and of reproduction of that labor force.[49] By demanding the right to bear arms, women were threatening a huge reduction in the wealth that a man could gain by raids, but they hoped through it to escape the sad fate that was theirs, as the following narrative illustrates. It was recounted to the caliph 'Umar by 'Amr Ibn Ma'dikarib, a bold horseman during the days of the *jahiliyya*:

I am going to tell you about an adventure that I have never before divulged to anyone. I went one day with some horsemen of Banu Zabid to make a foray on the territory of Banu Kinana. We came upon a band that was out on a night march . . . . I saw some horses' feedbags, some vessels full of food, some red leather tents, and a number of goats. After having captured our booty, I went to the largest of those tents, which was set slightly apart. In it I found a woman of great beauty, seated on a carpet. When she saw us, me and my horsemen, she broke down in tears. I asked her the reason. "It is not my own fate that I weep for," she said. "I weep with rage at the thought that my female cousins escaped the misfortune that has befallen me." I believed what she was saying and asked her where her cousins were. "Down there, in that valley," she told me. I immediately ordered my companions to remain there quietly until my return. I put the spur to my horse, who scrambled to the top of a dune. [When 'Amr got to the top of the dune, he saw that he had been hoodwinked.] Close by I saw a young man with blond hair and long eyelashes, who was mending his sandals; his sword lay in front of him and his horse was at his side. Upon seeing me, he dropped his work, stood up without the least anxiety, picked up his sword, and climbed up a hill. Seeing that his tent was surrounded by my horsemen, he mounted his horse, then rode toward me while reciting some verses.[50]

A duel followed between 'Amr and the young man, a peerless warrior named Rabi'a Ibn Mukaddam, who was in fact the husband of the young woman. 'Amr lost the duel but attacked again and "seized a rich booty and Rabi'a's wife. Rabi'a, being not far away, was informed of what had just happened. He immediately raced off in pursuit, riding bareback and armed only with an untipped spear. He overtook 'Amr and called on him to surrender his prisoner."[51] Rabi'a succeeded in recapturing his wife "as well as the abandoned booty, and returned to his tribe."[52]

Here we see what happened to a young woman in pre-Islamic Arabia when she was not surrounded by all the members of her own tribe or her husband's. And not all husbands had the courage of the matchless hero, Rabi'a. The women who were married to ordinary men ended up as prisoners or slaves of their abductor.

Asking Islam to change such a situation meant bringing down

the whole structure of the economy of capture. If the Muslim God gave satisfaction to women, war would no longer have any meaning. Moreover, all the details we can glean about food, housing, and clothing show us a society of frugality, even scarcity. A believer once asked the Prophet if one could say one's prayers in the same clothing or if one should change beforehand. "Do you think that everyone has two sets of clothes?" was the Prophet's response.[53] The Arabs were amazed when they saw the clothing of the Christian princes they conquered: "The Muslims looked with astonishment at the robe of Ukaydir, which was of brocade embroidered with gold; they had never seen anything like it."[54] So over and above the equality craved by women, there were crucial economic interests at stake.

Confronted with this problem of survival for the community, most of the women did not take the necessary political stand. The only one who did was Umm Salama, who defended the right to go to war, not to gain wealth, but to have the privilege of "sacrificing oneself for God" and the Prophet's cause. The others declared: "It is too bad that we are not men; if we were, we could go to war and gain wealth like them."[55] Lacking Umm Salama's political sagacity, they were not able to hide their material interests under the trappings of holy war, and this false step was fatal to them.

Being a prophet means maintaining a delicate balance between the probable and the impossible, between risks and successes that at first glance seem impossible. A prophet is by definition a man who gives his followers hope that their life will be better if they decide to stake everything on the new ideal. The Muslim God, like His Prophet, knew that earthly riches are a not insignificant motivator. After all, the new converts were good fathers with responsibility for members of their family, and Islam held out the promise of bettering their conditions of life, whether spiritual life or earthly life. The promises of booty fed the legitimate desire to grow rich among Allah's warriors: "Allah promiseth you much booty that ye will capture, and hath given you this in advance".[56]

Booty, along with the promised life in paradise, represented the fulfillment of the two legitimate ambitions of the believer. Muhammad, in his role as military leader, quickly realized that very few of his warriors would agree with his tampering with the rules of distribution of booty. The incident at Ta'if in year 8 illustrates this well. During this expedition, the Prophet was upset by the distress suffered by the conquered tribes, among whom were some persons very dear to him. He wanted to humanize the customs regarding booty and the status of prisoners of war. But his troops turned against him and he found himself facing a veritable mutiny.

Also during the Hunayn expedition, two events, one involving personal emotions, the other involving religion, caused the Prophet distress and prevented him from mechanically applying the rules of booty distribution. The Hunayn expedition took place after the conquest of Mecca in year 8 of the Hejira. Alarmed by the taking of Mecca and determined to come to its aid, the tribes of the region, who were still resisting Islam, flocked to Ta'if, some hundreds of kilometers away. Without contact with Ta'if, Mecca could not survive:

> Mecca and Ta'if were separated by a three-day march along the Yemen route. Ta'if was composed of several very large villages . . . . There were many orchards, cultivated fields, vineyards, and flowing streams there. The inhabitants of Mecca had to constantly be in touch with Ta'if, because at Mecca there were neither vines, trees, nor fruit. All the fruits to be had in Mecca came from Ta'if, which produced all known varieties of fruit. Every Meccan owned a vineyard or garden in Ta'if, and during the three months of summer no one except the poor could be found in Mecca.[57]

Whoever conquered Mecca would not delay in capturing Ta'if. Malik Ibn 'Awf, the chief of the Thaqif, the tribe that controlled Ta'if, took command of the defense of the city. He succeeded in recruiting troops everywhere except in a clan of the Hawazin, the Sa'd Ibn Bakr, because the Prophet had been entrusted to them when he was an infant. It was the custom of city people to place an infant with a wet nurse outside of the city in a healthier environment. This clan refused to give soldiers to Malik: "They answered: 'Muhammad is our nursling; he was nurtured among us. We cannot make war against him.' However, Malik put so much pressure on them that he did obtain a troop of fighters from them."[58]

Malik left Ta'if at the head of an army of 30,000 soldiers and halted on the plain of Hunayn at two days' march from Mecca. In order to force his coalition of warriors to fight against Muhammad to the death, he "ordered that every soldier should bring with him his wife, children, and animals."[59] The Prophet, informed of the massing of bedouin at Hunayn, raised an army of 12,000 men, 2,000 of whom were Meccans. He handed over the command of Mecca to one of his men, and set out with his army for Hunayn.

It was a hard-fought battle, and the Prophet himself was nearly killed. The Muslims finally won, despite their opponents' numerical superiority. Malik decided to fall back on Ta'if, feeling better able to mount a defense in a fortified city. In the mêlée of the retreat, his allied tribes took flight, leaving behind their wives and children. The Prophet gave the order, according to the custom, "to pursue the fugitives as far as three days' march . . . to kill those that could be caught, and to bring back the women, children, and animals."[60] The booty was enormous: "The Muslim troops collected all the animals the enemy had brought with them, so many camels and sheep that only God knew the true number. In addition there were 6,000 women and children."[61]

Among the captives was 'Usma, the foster-sister of Halima, Muhammad's wet nurse: "The Prophet recognized her and broke into tears. Then he took his cloak from his shoulders, spread it on the ground, took 'Usma by the hand, and made her sit on it. The next day he asked her what she preferred to do: to stay with him or to return to her tribe."[62]

She preferred to return to her own people. The Prophet sent her off with gifts: "Two slaves, a man and a woman, a camel, and a sheep taken as booty."[63] By thus disposing of booty of which 'Usma was a part, the Prophet committed a great offense in the eyes of his troops, who had no time for acts of pity. But the most serious offense was still to come. Malik, the commander in chief of the enemy force, who had fallen back on Ta'if, announced the decision to convert to Islam – for himself and his allies! By virtue of this he could recover all the booty – women, children, and possessions. It was the law and logic of holy war, which was not the same as for *ghazawa*.

Malik's decision turned the situation completely upside down. The Prophet could no longer dispose of the booty and had to prevent his soldiers from touching it: "He had all the prisoners rounded up and gathered together all the booty. Pending his departure, he put it all in the care of Mas'ud, the son of Amr, at the head of 10,000 men."[64] But war had its laws, and the Prophet could not decide anything without the consent of his troops. So he suggested to the Banu Sa'd clan that they use the occasion of Friday prayer to raise the problem in public.

This was a critical moment for Islam. Was booty or Allah more important for a Muslim soldier? "The next day the Prophet was saying the morning prayer with the whole army arrayed behind him. When he turned his back on the *mihrab* [prayer niche], the Hawazin, the Thaqif, and the Banu Sa'd rose to their feet and begged for the return of their women and children."[65] The Prophet, who had set the stage for this scene, turned to the gathering and declared: "These captives do not belong to me alone, but to all the Muslims."[66] He added that he himself was ready to renounce his share of the booty, but as for the rest, "It is up to the Muslim troops to decide."[67]

A heated debate then took place in the mosque. It was not the animals that the soldiers refused to give up, but the captives, as each human being was worth several animals. To the commanders who refused to renounce their booty, the Prophet said: "You have the right [to claim booty], but those of your men who give up their share of captives will receive from me six sheep for each captive."[68] During this Friday prayer session in year 8 (AD 630), holy war was reduced to sharp bargaining in which Muhammad gambled the future of his whole mission. Would he convince the troops to go beyond *ghazawa*, to see in a captive something other than booty? Especially, would they see a captive as a believer like themselves?

When the session ended, nothing had been settled. Muhammad had succeeded in controlling the psychological impact of the scene by advising the defeated people to come to the mosque, declare their conversion to Islam, and thus to get the troops involved. But once outside, the soldiers attacked the Prophet, calling on him to order the division of the booty: "They stayed close to him and insisted that he make the distribution right then and there. The Prophet promised them to do it. Then they placed a hand on him, saying: 'We will not let you go until you make the distribution.' They pulled off his cloak, shouted at him, and made an ugly scene."[69] The Prophet was forced to divide up the remainder of the booty on the spot, according to tribal custom.[70]

We can see that at this point the Muslim fighter did not have a clear idea of his duties as a believer, regarding women captives as his most precious possession. In such an atmosphere of political tension it is obvious that the equality of all believers preached by Muhammad had reached an impasse.

However, we must keep in mind the chronology of events. When the Battle of Hunayn took place, Islam was already victorious. But the women had brought up the question of war and booty well before, during the hard times, years 4 to 8 of the Hejira, between the defeat of Uhud and the taking of Mecca, the period when the morale of the troops was at zero, when Muhammad's credibility as a military leader was seriously impaired. We cannot understand the turning against women if we do not keep the military context in mind. We have already seen at Hunayn that a victorious Prophet is always more or less at the mercy of his troops. What power of negotiation does he have with his soldiers when he cannot even let them dream of booty? We have seen the Prophet imploring the aid of Allah during the Battle of Badr. Without military success there would be no Islam. The Prophet's margin for maneuver in a city dominated by a war economy was very limited.[71]

Applying the principle of social equality added the risk of even more trouble. It destabilized the family by giving women the right as believers to claim equality, since henceforth piety would be the only criterion for ranking in the hierarchy. "Lo! the noblest of you, in the sight of God, is the best in conduct."[72] Giving women the right to paradise posed fewer problems than giving them the right to inheritance and booty, which greatly increased the sacrifices that the male believer had to make to Allah. If men had need of God, God also had need of men.

Faced with this difficult choice – equality of the sexes or the survival of Islam – the genius of Muhammad and the greatness of his God shows in the fact that at least at the beginning of the seventh century the question was posed and the community was pushed to reflect about it. It is a debate that fifteen centuries later politicians are calling alien to the culture, alien to the Sunna, the Prophet's tradition. A prophet is above all a man who masters the art of the sacred dance between an idealistic God, who is far away, alien, celestial, and men who suffer as prisoners of a world in which violence and injustice rage. During Muhammad's lifetime, prophets – or rather false prophets, as they are called by Muslim historians – were found throughout the Arabian peninsula, as for example in Yemen, where there were "al-Ansi, and in the Yamama, where there was Musaylima, the most famous one. He was a man of great charm, of great eloquence, who knew how to express himself in beautiful, rhyming language."[73] Musaylima considered himself the rival of Muhammad, to whom he proposed a partnership: "I am a prophet like Muhammad", he declared to crowds in the Yamama, "and half of the earth belongs to me, the other half to him."[74] He often appealed to nationalist sentiment to convince his listeners: "You will not find a better prophet than me. Why do you follow a foreign prophet?"[75]

Women also took up the career of prophet, one of them being Sajah Bint al-Harith Ibn Suwayd, whom the poets of her tribe glorified in song: "Our prophet is a woman on whom we lavish our praise, While other people have men for prophets."[76] She committed the rash act – rash for a prophetess – of letting herself be guided by her feelings and falling in love with Musaylima to the point of marrying him:

When she first claimed prophethood, she denied that of the impostor Musaylima; later she believed in his mission. Before she claimed to be a prophetess, she was a diviner and asserted that she practiced the same art as Satih, Ibn Salama . . . and other diviners. She went to Musaylima, who married her.[77]

All the prophets, men and women, whom Muslim tradition calls false, failed because they did not master that dance between the divine and the human, that intense desire to soar to Heaven, to burst the earthly bounds, to go to God, to become God. If Musaylima failed miserably, it was because, like many politicians of our day, he confused prophecy and demagoguery, making the fatal error of believing that the success of a prophet lies in his ability to charm the mob:

> Musaylima gave religious institutions to his compatriots; he exempted them from praying and declared fornication and wine lawful. These laws pleased them, and they acknowledged him as a prophet and accepted his religion. He gave speeches that were rhymed, not rhythmic, speeches that he claimed to have received from Heaven.[78]

Contrary to what Musaylima believed, being a prophet means pushing people to the utmost, toward an ideal society. Being a prophet means teaching a Medina merchant, who cannot see beyond the lure of booty, that a woman can be something other than a captive. Being a prophet means showing a boorish man, the prisoner of his passions and egotism, new horizons, unsuspected relationships. And Muhammad was the ultimate prophet, a creator of horizons so vast that merely contemplating them makes one giddy. The worthy Companions of the years AD 624, 625, and 627 tried to cope with it; they staggered, one step forward, one step back. They made progress as best they could.

This matter of women, as disturbing as it was for the men, did have one positive aspect for them: it forced them to close ranks. More than ever they realized that they needed each other to defend themselves against attacks – in their own households as well as on battlefields. Discord and enmity evaporated, giving place to a revitalized solid front. But to form a serious opposition they needed a leader, someone who also was highly regarded by the Prophet. And to women's misfortune, they found a towering one – 'Umar Ibn al-Khattab, the Prophet's favorite Companion.

8

'Umar and the Men of Medina

Before becoming a Muslim, 'Umar belonged to the elite of the tribe of Quraysh, and was one of Muhammad's bitterest enemies.[1] He blamed Muhammad for "sowing dissension in the ranks of the tribe, finding fault with their cults, and insulting their deities."[2] The Prophet took great pride in 'Umar's conversion. With him he gained for his cause one of the ablest men of Mecca. Once converted, "'Umar turned against the Quraysh and fought them until he forced his way to the Ka'ba [the holy site]. He was the first to dare to say the *salat* [prayer] there, and we prayed with him."[3]

Muhammad, who had already admired him before his conversion, held him in special regard. He loved him for his intransigence in the face of injustice, and gave him the nickname of al-Faruq (he who has the power of discernment), because he had an infallible ability to sort out the true from the false, which was not an easy thing for new converts.[4] He also valued his critical spirit. According to 'Umar, an Arab "should ascertain for himself where his chief is leading"; he should not just blindly follow his orders.[5]

When 'Umar later became caliph, he was the exemplary caliph one who makes us love Islam in our first school history books. He was a governor who listened to the people he governed, and who, above all, pushed honesty and disdain for riches to the point of penury:

'Umar lived simply, wore coarse garments, and was very strict about everything concerning the worship of God . . . . His attire consisted of a woolen tunic [*jubba*] patched with pieces of leather and other materials, and a cloak [*abaya*] in which he wrapped himself. Despite his great dignity, he did not hesitate to carry a waterskin on his shoulder. His mount was customarily a camel to which he attached his baggage with a palm-fiber cord. These were also the customs of his representatives, notwithstanding the extent of the empire and the abundance of wealth that God had given them.[6]

Although 'Umar had many marvelous qualities, the Muslim chroniclers, who recorded everything about a historical personality, including faults, also depicted his fiery, violent character with women. Al-Tabari already noted that a woman refused to marry him when he was caliph with the imposing title of *amir al-mu'minin* (prince of believers), a title that he was the first to bear. She refused to marry him "because he was rough and harsh with women." The woman in question was 'A'isha's sister, Umm Kulthum.[7]

So it was not just by chance that he became the spokesman for the men's resistance to the Prophet's egalitarian project. A man of exceptional charisma, he supported the maintenance of the status quo in the domain of the family. For him, as for the many Companions that he represented, the changes that Islam was introducing should be limited to public life and spiritual life. Private life should remain under the rule of pre-Islamic customs, customs that Muhammad and his God rejected and condemned henceforth as out of step with the new system of Muslim values, which emphasized the equality of all, including equality of the sexes. The men were prepared to accept Islam as a revolution in relations in public life, an overturning of political and economic hierarchies, but they did not want Islam to change anything concerning relations between the sexes. In family matters and relations with women, they felt at ease with the pre-Islamic traditions. This was especially true of Meccans like 'Umar, who on their arrival in Medina were surprised by the freedom of thought and action of the women of Medina: "We men of

Quraysh dominate our women," he said. "When we arrived in Medina, we saw that the Ansar let themselves be dominated by theirs. Then our women began to copy their habits."[8] 'Umar had reason to be alarmed, because one of the admirers of the Ansari women was none other than his own wife.

One day 'Umar was having an argument with his wife and waited as usual for her to accept his shouting with bowed head, according to the custom of Quraysh. But she did nothing of the sort: "As I was railing at my wife, she answered me in the same tone of voice. Responding to my reproaches for her acting like that, she said: 'You reproach me for answering you! Well, by God, the wives of the Prophet answer him, and one of them ran away from him until nightfall.'"[9]

What 'Umar feared had happened. The autonomy of the Ansari women and their rejection of any supervision had invaded the households of Quraysh. His own wife, whom he had kept so well subdued in Mecca, now was standing up to him and justifying her behavior by citing the model man – the Prophet. And 'Umar could scarcely demand better treatment from his wives than the Prophet asked. If the wives of the Prophet raised their voices and freely expressed their anger in the presence of their husband, the Companions would have to adapt to the new situation. Those who had decided to follow the Prophet knew that they had chosen a difficult path. But to be expected to live with sedition at home was a demand that far exceeded their capacity for absorbing change.

'Umar was not content with just rebuking his wife. Concerned about the spread of the revolt, he hurried to his daughter Hafsa, who was one of the wives of the Prophet, to question her about the situation. 'Umar recalls the incident this way:

> "Oh, Hafsa," I cried, "is it true that yesterday one of you had a fit of anger with the Prophet and sulked until nightfall?"
> "Yes," she responded.
> "You are in the wrong and you will regret it," I went on. "Aren't you afraid that God will be vexed because of the anger of the Messenger of God and strike you down? Don't make demands on the Prophet, don't answer him back.

Don't be sulky with him. Come to me for what you want."[10]

But he did not just speak to his own daughter. He zealously preached to the other wives of the Prophet the model of docility toward their husband. He made the rounds of the Prophet's other wives, exhorting them to never raise their voice in his presence. There was no problem until he came to Umm Salama. She was offended by his attitude. How did he, 'Umar, dare to interfere in her private life, her relationship with her husband, and give her advice on that subject? She did not hesitate for a moment in putting him in his place. And she did it in front of the other wives of the Prophet, who were delighted with her courage:

> Why are you interfering in the Prophet's private life? If he wanted to give us such advice, he could do it himself. He is quite capable of doing it. If not to the Prophet, then to whom are we supposed to address our requests? Do we meddle in what goes on between you and your wives?[11]

'Umar had many good qualities, but subtlety and tact were not his strong points. When Abu Bakr became caliph after the death of the Prophet, he began to be concerned about his successor and asked the opinion of his entourage about 'Umar as a possible candidate. Many complained of his *ghilda* – an untranslatable mixture of rigidity, impulsiveness, and obtuseness.[12]

After the exchange between 'Umar and Umm Salama, the other wives of the Prophet came in a delegation to thank her. They admired her courage and would have liked to behave like her. But they did not have her strength of character.[13]

When 'Umar finally decided to inform the Prophet of his fears and the danger that men were running, the Prophet responded with a smile.[14] The Prophet's smile was more than a smile. It was his most persuasive weapon. Paradoxically, among the Arabs – who glorified the fierce warrior in their poems – the Prophet's smile and gentleness radiated a powerful charisma. "His face had such a sweet expression that one hated to leave his presence."[15]

The different attitudes of the Prophet and 'Umar about the danger of a potential revolt by the women of Quraysh –

nonchalance on the part of the former and great agitation on the part of the latter – reflected more than just differences in personality. It represented two totally different visions of marital relations – and especially the use of violence toward women. The Prophet astonished his entourage by his gentleness toward his wives. Many of the Companions, with 'Umar in the lead, did not hesitate to slap theirs. It was concerning this problem of physical violence that the clash between women's demands and men's stiff opposition came to a head. The split in the community that it implied put the survival of Islam in danger.

DEBATE ON SEXUAL PRACTICES

As 'Umar feared, it was the Ansari women who forced into the open the breach between the women supported by the Prophet (often, it is true, just by listening to them), and the male population with 'Umar as their spokesman. And this time God decided against his own Prophet, for the very survival of monotheism was threatened.

Two incidents sparked things off. The first concerned an Ansari woman's refusal to submit to certain sexual positions that her husband demanded. The second involved a marital dispute in which the husband used violence. In both cases, the women hastened to the Prophet and called on him to intervene as arbiter. As his arbitration was dependent on the divine will, Muhammad waited for a revelation from Heaven – and Heaven supported the men. Throughout these incidents, Umm Salama and 'Umar played the role of intermediary with Muhammad, she speaking for her sex and he for his, defending their interests.

What exactly was involved? The people of Quraysh "had sexual intercourse with their wives from in front and from behind," and this latter position was unknown among the Medinese.[16] An Ansari woman went to see Umm Salama and asked her to put the question to the Prophet. As was his custom, the Prophet summoned the person concerned in order to communicate the response revealed by Heaven. When the woman came, the Prophet/arbiter/legislator recited verse 233 of sura 2, which gives to men alone the right of decision regarding sexual positions: "Your women are a tilth for you (to cultivate) so go to your tilth as ye will."[17] Using an impressive collection of testimonia, al-Tabari shows us that this verse, far from closing the debate, did nothing but start it up again. Some people said that the verse permitted sodomy, others that it forbade it, and the argument also extends to vaginal intercourse, from behind.

We are faced – and al-Tabari along with us – with one of those ambiguous verses, susceptible to various interpretations, which require the imam who undertakes to explicate the Koran to be doubly vigilant. The fussy, hairsplitting al-Tabari takes every precaution: 41 testimonia, opinions, and views are minutely examined. Some of them maintain that the verse sanctifies men's right to sodomize their wives. No point of view is ignored. Even the most ridiculous have the right to be cited: "'Abd al-Rahman told me . . . someone had said to Yazid Ibn Aslam: 'Muhammad Ibn al-Munkadir advises men not to sodomize their wives.' Yazid said: 'By Muhammad, I testify that I heard Muhammad Ibn al-Munkadir say that he practiced it himself.'"[18]

What is certain is that with this verse Heaven supported the men. They had the right to use the positions that they wanted; women had no right to protest; they had only to submit to men's whims. In any case, this verse excluded women from the debate, and by so doing transformed the question, which was thus reduced to the following: Do men have the right to sodomize their wives?

Moreover, one explicit version of this debate rewrote the history of its origin, suppressing the Ansari woman's question and substituting for it a male problem. In this version, it was no longer women who initiated the debate, but men. While chatting with each other and exchanging confidences about different sexual positions, they stumbled onto the subject of sodomy. They noted that they did not know exactly what Islam's stand on this practice was. So they decided to go to the Prophet and put the question to him.

Another version brings a Medinese Jew onto the scene. He was having a discussion with a Muslim, who confided in him that he had intercourse with his wife from behind. Horrified, the Jew cried: "But you are like the beasts; we [that is, the Jewish community] have only one way of making love with our wives."[19] Still another version says that in fact Allah intervened because a Jew had told the Muslims: "When a man has intercourse with his wife from behind, the child who is born from such copulation will be blemished; it will be crosseyed."[20] With verse 223 of sura 2 Allah invalidated what the Jew had said (though here, of course, sodomy is not in question).

The particularly revealing debate concerning this verse allows us to grasp the depth of the problem that this book seeks to make clear: the use of the sacred by men to legitimize certain privileges, whether they be of a political or a sexual nature. Three centuries later, when al-Tabari in his role as imam was trying to help the believer clarify the meaning of the verse, the debate was still going! And still today they are arguing about whether a Muslim does or does not have the right to sodomize his wife! What seems important to me is that a debate in Islamic religious literature is never closed. Each generation takes it up where the previous one left it to discuss it again, although there has been no useful progress. Why? In brief, because a civilization that rules the life of millions of individuals must evolve general principles without letting itself be sucked into casuistry and empiricism. Al-Tabari, as brilliant as he was, did not help his contemporaries to resolve this question, leaving it bogged down in observations that are strangely reminiscent of the time of the *jahiliyya* (the era of ignorance). Observations like: "Yes, I have the right to sodomize"; and "No, you don't have the right to sodomize." He did not try to evolve principles that codified what is permitted and what is forbidden in the heterosexual sex act by recalling the equality of the partners as believers. He did not go beyond the incident to arrive at the principle that the sex act depends on two distinct free wills; that it is a relationship between two believers with needs and desires that do not necessarily coincide. It was this timidity on the part of the imam toward the necessity to evolve principles that makes the verses so malleable, and makes opportunism in their interpretation a structural, almost institutional, feature of Islam.

Al-Tabari did add a supplementary opinion, his own, which

said that the verse permits the man to have intercourse with his wife when he wishes, as he wishes, from in front or from behind, the essential point being that he must penetrate her through the vagina, the sole spot where insemination is guaranteed.[21] Thus, according to him, sodomy was formally forbidden. But the essential question remained without answer: what principle in Islam regulates the role of the woman during the sex act? Did or did not the free will of a woman as a Muslim person exist? And were there cases where this free will was affirmed and others in which it disappeared? It was the answer to this essential question that the woman tried to obtain from Heaven. The pre-Islamic laws on this matter were very clear: since a woman could be inherited or taken as a hostage and reduced to slavery (contrary to a man, who was in principle physically done away with after the defeat of his tribe), her free will could be suspended in certain situations.

The first Muslim women, by bringing up the questions of inheritance, the right to war and booty, sexual positions, and physical violence, pressed the Prophet to ask the Muslim God to make a declaration on the place of the free will of a woman as a believer in the new community. The imams, by remaining at the level of empirical cases, did not help Islam to develop a theory of the individual, of the sovereign, inviolable, changeless will that would not disappear in certain circumstances.

SLAVERY

Women were not the only ones to find themselves liberated and at the same time confined. Islam's attitude toward slaves is rather similar. The principle of the equality of all believers was set forth by the Prophet and regulated by the Koran, which condemned slavery. Whether the Muslims obeyed the orders of God and his Prophet regarding slavery is another story: "Islam, like its two parent monotheisms, Judaism and Christianity, has never preached the abolition of slavery as a doctrine, but it has followed their example (though in a very different fashion) in endeavouring to moderate the institution and mitigate its legal and moral aspects."[22]

Islam then set forth the principle of equality and took a position against slavery. First of all, "from the beginning to the end of the Preaching, it makes the emancipation of slaves a meritorious act: a work of charity."[23] Various verses encouraged the freeing of slaves as an act of faith, such as verse 177 of sura 2: "It is not righteousness that ye turn your faces to the East and the West; but righteous is he who believeth in Allah and the Last Day and the angels and the Scripture and the Prophets; and giveth his wealth . . . to set slaves free . . ."[24]

The same idea is found in verses 13 of sura 90, 60 of sura 9, and 92 of sura 4. The Prophet set the example by freeing a dozen slaves, among whom was Abu Bakra, whose history we recounted above. Let me simply add that at the siege of Ta'if, of the dozen slaves who responded to the Prophet's call and left the citadel to come and join him upon his announcement that if they converted they would become free men, only Abu Bakra remained with the Prophet. The others "scattered."[25] So it is not necessary to take Muhammad's offer at Ta'if as a mere recruitment tactic. It was a way of showing the egalitarian message of the new religion.

Next Islam affirmed the dignity of a slave as a human being by making rulings that affected "social relations concerning sexual matters," notably the banning of the practice of making women slaves prostitutes. In order to put an end to this prostitution, Islam encouraged the Muslim man to marry "virtuous" slaves. But the most spectacular decision was that authorizing the marriage of free men and women with slaves (Muslims obviously). The Prophet set the example by freeing, before marrying them, some of his wives who had been prisoners of war. This was the case with Juwayriyya Bint al-Harith. After the defeat of her tribe, as a prisoner of war she became part of the booty that fell to the victorious Muslim army. Following the distribution of booty according to the established rules, she became the property of one of the Muslim soldiers, Thabit Ibn Qays. However, as she was of aristocratic origin, she negotiated with him for her release in exchange for a ransom that she was to pay him. When she came to the Prophet to explain her case to him, he was so attracted by her that he proposed another solution: he would pay the ransom that she owed to Thabit, and then he would free her and marry her when she had become a free woman.[26] He did the same with Safiyya, a Jewish prisoner of war who came to him as part of his booty after the expedition against the Jews of Khaybar.

As in the case of women, so in the case of slaves Islam interfered in the private life of individuals and overturned ancient customs. Freeing slaves was one thing, but treating them as equals was quite another. When the Prophet decided to entrust a military command to Usama, the son of Zayd, a slave freed by the Prophet, the troops objected. In fact, the opposition was as fierce as when the women sought to challenge men's prerogatives:

> The Prophet was informed that there was massing and movement of Roman troops at the Syrian border. Despite his illness, he ordered the Muslims to prepare to go to Syria, and he named Usama, the son of Zayd, leader of the expedition. Usama set up camp at the gates of Medina, and the troops began to prepare to go. However, the soldiers complained, saying: "He made the son of his freedman the leader of the Muhajirun, Quraysh, and the Ansar." The Prophet, hearing these words, said: "He is worthy of command. When I placed his father Zayd, the son of Haritha, at the head of the army of Mu'ta, they said the same thing." When Usama came to the Prophet, the Prophet drew him close and told him: "Don't worry about what the men are saying: they said the same thing about your father, and he was most worthy of command. And you are too." He lavished praise and honors on him. Usama returned to camp, and the soldiers, after having finished their preparations, also reported there.[27]

During the Prophet's lifetime, the opposition to his egalitarian project – that all people be free – was strong and persistent. After a generation, the son of a freedman did not seem worthy of military command. Asserting the equality of slaves, as in the case of women, threatened enormous economic interests: "The institution is kept going by only two lawful means: birth in slavery or capture in war."[28] The new religion sought to intervene in both these instances. As for capture, we have already seen at the time of the Battle of Hunayn that a Muslim could not be reduced to slavery by another person. But it was by acting on the question of birth in slavery that Islam overturned the system in a definitive fashion: it declared free a child born of a union between a free man and a slave woman. However, despite all the declarations of principle clearly defined in revealed verses and despite the example set by the Prophet, Muslim society remained a slave society for centuries and only renounced it under pressure from the colonial powers in the twentieth century. It is important to follow this history of slavery in order to understand the attitude toward women that has persisted right up until the present day.

Since Islam condemned slavery, how was it able to continue to exist? Through linguistic and legal tricks, as always. There would be quibbles about the identity of a slave. Islam forbids that a Muslim be reduced to slavery? Never mind, we will look elsewhere. It will be non-Muslims who will be made slaves. The era of the great Muslim conquests was used to reduce conquered peoples to slavery. Slavery in Islam could only subsist through "the constantly renewed contributions of peripheral or external elements, either directly captured in war or imported commercially, under the fiction of Holy War, from foreign territory."[29] The "foreign territory" was designated by the name *dar al-harb*, the house of war, as distinguished from the house of peace, the land of Islam. Because of the contradiction they pose for the principle of equality, slavery and the fate of the slave are constant themes in studies by philosophers and historians as well as the *fuqaha* (religious scholars).[30]

Forty years after the death of the Prophet, the caliph Mu'awiya bought some women slaves (who at that time were usually called *jariya*) to give as a bribe to his political rival, Husayn, the son of 'Ali. The case of Hawa, that *jariya* whom the Muslim caliph gave as a gift some decades after the death of the Prophet, is all the more revealing since she was acquainted with the Koran. What is even more troubling is that here we have a woman who was acquainted with the holy book, but who had not been encouraged to become Muslim. "Someone brought a *jariya* to Mu'awiya, and he found her pleasing. He asked her price. They told him she cost a thousand dirhams. He bought her . . . and he gave her to Husayn, the son of 'Ali. He sent her to him laden with money and clothing."[31] Husayn was a fervent believer, who practiced his religion. When he received the slave as a gift, he asked her some preliminary questions and immediately decided to free her. Their dialogue, in its very simplicity, condemns Mu'awiya as caliph, as the successor to Muhammad at the head of the Muslim community. The historical record specifically mentions that Husayn was "extremely taken with the beauty of the *jariya*." Their dialog went as follows:

Husayn: What is your name?
Slave: Hawa [desire].
Husayn: Your name suits you well. What can you do?
Hawa: I read the Koran and I recite poetry.
Husayn: Read me something from the Koran.
Hawa: "And with Him are the keys of the invisible. None but He knoweth them." [Sura 6, verse 59.]
Husayn: And now can you recite some poems?
Hawa: May I speak freely? Do you guarantee my safety?
Husayn: Yes.
Hawa: Your company would give perfect happiness, if you could last forever. But it is certain that a human is by nature ephemeral.[32]

Husayn, the historian tells us, began to weep and said to Hawa: " 'You are free, and all the riches that Mu'awiya sent belong to you.' . . . And he rose to say his prayers."[33]

It would be an exaggeration to say that all Muslims continued to be slave owners. To understand the evolution of a given phenomenon in a society, whether in the past or the present, it is always necessary to be able to distinguish the different social levels of that society, the interactions between them, and their relationship to power. Husayn Ibn 'Ali renounced the caliphate because he did not have the cynicism necessary to succeed in politics. His attitude toward Hawa, that slave who handled the sacred text and poetry with intelligence, is a reflection of his personality in general, just as Mu'awiya's attitude toward that same Hawa expresses his. The story of slavery ends when, the colonizers having had to strongly pressure the Muslim states to make them permanently ban slavery, the Geneva international convention of September 25, 1926 was submitted to the states for signing. Almost all signed. Almost all, because among those who refused to ratify it were Saudi Arabia and Yemen. Only in 1924 did Iraq ban slavery; Egypt guaranteed individual freedom in its constitution of 1923. And finally Morocco abolished slavery in a memorandum of the French administration during the Protectorate.

So we see that Muslims, beginning in the seventh century, could have started elaborating laws that would have realized the Prophet's dream of an egalitarian society. But it was not until the twentieth century that with much anguish – and under pressure from the "immoral infidels," otherwise known as the colonizers – they renounced slavery.

VIOLENCE TOWARD WOMEN

The first Muslims did not live an exclusively earthly life as we do today. They lived in a time when Heaven and earth together constituted the horizons of the human adventure. Medina in the years AD 622 (the year of the Hejira) to AD 632 (the death of the Prophet) was a city where Heaven was accessible to all.

The Prophet was constantly importuned. Al-Bukhari reports a Hadith in which the Prophet was so sought after and petitioned by men and women in search of knowledge that he begged them to leave him in peace: "'Umar said: 'When the conflicts and disputes brought to the Prophet grew in numbers, he, feeling harassed, said to them: "Go away! Leave me in peace." ' "[34] Ibn Sa'd reports that "when the Prophet rose to go home, the people crowded around him and followed him."[35] Allah was obliged to intervene to protect the tranquility of His messenger, pursued by a community avid for knowledge and intoxicated by direct contact with the God of power, the God of law, the ideal God: "Lo! those who call thee from behind the private apartments, most of them have no sense./And if they had had patience till thou camest forth unto them, it had been better for them."[36] God could be approached at any moment, questioned about this or that conflict, and called upon to settle it. And His messenger on earth was besieged by a crowd of believers who shouted at his door, probably angry over conflicts in a society that was in a state of revolution: "O ye who believe! Lift not up your voices above the voice of the Prophet, nor shout when speaking to him as ye shout one to another."[37]

The Prophet was in his sixties when he died in the year AD 632. The suras we are discussing were revealed during the last eight years of his life. At that time he had to deal with serious military problems and often went off on expeditions. When he returned home, instead of finding rest, he was harassed by hordes of women and men who came to shout about their conflicts at his door. He no longer had the energy and vigor of youth. By contrast, 'Umar, who was twelve years younger than the Prophet (like the Prophet, he died at the age of 63, in AD 644),[38] was in the prime of life, and his influence on the Prophet was growing.

While the debate on sexual positions was stirring up Medina and pitting women and men against each other, with God and His Prophet as arbiters, a new subject of scandal swept the city: a man had beaten his wife.

The imams, who devote their life to explaining the divine will, could have developed an egalitarian Islam based on the verse that Umm Salama obtained from Heaven (sura 33, verse 35), which established the principle of equality between the sexes. But instead of citing that verse, they brandished verse 34 of the sura on women, which is a verse in flagrant contradiction to the one we will henceforth call Umm Salama's verse, doubly so, since it introduces access to wealth as a factor in establishing social hierarchies, a very disputed question in the Islamic community: "Men are in charge of women, because Allah hath made the one of them to excel the other, and because they spend their property (for the support of women)."[39]

How are we to explain this double retreat from the initial egalitarian message? Not only is the inequality between the sexes reestablished, but in addition it is justified by the access of men to wealth, from which women are excluded. Before examining the circumstances surrounding the revelation of this verse, we need to recall that pre-Islamic Arab society was one of unparalleled violence toward women, with the degree of the violence varying by class and treatment differing between the slave and the Qurashi aristocrat.[40] If we continue the reading of this verse, we realize that it sanctifies the right of men to strike their wives in case of *nushuz* – that is, rebellion against male authority: "As for those from whom ye fear rebellion [*nushuz*], admonish them and banish them to beds apart, and scourge them. Then if they obey you, seek not a way against them."[41]

During a violent dispute an Ansari man slapped his wife. The injured woman hurried to the Prophet and demanded that he, as *hakam* (that is, arbiter in the legal sense), apply the law of retaliation, and that he take action on the spot. Muhammad was preparing to make his decision to fulfill her request when the verse was revealed. God had decided otherwise. Muhammad realized that as an individual he could be in conflict with God. So the Prophet summoned the husband, recited the verse, and told him: "I wanted one thing, and God wanted another."[42] But alongside this difference between God and His Prophet, we must point out another, one that put the Prophet in conflict with 'Umar.

On the question of women there were apparently two very distinct opinions in Medina: that of the Prophet, who advised against the use of violence toward women; and the contrary opinion represented by 'Umar. How was it that this difference in the two men's opinions was not resolved in the long run by an affirmation of the Prophet's attitude in the spirit of Muslim laws? How can we account for the fact that such an important disagreement between the Prophet and 'Umar, on violence toward women, was not made the subject of syntheses and treatises of *fiqh* which put the Sunna (the Prophet's tradition) into perspective for the believer? There are so many questions that lead us to think that a thorough, methodical study of the religious literature remains to be done, a study that will enrich our vision of the ancient texts, which up until now have been left solely to the theologians and legal scholars. The majority of these, especially today, talk in terms of power and as a result are not interested in egalitarian perspectives, which are the ones that interest us here. In any case, what is certain is that the Prophet abhorred violence toward women and stubbornly adhered to that attitude:

The Prophet said: "Do not beat women." And in fact people renounced it. And then 'Umar came looking for the Prophet and said to him: "Messenger of God, women are rebelling against their husbands." The Prophet authorized them to beat them, but he said: "A crowd of women is gathered tonight around Muhammad's family. There are seventy women who have come to complain about their husbands."[43]

What is implied by the concept of *nushuz* that we have seen in verse 34 of sura 4? It is such a dangerous rebellion on the part of women that it entitles men to use violence against them when all violence between believers is formally forbidden.

Muslim commentators explain that *nushuz* means a rebellion by women, a refusal to obey their husband in the matter of the sex act. It is not just infidelity that is meant here. The most grave offense, according to them, is women's refusing themselves to their husband. In his attempt to elucidate this verse, al-Tabari says:

> *Al-nushuz* means that the wife treats her husband with arrogance, refuses to join him in the marital bed; it is an expression of disobedience [*al-ma'siya*] and an obvious unwillingness to any longer carry out what obedience to the husband requires. It is a way of showing hatred [*bughd*] and opposition [*i'rad*] to the husband.[44]

A verse that is taken literally by the imams of today as authorizing violence against female Muslims posed a very grave problem for al-Tabari. He felt it necessary to clarify its context and limit its scope in order to be certain that it did not constitute a pretext for *fitna*, violence among Muslims. He devoted 27 pages of commentary to it, and included not less than 200 conflicting opinions on the meaning of it. Al-Tabari, who wrote a century after Ibn Sa'd and often referred to his work, knew that beating a woman was not part of the Prophet's tradition.

"The Prophet never raised his hand against one of his wives, nor against a slave, nor against any person at all."[45] The only time when the Prophet was confronted with a domestic revolt, a rebellion by some of his wives, not only did he not beat them, but he preferred to leave his home and, to the great surprise of the city, to move for almost a month to a room adjoining the mosque: "The Prophet stayed away from his wives for 29 nights. He was so angry with them that he declared that he would not go back home for a month, and God censured him for this."[46] Apparently such an attitude did not become commonplace, and the split between the Prophet and his Companions on the subject of violence toward women was already taking shape: "The Prophet was always against the beating of women, and people used to say to him: 'Prophet of Allah, they [the women] are sowing disorder.' "[47] The Companions still did not understand why the Prophet acted with such clemency, not to say weakness; he told them: "Very well, beat them, but only the worst ones among you will have recourse to such methods."[48]

'Umar had no scruples about seizing this opportunity, and history has retained at least two examples of his acting in this manner. He beat his own sister Fatima so violently that he left marks on her[49] when he learned that not only had she been converted to the alien religion of Muhammad, but that she was organizing meetings at her house where fervent readings and explanations of the Koran were taking place.[50] The second time that 'Umar resorted to violence was against his wife, Jamila Bint Thabit. He confided to the Prophet that he had given her a slap "that knocked her to the ground."[51] Jamila was an Ansari woman who belonged to the tribe of Aws.[52]

Ibn Sa'd, who lived four generations before al-Tabari,[53] emphasized the Prophet's refusal to give in on the question of violence:

> The Prophet had always persisted in his opposition to the beating of women. And men came to the Prophet to complain about women. Then he gave them permission, while saying: "I cannot bear seeing a quick-tempered man beat his wife in a fit of anger."[54]

Knowing the Prophet's categorical attitude toward physical violence, how does al-Tabari interpret that very problematical verse 34 of sura 4?

He begins, as always, by lining up the testimonials and opinions, and then concluding: "The verse saying that 'Men are in charge of women' means that they can discipline them, put them in their place when it comes to their duties toward God and toward their husband, and this is because Allah has given authority to some of you over others."[55] The authority, he tells us, results from the *sadaq* (dowry) that men pay to their wives when the marriage contract is concluded, and from the *nafaqa* (providing for them during marriage). It is because they spend their wealth on them that men have authority over women. But although all the experts cited agree on men's supremacy over women, there is no unanimity on the extent of that power, particularly when it is a question of *nushuz*, rebellion in the matter of sex.

If a woman refuses to give herself in sexual relations, should the man force her or simply treat her with coolness? Should he be cool toward her while still sharing the bed with her? Or should he sleep separately, expelling the subversive woman from his bed? Should he stop speaking to her but nevertheless share a bed with her? Or, on the contrary, should he continue to speak to her while evicting her from his bed? Finally, should he stop speaking to her but force her to have sexual relations anyway? Totally perplexed, the poor *fuqaha* were in a dither.

Let us continue with al-Tabari, who analyzes the verse phrase by phrase in his usual way. What is the meaning of "As for those from whom ye fear rebellion [*nushuz*], . . . banish them to beds apart"? Some say that "the man should share the wife's bed after having verbally persuaded her to reconsider her decision [to refuse herself], but he should turn his back on her, and if he 'mounts' her, he should do it without saying a word to her."[56] Others find that this interpretation is completely wrong and that the verse clearly says that they must be banished from the bed (*al-hajr*). So it is not just a question of merely ceasing to speak to the rebel; she must be deprived of the joy of the shared bed: "You must not go near their bed, at least until they make a retraction and return to their initial attitude and adopt the behavior that you wish."[57] But one of the authorities cited, Qatada, does not view it like this. According to him, you must proceed by stages: "You begin with verbal persuasion: 'Listen, descendant of Adam . . .' [etc.]. If she persists in her refusal, you banish her from your bed."[58]

Al-Tabari keeps for himself the privilege of the last word: "The Prophet told us: 'A Muslim is forbidden to use the refusal of verbal communication with another person as a punishment for a period exceeding three days.'" So, he concludes, the banishment that the verse speaks of cannot refer to verbal communication. And, he adds, "if the wife is in open rebellion and repudiates her husband's authority, not talking to her and avoiding seeing her will fill her with joy."[59] What advice can he give the rebuffed husband? Al-Tabari, so serious, so pious, so respectful of the Prophet's intention, commits what many *fuqaha* and imams acknowledge to be a mistake. He advises the believer to just simply tie up the rebel: "'Banish them to beds apart' means tying them to their bed." His argument is a linguistic one: "*Al-hijar*," he explains, "is the rope with which the Arabs tie up their camels."[60]

Mahmud Shakir, who died recently, was an erudite scholar who edited, annotated, and prefaced the new edition of al-Tabari's work, and who stated that he did it in order to keep Islam from being used by the fanaticism of our contemporaries. And he could only disavow al-Tabari on this point: "Al-Tabari's interpretation of the meaning that should be given to the word *hajr*, linguistically reducing it to the root meaning 'attach' . . . is most decidedly a strange interpretation!" And he cites a long list of *fuqaha* and imams who found al-Tabari gravely in error: "What a failing on the part of a great expert on the Koran and the Sunna," concludes Shakir. "What a failing on the part of a man so expert in religious scholarship and the Arabic language."[61]

This gives us an idea of the difficulty that the interpretation of verse 34 of sura 4 poses and of why modern politicians, who have not succeeded in assimilating the concept of democracy, use it to legitimize their fanaticism, never stopping for a moment to consider the enormous difficulty it has posed, and still poses, to those who make some effort to respect the divine will. They use it today to affirm male supremacy, as if this were a verse without ambiguity, without differences in interpretation, without conflict.

The Prophet, beset by Companions of both sexes and their contradictory demands, troubled by divine revelations that went counter to his aims, influenced by 'Umar, who represented tradition, deep-seated reflexes, and customs, knew that he had to use his influence in the most reliable manner – that is, the one least likely to be challenged. He had to win military victories, channel the energy of the believers into religious war, and regain his position as leader of the community.

9

The Prophet as Military Leader

Many of us have an idyllic picture of Medina in our minds, a distortion fostered by the lessons in *tarbiya islamiyya* (Islamic education) that we studied in primary school, which simplified for us the story of the Prophet. We were taught that, opposed by his own people, he was obliged to emigrate to Medina. When he arrived in Medina, he was joyfully received by the people, with young girls coming to meet him singing the famous "The moon has risen over us" (*tala'a al-badru 'alayna*), the moon being Muhammad, the new arrival who was going to transform everything with his gentleness and wisdom.

The end of the school year during which we studied the life of the Prophet was celebrated at a fête organized by our teacher. Standing on a shaky platform decorated for the occasion, and with our heads encircled with jasmine, we sang for an audience of proud parents "The moon has risen over us." And a moonlit Medina was for ever inscribed in our memory, along with the national anthem and all the songs in which Morocco, the Atlas mountains, the sun, happiness, and the future are magically (and tightly) entwined to shape our childhood. Together they form the poetry that is the basis of our political consciousness.

But as an adult, when you look at the city to which for ten years Muhammad strove to bring his enlightenment, you see the narrow streets of a city like any other, a city at war with progress and freedom, a city in which Muhammad suffered, as the history books written for adults tell us. He suffered because of rumors circulated about him, whispers that his young, beautiful wives would marry younger husbands after his death. They said that he was no longer as sexually vigorous as before. They said that his favorite wife was deceiving him. They hit at his most vulnerable point a man who wanted to be as successful in his private life as in his public life and who insisted on the impossibility of separating them.

I want to suggest here that during the years that interest us – from year 3 (the defeat at Uhud) to the beginning of year 8 (the conquest of Mecca) – the Prophet's project for equality of the sexes foundered because he refused to minimize the sexual aspect of life, to hide it, to consider it marginal or secondary. The Prophet was in a vulnerable position. His aims came to nothing because he always refused to separate his private life and public life. He could only conceive of the sexual and the political as being intimately linked. He would go to prayer directly upon leaving 'A'isha's bed, using the small door that linked her room to the mosque. Despite 'Umar's advice, he continued to go on expeditions accompanied by one or two of his wives, who, accustomed to being directly involved in public affairs, moved around freely and inquired about what was going on. One scene in al-Tabari depicts 'Umar as being beside himself at seeing 'A'isha strolling around the battlefront beside the trenches: "But what brings you here?" he cried out. "By my life, your boldness borders on insolence! What if a disaster befalls us? What if there is a defeat and people are taken captive?"[1]

The Prophet's wives did not seem to regard political or military problems as being alien to them. They were as much concerned with the liberation of prisoners, an eminently political matter, as with domestic questions. In that same year, year 5 of the Hejira, before the descent of the *hijab*, during the expedition against the Jewish tribe of Qurayza, Umm Salama intervened in a case involving the liberation of a political prisoner who was tied up in the courtyard of the mosque. It was not that she made the decision to release him, but she made her opinion about it known to those who had the decision-making power and awaited their reaction. And the source who reports this incident specifically states that it took place "before the descent of the *hijab*." After having ascertained the Prophet's judgment in the matter, Umm Salama took it upon herself to go inform Abu Lababa of his liberation.[2] So she behaved as if this were a matter in which women had a say. The household was not their sole legitimate domain.

It seems to go without saying that if the verse of the *hijab* came to separate the world of women from that of men, to confine the former to the household and forbid their access to the public sphere, the previous situation was different. The instituting of the *hijab* would have been unnecessary in a situation in which the sexes were already separated and women were excluded from public life. By its very advent, the *hijab* reveals to us a social reality contrary to that which it came to put in place. The descent of the *hijab* during Zaynab's wedding festivities is only understandable if we remember the extraordinary freedom of the Prophet's wives in the public sphere. A woman encouraged by her husband to regard the mosque and the battlefield as fields of action is going to behave differently from a cloistered woman isolated from the world. By acting contrary to the customs of the strongly homosexual armies where the men lived among themselves from morning to night, Muhammad, who retired in the early evening to his tent/household, was bound to disappoint his commanders. His determination to live his relationship with women as a constant and privileged experience was used by his political enemies to attack him, to wound him, to humiliate him, and finally to make him give up his aims for equality of the sexes. His political opponents used his private life as a political weapon against him. They sexualized their political attacks aimed at weakening the Prophet. And all this was happening at a time when he was living through two new and trying experiences: uncertainty in his military career and physical decline due to increasing years.

He was a man of almost 60 and he was surrounded by remarkable and distinguished women like Umm Salama, 'A'isha, and Zaynab. They were women who were younger than he, intelligent, and, above all, actively involved in political life and demands for a different status for women. 'A'isha, his best beloved, was to be the prey that his enemies seized upon to make him suffer, to make him taste the bitter fruit of loss of confidence by accusing her of adultery. Hurt and weakened, he lost his ability

163

to stand up to 'Umar, and he agreed to the confinement of women. He gave his consent to the *hijab*. He gave his consent to the reestablishment of male supremacy.

Year 5 (AD 627) is the one that must be especially brought to mind. The events that relate to it can be easily found in two key suras, where the Prophet's military difficulties and the attacks against his wives are symbolically presented to us as entangled. I refer to sura 4, *An-Nisa* ("Women"), and sura 33, *Al-Ahzab* ("The Clans"). They contain the debates that took place in Medina about equality of the sexes, especially the verses concerning the inheritance rights of women and young girls, the accusation of adultery against 'A'isha, and the descent of the *hijab*; and about the "prayer of fear" (*salat al-khawf*), which the Prophet uttered for the first time during the Battle of Dhat al-Riqa' (at the beginning of year 5), and the famous Battle of the Trench during the siege of Medina (year 5).

It might be useful to recall here that the order of the suras in the Koran is not chronological. Even within the same sura there may be verses that belong to the Meccan period (AD 610–22) and others that belong to the Medinese period (AD 622–32). I agree with what Régis Blanchère, one of the French translators of the Koran, says: "To a certain extent it can be said that today we read the Koran in a reverse fashion, since the first suras, the longest ones, are in general formed from revelations that came to Muhammad near the end of his preaching career."[3] The version of the Koran that we currently read is the version officially established under the third caliph, 'Uthman. We know that the transcription of the Koran was begun during the lifetime of the Prophet,[4] and that the ordering of the suras in 'Uthman's text does not follow the chronology of the revelations. Rather, the version we have today is ordered in a way that the experts tried to justify as responding to a pedagogical need. The Meccan suras, al-Suyuti tells us in his book *The Mysteries of the Ordering of the Koran*, were revealed in a polytheistic context, while the Medinese suras were revealed in a Muslim community that asked questions about the practical details of life. According to him, this explains why many Medinese suras come first in the Koran, because the book is addressed to a Muslim and not to a polytheist.[5] Nevertheless, one problem remains for the experts: how does one find one's bearings if the verses cannot be linked to the events they were meant to clarify, there being no chronological ordering? The chronological order of the revelations is also extremely important in determining the *nasikh* (that which abrogates) and the *mansukh* (that which is abrogated) in cases where there are two contradictory verses concerning the same fact. For example, this is the case concerning the correct attitude toward non-Muslims, especially Jews and Christians. In the Koran there are some verses counseling tolerance toward them, and others counseling holy war and constant struggle. The experts on abrogation devote detailed analyses to the contradictory verses and come to the conclusion that the last revealed verses are the ones that should be taken into account, and therefore it is necessary to situate the verses in time.[6]

The two suras that interest us – 4 and 33 – were revealed at Medina during that pivotal year, year 5 of the Hejira. Not only is this the indication of the 'Uthman text, but also all the experts agree on it. I will refer particularly to al-Suyuti's and Ibn Hazm's ordering of the suras.[7] In the chronological ordering of the 114 suras of the Koran, the sura "The Clans" is number 90 and that called "Women" number 92. We know that the first sura revealed at Medina after the Hejira in 622 is "The Cow," which is number 87 according to the chronological numbering (and number 2 in the textual ordering). The two suras that concern us are placed some years later. So the ordering by the chronology of the revelations, like the ordering by historical events, places sura 4, "The Women," and sura 33, "The Clans," about year 5 of the Hejira – the year of military vicissitudes, the year of the prayer of fear.

According to Ibn Hisham, the first "prayer of fear" (*salat al-khawf*) took place during the Battle of Dhat al-Riqa' in the fifth month of year 4.[8] The Prophet started off on the expedition to Dhat al-Riqa' in the hope of redressing the military situation and living down the defeat at Uhud. But when he came face to face with the enemy, he preferred to avoid a direct challenge: "He met there an enormous massing of the Ghatafan tribes. The two forces drew near, but there was no battle, as the Muslims, like their enemies, were overcome by fear. The Prophet led 'the prayer of fear' and withdrew."[9]

One of the reasons for this fear was that the Muslims could not afford an encounter that would lead to defeat. At the same time they could not afford the luxury of not engaging in battle. They could not fail to act, and yet they knew they were too demoralized by the defeat at Uhud to be able to win any victory at all over their enemy. So the Prophet, in his role as strategist, played an extremely cautious game, in a situation in which the only margin for maneuver that he had was of a symbolic nature. The prayer of fear expressed this perfectly: using symbolism, for lack of being able to use force. We must remember that the first principle of Muhammad's strategy was not to put his soldiers at risk unnecessarily. He wanted to win battles without loss of life.

The Prophet stayed for three days face to face with the enemy army, without deciding to launch his men into battle, haunted as he was by the memory of the disaster at Uhud when "weeping and lamenting, the people of Medina came out of the city searching for dead relatives. They wanted to bring the corpses to Medina. But the Prophet ordered them to be buried there where they had fallen."[10] Since then his troops had not regained that self-confidence that would assure success. The tribal enemies that Tabari calls *A'rab* – that is, bedouin who were non-Muslims – were also demoralized:

> They were camped not far from the army of the Prophet. Then God filled their hearts with fear and they dared not leave their camp. They dreaded the thought of fighting. The two armies, each fearing the other, remained two days facing each other. Then the bedouin [the non-Muslims] fled without giving battle. For three days the Prophet said the prayer of fear, and the following verse was revealed in those circumstances: "And when thou (O Muhammad) are among them . . ."[11]

The prayer of fear is described in verse 102 of sura 4, "Women." It advises the Prophet to cut prayer short when there is an emergency, as, for example, fear of being surprised by the enemy. The prayer of fear consists of organizing the troops so that they will not be in a vulnerable position – for example, all bowing their heads at the same time, as ritual requires. Allah gave precise orders on this subject:

> And when thou (O Muhammad) art among them and arrangest (their) worship for them, let only a party of them stand with thee (to worship) and let them take their arms. Then when they have performed their prostrations let them fall to the rear and let another party come that hath not worshipped and let them worship with thee and let them take their precaution and their arms.[12]

The prayer of fear illustrates the pragmatic dimension of the Muslim God. The believer does not have to carry out a ritual automatically without paying attention to the context, that is, the situation he is in. He should use his judgment in every circumstance, and when he has to choose between prayer and survival, he should not hesitate to choose survival: "Those who disbelieve long for you to neglect your arms and your baggage that they may attack you once for all."[13] One can always find time to think about God when one is out of danger. During the battles the Prophet engaged in after Uhud, his objective was not so much offensive as a defense minutely calculated to maintain his credibility in the eyes of his enemies without giving them the opportunity to take on his troops in hand-to-hand combat. Faced with the strong coalitions that the Meccans were organizing throughout Arabia, Muhammad had to respond to attacks and assert himself as a credible force while never taking the risk of a military engagement that could prove fatal to him.

The Battle of Dhat al-Riqa' ended as the Prophet wanted – it just fizzled out. There was no engagement. The two facing armies did not recklessly throw themselves into battle. Apparently it was a time when the life of a soldier was highly valued, both by Muhammad and by his enemies. This pragmatic approach, which we find in the verse of the prayer of fear, also figures in the tactics that Muhammad adopted during the Battle of the Trench described in sura 33 ("The Clans").

Medina was under siege. The Prophet's enemies and the local opposition against him were increasing. Insecurity prevailed in the city. It was an insecurity that kept all women from going out, even the free women and even those who belonged to the ruling elite, including the wives of the Prophet. For the first time it was not the Prophet who decided the site of confrontation between Meccans and Muslims. In the spring of AD 627 Abu Sufyan, the military leader of Quraysh, at the head of a coalition of 10,000 men, besieged Muhammad in Medina. After intense negotiations Muhammad could only mobilize 3,000 men, and even this only after much effort.[14] The siege promised to be long and relentless, because the nearest neighboring tribes, like the Qurayza (the Medinese Jews), had joined the distant tribes from the Najd in the camp of the enemy under the command of the Meccans.[15] The Prophet decided to use his favorite tactic when the enemy's numerical superiority was indisputable – avoid contact. But how was he to avoid it this time, when the enemy was at the gates of the city? He had recourse to a tactic absolutely unknown at that time among the Arabs – digging a trench around the city to protect it.

Without doubt the idea came to him during a conversation with Salman, a Persian slave whom he had freed. Salman explained to the Prophet that "in Persia when we are besieged, we dig a trench around the city."[16] When the Prophet gave the order to dig the trench, many people were astonished at such an idea, and the *munafiqun*, those Hypocrites among the inhabitants of Medina who were hostile to any idea coming from the Muslim leader, used it to ridicule him. But neither the surprise of his entourage nor the ridicule of the Hypocrites made him give up his project. He commanded the soldiers to exchange their swords for shovels and to put a gap between themselves and the enemy instead of going out to meet them:

> The Prophet gave the order to dig a trench around Medina as deep as twenty cubits and also as wide as twenty cubits. The work was assigned to ten men. The Hypocrites mocked the Prophet for shutting himself up in the city. Nevertheless, he came each day to oversee the work, seated in a tent built for him, so that the men, watched by him, would work with more zeal.[17]

One month later, the work was finished. The enemy soldiers were taken aback at seeing the trench:

> When the infidels saw the trench surrounding Medina, they were astounded, because they had never seen such a thing before. Being unable to cross it, they came each day to the verge of the city. The Prophet remained beside the trench, and no one left the city to fight. He even spent the nights there, while the Hypocrites went back into the city to sleep, saying: "If an accident befalls Muhammad during the night, at least we will be safe in our houses."[18]

The Hypocrites thought that the Prophet had misled them. He had promised conquests, and all he had done was draw the enemy to the gates of the city, which he was about to bring to ruin. Verse 12 of sura 33 describes their fear and their disappointment: "Allah and His messenger promised us naught but delusion."[19]

But they were not the only ones to be terrified. The good believers were also, as verses 9 and 10 of the same sura describe: "O ye who believe! Remember . . . . When they came upon you from above you and from below you, and when eyes grew wild and hearts reached to the throats, and ye were imagining vain thoughts concerning Allah."[20]

After 27 days of siege, the city still held fast. The enemy had lost three men, for from time to time "the two armies shot arrows at each other."[21] However, the siege seemed endless, seriously threatening the psychological stability of the city. It became necessary to take some quick action, in the only way possible for someone with numerically inferior forces. Muhammad decided to engage in psychological warfare by creating some false and some true intelligence and disseminating it to the central command of the enemy forces as well as to their most distant allies. To do this, Muhammad used the services of a new convert in the enemy ranks whom he had secretly contacted. Thanks to this spy, who spread the false rumors in the enemy camp, playing on their suscept-ibilities, the rivalries among allies, and especially the insecurities of the Jewish command, discouragement and mistrust spread among the Meccans.[22] The event that led to the lifting of the siege was a providential storm sent by Allah: "At nightfall God unleashed over the camp of the infidels a wind which overturned all their tents. The enemy was filled with terror."[23] The next day Abu Sufyan lifted the siege and vanished, leaving behind him a city very different from that which existed before the siege. The Prophet knew that a new war was beginning – the kind of war he considered the worst of all – internecine war, internal disorder in the city, *fitna*.

The Koran is a faithful mirror not only of the Prophet's military difficulties, during the siege of Medina for example, but also of the personal attacks on him in which his private life was dissected and criticized by a Medinese opposition that became more and more virulent. Although the Prophet succeeded in avoiding a massacre of the Muslims, the siege of the city sorely tested the inhabitants by the sacrifices required of them for the provisioning and maintaining of an army of 3,000 men.[24] The hostility of one section of the Medinese population led the city to the brink of civil war and a state of the most primitive insecurity. It became impossible for a woman to walk around the city without being harassed. This was even true for the Prophet's wives, who were subjected to harassment when they went out, and even sometimes at home under the very eyes of the Prophet. It is in the light of these events that it is now necessary to reinterpret the verses concerning the *hijab* and al-Tabari's explications of them.

According to al-Tabari, the second part of the verse of the *hijab* – "And it is not for you to cause annoyance to the messenger of Allah, nor that ye should ever marry his wives after him. Lo! that in Allah's sight would be an enormity" – was revealed after a man came to see the Prophet and later began to say that "he intended, after his death, to marry one of his wives, whom he moreover named."[25] In this version the words were not spoken in front of the Prophet but were circulated throughout the city. In another commentary on the Koran, that of Nisaburi, the name of the coveted wife is given, and the man in question is supposed to have been boorish enough to express his wish out loud in front of the Prophet himself and in the presence of the woman concerned. He was 'Uyayna Ibn Hisn, chief of an Arab tribe known for its bad manners. After his conversion to Islam he saw 'A'isha during a visit to the Prophet:

> It is recounted that 'Uyayna Ibn Hisn came to see the Prophet and that he pushed the door open and walked in without asking permission. The Prophet said to him: "'Uyayna, don't you know that good manners require one to ask permission before entering someone's house?"
> "In my whole life, as far as I can remember," responded 'Uyayna, "I have never asked permission from any man."
> Then 'Uyayna said to the Prophet, "Who is that beautiful woman seated beside you?"[26]

When the Prophet told him that she was 'A'isha and that she bore the title of Mother of the Believers, a title that made her forbidden to other men, 'Uyayna put forward a proposition: he would take 'A'isha and as compensation he would give the Prophet an even more beautiful wife, his own. The Prophet coldly told him that "Allah forbids such practices" for Muslims.[27]

Another version informs us that 'A'isha, shocked at hearing 'Uyayna tell the Prophet that he was prepared to give up "the mother of his children" in exchange for herself, could not restrain herself from exclaiming: "But who is this individual?"[28] The Prophet, maintaining his usual calm, explained to 'A'isha that the man in front of her had been chosen by his own people to lead them: "That man you see is the leader of his tribe!"[29]

Some historians report that only one of the Prophet's wives actually remarried after his death, usually known as 'Aliya Bint Zabyan. The Prophet had married her, she had stayed with him for some time, and then he had rejected her. She remarried, say the *fuqaha*, before the verse that forbade remarrying was revealed. However, the historians do not agree on the name of that wife of the Prophet who dared to seek another husband. Some say that she was called 'Alia, others that she was known as Qayla. In any case, embarrassed as they are by this marriage, the Muslim historians do not hide it. According to al-Tabari, she was Qayla Bint al-Ash'ath. She is supposed to have married 'Ikrama Ibn Abi

Jahl after the death of the Prophet during the reign of Abu Bakr. The latter was very distressed, al-Tabari tells us, by this remarriage, which he considered scandalous. But 'Umar reasoned with him that, after all, she was divorced – she was no longer "really" the wife of the Prophet since she had opted to leave him at the time of the verse of choice. This choice given to his wives by the Prophet, to leave him if they wished to, put an end to an intense dispute between the Prophet and his wives.[30] As the leader of the Muslim community, the Prophet was obliged to receive delegations from every corner of Arabia, delegations of people with different outlooks and strange customs and practices, such as the exchange of wives.[31] He used to receive them at home, occasionally in the presence of his wives. Al-Tabari explicitly says that the incident with 'Uyayna took place before the descent of the verse of the *hijab*.[32]

This insistence by the Prophet on not setting up boundaries between his private life and his public life, which allowed his wives to be directly involved in the affairs of the Muslim state, little by little turned against him. It was the breach through which, during the years of crisis, the attacks against him would be launched. People pestered him; they came to his house without permission: "A visitor came to his house without his permission and said, 'May I enter?' The Prophet said to his slave named Rawda: 'Have him leave and teach him some manners. Tell him he should say: "Peace unto you! May I enter?" ' "[33] Sometimes men followed him when he was going home and crowded so close around his table that you could not even reach out to pick up a morsel of food.[34]

It can be argued that it was only the appearance of two new factions among the Hypocrites – namely, *al-ladhina fi qulubihim maradun* (those in whose hearts is a disease) and *al-murjifuna fi al-madina* (those who spread disorder) – that made the Prophet ready to think about the public/private separation instituted by the descent of the *hijab*. If we take the Koran and the standard texts of religious history as references, we find that, up until that time, women were not cloistered and were not in the habit of living shut up in their houses. They used to go out to attend to their personal affairs. Before the harassment began, they usually went out at night, probably because the city, which was sleepy during the day because of the heat, woke up at night: "The wives of the Prophet went out at night to attend to their personal affairs, and some of the Hypocrites placed themselves along their route and harassed them."[35] Verse 60 of sura 33 ("The Clans") suggests that the attacks had reached such a state that God decided to intervene by launching anathemas and threats of punitive measures against the new categories of Hypocrites: "If the hypocrites, and those in whose hearts is a disease, and [those who spread disorder] in the city do not cease, We verily shall urge thee on against them, then they will be your neighbours in it but a little while."[36]

According to al-Tabari, the first category – "those in whose hearts is a disease" – refers to men who exhibit obsessive sexual behavior. In the paragraphs he devotes to verse 60 of sura 33 he says that the verse refers to "those who have obsessive relations with women," to "those who suffer from an uncontrolled desire to fornicate and from a passion to indulge in illicit sex acts."[37] The people in the second category – those who spread disorder – played a pernicious role, especially in the case of the accusation of adultery against 'A'isha, as we will see.

There are thus two kinds of attacks: physical attacks, the harassing of the Prophet's wives when they go out into the streets; and verbal attacks, spreading rumors about them or the Prophet. According to al-Tabari, verse 63 of sura 33 – "O ye who believe! Be not as those who slandered Moses, but Allah proved his innocence of that which they alleged . . ."[38] – refers to the accusation that the people of Moses made against him, that he was *adar*. The *Lisan al-'Arab* dictionary informs us that *adar* is a characteristic of a person who has a testicular hernia, a "swelling of one of the two testicles." In any case, for al-Tabari the verse refers to an accusation of an intimate nature.[39]

Accusations of this kind doubtless originated in the incident already related concerning a dispute between the Prophet and his wives which drove Muhammad to withdraw from them for some days. This incident produced the verse that the imams called "the verse of choice" (*ayat al-takhyir*). Some of the commentaries that have tried to analyze the reasons for the dispute indicate that the dissatisfaction of at least half of the Prophet's nine wives was of an

173

economic kind, and others say it was of a sexual nature.[40] According to the Muslim law of polygyny, the man has to share his nights equally among all his wives, with it being understood that he must not simply sleep peacefully during the nocturnal period. The polygynous husband must be able to sexually satisfy his wives. A frustrated Muslim wife is considered to be a wife who will create *fitna* by seeking satisfaction elsewhere. Al-Tabari explains that verse 51 (of sura 33) exempts Muhammad, by order of Allah himself, from sharing the bed of those of his wives for whom he no longer feels desire. This is obviously an exceptional measure. Moreover, Allah himself cannot force a sexually unsatisfied wife to stay with her husband. The verse of choice, then, gives to those of the Prophet's wives who complained of his recent coldness the choice of leaving him if they so desired.

According to such accepted authorities as al-Tabari and Ibn Sa'd, five of his wives were affected by this verse and only four of the nine continued to enjoy his favors, 'A'isha and Umm Salama obviously being among them.[41] The Prophet, who was in his sixties, had nothing of the old man about him. Despite his age, his hair was still black, he enjoyed good health, and he had undeniable physical charm:

> His nose was straight, his teeth were even. Sometimes he let his hair fall naturally loose, and other times he wore it twisted into two or four locks. At 63 years old the only traces of age that his body showed were 15 white hairs on his head and 10 to 20 white hairs in his beard.[42]

Arab historians accord great importance to the physique of political personalities, which they believe can explain behavior.

Other descriptions emphasize "his walk that was so energetic that one would have said that his feet did not touch the ground, and at the same time so light that he seemed to float along." But, al-Tabari stipulates, "he did not walk haughtily as princes do."[43] So it is not surprising that, when the verse of choice gave permission to leave to those of his wives who were frustrated by the unequal treatment he accorded them and the fact that he did not give them as much affection and caressing as before, only one decided to leave.[44] In terms of this incident, it might be said that the rumors of the Hypocrites were put to rest by a plebiscite on the Prophet by his own wives. When he decided to leave the shelter of the mosque where he had barricaded himself, he returned home and repeated to each of his wives the verse of choice, asking that they make their decision separately. Those who wished to remain had to accept that the Prophet was not obliged to satisfy them sexually and economically. He advised 'A'isha, the youngest, to consult her parents before deciding. She took offense at this and answered that she never asked the opinion of her parents in such matters.[45]

In addition to the rumors that circulated about his sexual performance, there were others that concerned either his marriages or 'A'isha, who was the object of envy and jealousy. Two of the Prophet's marriages – one contracted in year 5, the other in year 7 – were considered scandalous by some.

The first marriage that scandalized Medina was that with Zaynab, his own maternal cousin, after he had insisted that she marry his former slave, Zayd Ibn Haritha. Zaynab, who had always been interested in the Prophet, rebelled when he suggested to her the marriage with Zayd, his former slave whom he had freed and to whom he now was entrusting military commands. He had adopted Zayd and treated him with such fatherly devotion that people called Zayd the son of Muhammad.

According to pre-Islamic customs, adoption established an almost biological parental relationship between an adopted son and his father. When Zayd divorced Zaynab and she married the Prophet in year 5, many people of Medina deemed that marriage incestuous and cried scandal. This would explain why the Prophet insisted on inviting "the whole community" to the wedding feast, as related by Anas Ibn Malik, the Companion who witnessed the revelation of the *hijab*. Moreover, the fact that today most modern Muslim family codes do not recognize adoption as an institution is a result of the verses revealed on the occasion of Zaynab's divorce and in response to rumors circulating in Medina saying that adoption created a relationship of effective parenthood.[46] Most of these codes stipulate that adoption does not create and can never create a parental bond like that created by biological parenthood.

An adopted child, in principle, can never inherit like a biological son. Tunisia, which has legalized adoption, is regarded as an eccentric case very much affected by the pernicious influence of the West.

The other marriage of the Prophet that was controversial was the one with Safiyya Bint Huyayy, a young Jewish captive whom he married after the taking of the city of Khaybar in year 7 of the Hejira.[47] "Khaybar was held by the Jews; it was the strongest of their fortresses. It was composed of seven forts of different sizes surrounded by date groves."[48] Safiyya was the wife of Kinayna, one of the chiefs of the Jewish tribe of Banu Nadir. Safiyya's relatives had fought at the Battle of the Trench on the side of the Meccans.[49] Attracted by the beauty of Safiyya, who had fallen to him as part of his booty, the Prophet "suggested to her that she convert to Islam"; he freed her and married her when she agreed to this condition.[50] According to al-Tabari and Ibn Sa'd, when the Prophet threw his cloak over the new captive after the taking of one of the forts, his entourage understood that he intended to keep her for himself. But Ibn Sa'd adds that "the people asked if he was going to marry her or keep her as *umm walad*." *Umm walad*, "mother of a child," is a slave with whom the master officially maintains sexual relations and whose children will be free.[51] Apparently Safiyya was the exception because her religion was Judaism. The two other women who were not Muslim and with whom the Prophet had a sexual relationship were Maria the Copt, who was given to him by the governor of Alexandria, and Rayhana of the Jewish tribe of Banu Qurayza. Despite the fact that Maria had borne the Prophet a son, Ibrahim, who died at a young age, she was classed with Rayhana among the Prophet's *saraya*, wives who had the status of slaves.[52]

What was surprising in the case of Safiyya was that the Prophet's behavior toward her was not what would be expected in such a case: "The people said to themselves: 'If he imposes the *hijab* on her, we will know that he intends to make her his wife; if not, he will go on treating her as just an *umm walad*.' "[53] *Umm walad* was one of those new legal categories that Islam had instituted to combat the reproduction of slavery, and according to which the children born of a marriage between a free man and his slave were inevitably free beings, whatever their sex. Before Islam, children born of a slave woman and a free father were slaves. One of the reasons why men used their slaves as prostitutes, as we shall see, was that it enabled them to obtain children that they could eventually sell. The status of *umm walad* gave a woman slave the right to have freeborn children who then might inherit everything that could be inherited in the way of wealth and power. This ruling allowed some women to be very ambitious for their children, and some even pushed them to become caliphs.[54]

Coming back to Safiyya, we must not forget that in the middle of a revolution in customs the smallest action of the Prophet had enormous symbolic importance. It was he who showed the Sunna, the way, the new manner of doing the things that were specific to Islam in terms of a break with the past. When the Prophet helped Safiyya onto his mount, he took care to veil her, and then the people knew that he definitely intended to marry her. Freeing a Jewish captive and marrying her, instead of keeping her as a slave, was bound to surprise Medina and especially the Hypocrites, who were looking for things to criticize.

However, between the marriage with Zaynab (year 5) and that with Safiyya, there was an even more serious scandal, which unleashed the tongues of the Hypocrites, who had been relentlessly attacking the Prophet since the defeat at Uhud and the siege of the Battle of the Trench. In year 6 'A'isha was accused of adultery by the Hypocrites. The Muslim *fuqaha* and imams call this incident *al-ifk* (the lie), and the orientalists, looking for the sensational, call it "the affair of the necklace."

During an expedition against Banu al-Mustaliq, on which 'A'isha accompanied the Prophet, she lost a shell necklace from Yemen that she was very attached to. When she learned that they were to leave in a few hours, she began to look for it. When she found it, the caravan had already left. Those who were in charge of placing her litter on the camel believed that she was already in it, because she was so light. When her absence was discovered, the Prophet ordered a halt to wait for her. He began to worry until she appeared on the horizon, accompanied by Safwan Ibn al-

Mu'attal, a young Companion who, having found her *en route*, escorted her.

This was enough to unleash a veritable campaign of defamation against 'A'isha, orchestrated by the leader of the Hypocrites, 'Abdallah Ibn Ubayy, who, as we will see, earned his living by forcing his women slaves to become prostitutes. He is supposed to have exclaimed upon seeing 'A'isha arrive with Safwan: "'A'isha can be excused for what she just did; Safwan is handsomer and younger than Muhammad."[55] The matter took on such importance that the leader of the young Muslim state decided to broach the subject publicly. He mounted the *minbar* and spoke thus to the assembled believers in the mosque: "How does somebody dare to throw suspicion on the house of the Prophet of God?"[56] It was one of the rare occasions in our Muslim history on which a political man came to the defense of his wife instead of taking sides with her accusers. He made the Medinan tribes, the Aws and especially the Khazraj (to which 'Abdallah Ibn Ubayy belonged), face up to their responsibility. With his action in the mosque he transformed a simple rumor into a matter of tribal responsibility: the tribe to which the defamer belonged had to take charge of punishing him. Finally, Heaven intervened: "God revealed seventeen verses on the subject of 'A'isha's innocence."[57]

The affair of the *ifk*, which turned a trivial incident into an affair of state and which came close to introducing *fitna* into Medina, is a good illustration of the desire to humiliate women and put them in their place, which often follows periods in which they acquire some rights and make some gains. 'A'isha, like any intelligent, beautiful woman loved by a powerful man, was not likely to be lacking in egotism and insolence. As a result, she was bound to be the focus of envy, to arouse hate, and to provide an easy means by which to attack the one who held power. Combined with the lack of security that reigned in the streets, the slanders against 'A'isha were to shake the Prophet's faith in the project that was so dear to him – that of a private life open and mingled with public life, with the two of them existing side by side without conflict or barriers. In the face of the insecurity and rumors, his entourage presented a slaveholding solution to him: protect women – free women only – by veiling them. The slaves remained unveiled. This was an implicit acknowledgment that they could be approached and attacked.

In a city on the brink of civil war, in which the number of the Hypocrites had increased dangerously since the siege, the anti-slaveholding policy that Islam sought to promote was officially abandoned – at least as far as women were concerned. Since the security of all, including slaves, could no longer be assured, protection would be limited to those who were free. And the *hijab* incarnates, expresses, and symbolizes this official retreat from the principle of equality. Symbolically, regression on social equality became entangled and implicated in regression on sexual equality in the case of the female slave. The *hijab*/curtain descended on them both, mingling and confusing the two ideas in the consciousness of Muslims during the fifteen centuries that followed.

10

The Hijab *Descends on Medina*

Islam, put to the test militarily and challenged by the Medinese civilians, sacrificed women slaves in order to protect women aristocrats. Women, whatever their status, were being harassed in the streets, pursued by men who subjected them to the humiliating practice of *ta'arrud* – literally "taking up a position along a woman's path to urge her to fornicate," to commit the act of *zina*. At this point the Prophet's problem was no longer freeing women from the chains of pre-Islamic violence, but simply assuring the safety of his own wives and those of other Muslims in a city that was hostile and out of control.

In order to deal with the problem, he began by looking into the immediate causes of what was going on, employing his usual method of information gathering: he sent some emissaries to question those who were acting in this manner. And they explained their behavior by saying: "We only practice *ta'arrud* with women we believe to be slaves"[1] – thus excusing themselves by claiming confusion about the identity of the women they approached. This was the reason Allah revealed verse 59 of sura 33, in which He advised the wives of the Prophet to make themselves recognized by pulling their *jilbab* over themselves. It was not a question of a new item of clothing, but of a new way of wearing a usual one, distinguishing themselves by an action.[2] According to the *Lisan al-'Arab* dictionary, *jilbab* is a rather vague concept. It can designate numerous pieces of clothing, ranging from a simple chemise to a cloak. One of the definitions in this dictionary describes the *jilbab* as a very large piece of cloth worn by a woman; another describes it as a piece of cloth that a woman uses to cover her head and bosom.

That women slaves had been reduced to prostitution is a fact established by the Koran itself, in its mirroring of pre-Islamic social life and practices. Verse 33 of sura 24 ("Light"), which deals with the problem of *zina*, verifies the existence of organized prostitution in Medina: "Force not your slave-girls to whoredom that ye may seek enjoyment of the life of the world, if they would preserve their chastity."[3] And for those who were indulging in this kind of business Allah had this advice: "And such of your slaves as seek a writing (of emancipation), write it for them . . ."[4]

The *Isaba*, the collection of biographies of the first Muslims, gives us details about the life of Umayma and Musayka, two slaves belonging to 'Abdallah Ibn Ubayy "whom he forced into prostitution and who came to complain to the Messenger of God." It was in response to their complaint that Allah revealed the verse saying "Force not your slave-girls to whoredom."[5]

'Abdallah Ibn Ubayy is that same Hypocrite of the tribe of the Khazraj who circulated slanders about 'A'isha and Safwan, the young man who brought her to the camp at the time of the affair of the necklace. He was used to treating his slaves with force and violence: "'Abdallah Ibn Ubayy beat Musayka to force her to give herself to him in the hope of getting her pregnant and of later having the disposition of the child that would be born from such a union." Al-'Asqalani emphasizes that the "enjoyment of the life of the world" that 'Abdallah Ibn Ubayy sought through Musayka was, in addition to sexual pleasure, the slave child that might be born.[6] As Musayka was a Muslim, the Muslim God was obliged to intervene, and He did so in the verse quoted above, which condemned both prostitution of, and violence toward, women slaves. Musayka "refused to lend herself to the act that 'Abdallah was forcing her to perform." It is understandable why this man was so hostile to Muhammad and was one of the most virulent leaders of the Medinese opposition. Muhammad's ideas on granting women the same rights that men have, deprived men like 'Abdallah Ibn Ubayy of the considerable financial resources accruing from the enslaving of women. Islam could only make a real break with the customs of the polytheistic era if it succeeded in shattering the prerogatives of the tribal aristocracy and taking a position against slavery for either sex, thus making the idea of the believer as an individual not only logical but necessary.

This nation of equals, the Muslim *umma*, could not come into being without condemning slavery, and especially the enslaving of women, where the abuses were so obvious. But there was another reason, much more pragmatic, that led Islam to change the status of women slaves. The Muslim family represented something new, in the restrictions it imposed on the great sexual liberty that had previously existed. It is difficult for us to understand this when today the Muslim family looks like a unit that, being polygynous, is even now particularly permissive for the man, who also has that miraculous right to repudiate his wife on the spot by simply pronouncing the words "I repudiate you," with the judge having only to register the wish of the man. But the pre-Islamic man's sexual practices were so permissive that two Muslim regulations seemed to be huge restrictions. They were: (1) the rule of the *'idda* period that obliges a widowed or divorced woman to wait several menstrual cycles before remarrying; and (2) the rule of paternity, linking the child to the biological father. Although our knowledge of the pre-Islamic period is far from adequate, it can be argued that any woman who was not an aristocrat, who did not belong to a tribe that could ransom her in case of war, and who in daily life did not have the protection of a husband who handled a sword with dexterity, was a woman in perpetual danger – danger of capture, danger of *ta'arrud*, danger of being subjected to slavery by an abductor. Islam could not establish the patriarchal Muslim family, in which the minimal rule is to know who is the father of a child, without dealing with the lot of women slaves. I emphasize this point because I believe that having recourse to the *hijab* as a method of controlling sexuality and protecting a certain category of women at the expense of another expresses that mentality and allows it to be perpetuated.

If the *hijab* is a response to sexual aggression, to *ta'arrud*, it is also its mirror image. It reflects that aggression by saying that the female body is *'awra*, literally "nudity," a vulnerable defenseless body. The *hijab* for women, as defined by a Medina in a state of civil war, is in fact a recognition of the street as a space where *zina* (fornication) is permitted. The expression *ta'arrud* contains the idea of violence, of pressure, of constraint. Ibn Sa'd reports:

> In Medina slaves where being solicited by some foolish men (*sufaha*) who approached them in the public street and harassed them. At that time a free woman who went out into the street and whose clothing did not distinguish her from a slave was confused with the latter and subjected to the same treatment.[7]

Ibn Sa'd is one of the rare historians of the first centuries who puts some distance between himself and the material he is dealing with, and who makes an attempt at a synthesis. He perceives in the incident during which the *hijab* was revealed (Zaynab's wedding) some profound reasons that led the lawgiver, Allah himself, to resort to such a solution.

The recourse to the *hijab* can only be understood if we realize the significance of *zina*, that "illicit" sexuality that Islam was struggling against. And to do this we have to look back to the pre-Islamic era and its laws. Al-Bukhari describes four kinds of pre-Islamic marriages:

> The first of these marriages is like the marriage of today: the man asked the father or guardian for the woman's hand in marriage; he gave the dowry and then consummated the marriage. The second kind took place in the following way: the man said to his wife, "When you are purified of your periods, send a message to So-and-So that you want to cohabit with him." The husband then stayed away from his wife and did not touch her at all so that she would not show evidence of a pregnancy coming from cohabitation with him . . . . The third kind of marriage was practiced like this: a group of individuals, ten at the maximum, all had relations with the same woman. When that woman became pregnant and then bore a child, a few days after her confinement she sent for those individuals and all of them were required to come. Then, when they were all gathered around her, she

said to them: "You know what has resulted from your relations with me. I have just borne a child. This child is yours, O So-and-So. Give it whatever name you wish." . . . The fourth kind of marriage was practiced as follows: a large number of individuals had relations with the same woman, who did not refuse herself to any of them who came to her. These prostitutes put a flag at their door which served as a sign. Anyone who wanted to might enter. When one of these women became pregnant and bore a child, all her clients gathered at her house. Physiognomists were called in, and they attributed the child to the one they judged to be the father.[8]

Al-Bukhari uses the word *marriage* in the above without making it known if he was opposed to using the word *union*. He gives no indication of the social importance of these marriages or of the social origin of the parties concerned (the last two categories certainly must be called prostitution). For example, was 'Abdallah Ibn Ubayy's relationship with Musayka considered to be a "marriage"? There are no answers to many sorts of questions that future research needs to clarify so that Islam can become again what it aspired to be at the beginning: an experiment in living rooted in a reality in which knowledge plays an important role. It is true that rigorous research would very much upset official Islam, because some Muslim heads of state have preferred to subject prostitution to a tax instead of forbidding it and fighting against it, to the consternation of the *fuqaha*. This was the case with the Fatimid dynasty, for example.[9]

Islam as a coherent system of values that governs all the behaviors of a person and a society, and Muhammad's egalitarian project, are in fact based on a detail that many of his Companions, led by 'Umar, considered to be secondary: the emergence of woman's free will as something that the organization of society had to take into account. For 'Umar the solution was simple: "'Umar strongly wished that the *hijab* be instituted for women. He repeated to the Prophet: 'Messenger of God, you receive all kinds of people at your house, moral as well as evil. Why do you not order the *hijab* for the Mothers of the Believers?' "[10] Despite all the criticism of him, the Prophet persisted in not consenting to the *hijab*, not being of the same frame of mind as 'Umar. 'Umar was brave, just, honest, unselfish, pious, but he did not share with Muhammad a belief in such virtues as gentleness and nonviolence as both practice and theory – key elements of the new message, the new religion. As practice, these virtues meant civility and politeness in daily life. As theory, they meant the emergence of the individual as the locus of a sacred will that renders violence illegitimate and makes supervision superfluous. Muhammad put great emphasis on politeness. He himself was very shy. Several verses attest to this aspect of his character, which, as we have seen, in the absence of tactfulness on the part of some men of his entourage forced him to adopt the *hijab*. He did not consider that having a house open to the world had to mean that people would invade his privacy. The *hijab* represented the exact opposite of what he had wanted to bring about. It was the incarnation of the absence of internal control; it was the veiling of the sovereign will, which is the source of good judgment and order in a society. 'Umar, who had never reflected about the principle of the individual that the new religion emphasized, could not understand this. To him, the only way of reestablishing order was to put up barriers and to hide women, who were objects of envy. Unfortunately for Islam, the conflict and debate on this question took place at the end of the Prophet's life, when he was growing old and when he was being militarily tested and challenged in the city where he had hoped to realize all his aspirations. The reaction of 'Umar, for whom barriers constituted the only way to control the violence, reflected the horde mentality that was the pillar of the ethics of the Arabia of the period of ignorance (*al-jahiliyya*). Despite his love for the Prophet and his God, whom he served in a spirit of devotion admired by all, he was unable to visualize the Prophet's dream. A fighter, like most men of action he did not reflect long on the impact of every act nor on the reactions that might be produced in an enemy. We find many examples in which, when the Prophet is consulting his entourage before making a decision, it is 'Umar who speaks up first and gives such ridiculous and strategically dangerous advice that the Prophet merely turns to the other Companions to ask them to continue to think about the situation from all points of view. For example, during the Battle of Hunayn 'Umar advised killing the prisoners, while the Prophet, more far-seeing, intended to use them as a weapon of persuasion to force the enemy to convert to Islam.

The Islam of Muhammad banished the idea of supervision, of a police system of control. This explains the absence of clergy in Islam and the encouraging of all Muslims to get involved in understanding the written word. Individual responsibility came into play to balance the weight of aristocratic control, finally making it ineffective in an *umma* of believers whose behavior followed precise, internalized rules. Recognizing in women an inalienable will fitted into this scheme of making everyone individually responsible. 'Abdallah Ibn Ubayy knew very well that he could not continue to violate his slaves if 'A'isha and Umm Salama continued to demand the liberation of women and to move freely about the streets, symbols of the liberty and autonomy that they demanded for all. And 'Abdallah Ibn Ubayy was right. If woman's sovereign will was accepted, she would no longer be a private sex object that could be kidnapped, exchanged, stolen, bought, and sold. To prevent this from happening, it was necessary to attack the Prophet's wives and show that they could not escape the immemorial female destiny of being a creature deprived of judgment, of will, an object on which the will of another is exerted.

The philosophy of the veil, which 'Umar advocated, is clear. When the Hypocrites who attacked women were summoned to explain, they gave as justification the fact that "they are taken for slaves" and "God ordered women to change their clothing to distinguish it from that of slaves and to do this by covering themselves with their *jilbab* [cloak]."[11] They had to find a way of separating slaves, the only ones to be put in a situation where *zina* was thinkable, from free women, the wives of aristocrats and powerful men toward whom such approaches were forbidden. Free women "made themselves recognized in order not to be harassed. It was better for them to be recognized . . . . Women veiled their faces and allowed only one eye to be visible."[12] The verse soon descended from Heaven – it veiled free women: "O Prophet! Tell thy wives and thy daughters and the women of the believers to draw their cloaks close around them (when they go abroad). That will be better, that so they may be recognized and not annoyed."[13]

In the struggle between Muhammad's dream of a society in which women could move freely around the city (because the social control would be the Muslim faith that disciplines desire), and the customs of the Hypocrites who only thought of a woman as an object of envy and violence, it was this latter vision that would carry the day. The veil represents the triumph of the Hypocrites. Slaves would continue to be harassed and attacked in the streets. The female Muslim population would henceforth be divided by a *hijab* into two categories: free women, against whom violence is forbidden, and women slaves, toward whom *ta'arrud* is permitted. In the logic of the *hijab*, the law of tribal violence replaces the intellect of the believer, which the Muslim God affirms is indispensable for distinguishing good from evil. Islam asserts itself as the religion of the *ayat*, which is customarily translated as *verses*, but literally means *signs*, in the semiotic usage of the word. The Koran is a group of signs to be decoded by *al-'aql*, the intellect, an intellect that makes the individual responsible and in fact master of himself/herself. In order for God to exist as the locus of power, the law, and social control, it was necessary for the social institution that had previously fulfilled these functions – namely, tribal power – to disappear. The *hijab* reintroduced the idea that the street was under the control of the *sufaha*, those who did not restrain their desires and who needed a tribal chieftain to keep them under control.

In the circumstances of the military crisis in Medina in years 5, 6, and 7, the Prophet did not have many choices for coping with the insecurity in the city. He could either accept and live with this insecurity while waiting for the new source of power, God and His religion, to become rooted in the people's mentality, or he could reactivate the tribe as the police force of the city.[14] The first option meant living with insecurity while waiting for God to show His power through military successes. With the second option, the tribe would assure security in the city immediately, but Allah and his community would disappear forever – at least in their original perspective. Muhammad's message – his dream of a community in which individuals are respected and have rights, not because they belong to a tribe, but simply because they are able to believe they have a link with a God – was dependent on the role that the tribe was called on to play during this transitory phase. Tribal power was the danger. Tolerating it, under any form whatever, as a means of control was a very grave compromise with the Muslim idea of a reasoning human being who exercises self-control.

'Umar's solution, imposing the *hijab*/curtain that hides women instead of changing attitudes and forcing "those in whose heart is a disease" to act differently, was going to overshadow Islam's dimension as a civilization, as a body of thought on the individual and his/her role in society. This body of thought made *dar al-Islam* (the land of Islam) at the outset a pioneering experiment in terms of individual freedom and democracy. But the *hijab* fell over Medina and cut short that brief burst of freedom. Paradoxically, 15 centuries later it was colonial power that would force the Muslim states to reopen the question of the rights of the individual and of women. All debates on democracy get tied up in the woman question and that piece of cloth that opponents of human rights today claim to be the very essence of Muslim identity.

Conclusion

To make a journey to Medina, and then to leave it when it is in the middle of civil war, is perhaps not the best way to terminate a pilgrimage back to the sources of our history. We could have waited until year 8 (AD 630) and Muhammad's triumphal entry into the Ka'ba after the taking of Mecca. We could have celebrated with him his success as a man who knew very well that "a prophet is not without honor save in his own country." We could have been there when he smashed the idols, the symbols of pagan Arabia:

> The Prophet made his entry into the city, mounted on a camel and wearing a black turban. He was preceded by 'Ali, bearing his standard, and surrounded by Muhajirun and Ansar. When he arrived at the gate of the city, he ordered that his leather tent from Ta'if be pitched on the heights where Zubayr had planted his flag . . . . On the twentieth day of the month of Ramadan the Prophet made his solemn entry into the temple. At the door he dismounted from his camel, entered the courtyard, and made the ritual circuits of the Ka'ba. During this time the inhabitants had been told there would be no massacre. They left their houses and proceeded to the temple. After completing his circuits, the Prophet ordered that the door of the temple be opened and all the idols be taken down and smashed. As he was going out, he stopped at the door and looked at the

courtyard, which was filled with a crowd of inhabitants of Mecca. He seized the ring of the door, turned to the crowd, and, standing on the doorsill, spoke thus: "Praise be to God, Who made His servant triumph and Who fulfilled the promise He made to him. He promised to bring me back to Mecca; and He routed my enemies."[1]

We could have waited for the following day, when on the hill of Safa he received the male Meccans, who came, following their chieftains, to recite the declaration of faith and take the oath of allegiance.

We could have waited until the fourth day after the taking of Mecca and been present for the women's swearing of allegiance, which began with an incident that was so symbolic! The women, under the leadership of Hind Bint 'Utba, the wife of Abu Sufyan (the former leader of Mecca and commander in its battles), refused to swear the oath to 'Umar, as the Prophet had arranged. Hind pushed him aside and approached Muhammad: "It is to you that we want to swear allegiance and it is with you that we want to enter into agreement." When Muhammad came to the part of the oath of allegiance specific to women, Hind could not restrain herself, despite the solemnity of the occasion: "You are imposing obligations on us that you have not imposed on the men; but we accept them; we will not be infidels."[2] The Prophet asked the women to swear to "not kill their children." Hind pointed out that he, a military leader who originated battles in which blood was shed, was going too far in asking such a thing from women, who are the ones who give birth: "We have brought children into the world and we have raised them, but you have killed them on the day of Badr." Why was such a clause inserted into the women's oath of allegiance? The historical sources do not agree on this point. Was it an allusion to abortion or to the infanticide of girl babies? Many Muslim authors exaggerate the importance of infanticide, which they link to honor. According to others, infanticide is supposed to be vestige of the practice of human sacrifice in the pagan cults and was extremely rare.[3]

The incident with Hind shows not only that the women of the Qurashi aristocracy were highly enough esteemed as a social group to come, like the men, to swear allegiance and to take part in the negotiations with the new military leader of the city, but also that they could express a boldly critical attitude toward Islam. They were not going to accept the new religion without knowing exactly how it would improve their situation. This critical spirit on the part of women toward the political leader remained alive and well during the first decades of Islam. It only disappeared with the onset of absolutism, with Mu'awiya and the turning of Islam into a dynastic system. This meant, on the one hand, the disappearance of the tribal aristocratic spirit with the formation of the Muslim state, and, on the other hand, the disappearance of Islam as the Prophet's experiment in living, in which equality, however merely potential it might be, opened the door to the dream of a practicing democracy.

We could have strolled around Medina until the Prophet's return after the taking of Mecca and participated in the celebration of the conquest. With the help of this military success, security had returned to the streets, and the people "in whose hearts is a disease," the *sufaha*, had made a prudent and circumspect withdrawal.

Alas! We really do not choose the ending of a journey, especially journeys that transform our lives. For women, security would never return to the city. No more than dreams, can a journey back in time change the fact that the Medina of women would be forever frozen in its violent posture. From then on, women would have to walk the streets of uncaring, unsafe cities, ever watchful, wrapped in their *jilbab*. The veil, which was intended to protect them from violence in the street, would accompany them for centuries, whatever the security situation of the city. For them, peace would never return. Muslim women were to display their *hijab* everywhere, the vestige of a civil war that would never come to an end.

Nevertheless, some of them did try to resist; some rejected the *hijab*. They claimed the right to go out *barza* (unveiled), a word which they added to the *Lisan al-'Arab* dictionary: "A *barza* woman is one who does not hide her face and does not lower her head." And the dictionary adds that a *barza* woman is one who "is seen by people and who receives visitors at home" – men, obviously. A *barza* woman is also a woman who has "sound judgement." A *barz* man or woman is someone "known for their *'aql* [reasoning]." Who are they, these Muslim women who have resisted the *hijab*? The most famous was Sukayna, one of the great-granddaughters of the Prophet through his daughter Fatima, the wife of 'Ali, the famous 'Ali, the ill-fated fourth orthodox caliph who abandoned power to Mu'awiya and was assassinated by the first Muslim political terrorist. His sons' fates were as tragic as his own, and Sukayna was present at the killing of her father at Karbala. That tragedy partly explains her revolt against political, oppressive, despotic Islam and against everything that hinders the individual's freedom – including the *hijab*.

Sukayna was born in year 49 of the Hejira (about AD 671). She was celebrated for her beauty, for what the Arabs call beauty – an explosive mixture of physical attractiveness, critical intelligence, and caustic wit. The most powerful men debated with her; caliphs and princes proposed marriage to her, which she disdained for political reasons. Nevertheless, she ended up marrying five, some say six, husbands. She quarreled with some of them, made passionate declarations of love to others, brought one to court for infidelity, and never pledged *ta'a* (obedience, the key principle of Muslim marriage) to any of them. In her marriage contracts she stipulated that she would not obey her husband, but would do as she pleased, and that she did not acknowledge that her husband had the right to practice polygyny. All this was the result of her interest in political affairs and poetry. She continued to receive visits from poets and, despite her several marriages, to attend the meetings of the Qurashi tribal council, the equivalent of today's democratic municipal councils.[4] Her personality has fascinated the historians, who have devoted pages and pages, sometimes whole biographies, to her. Her character was deeply affected by history's harsh reality – particularly the killing of her father, Husayn Ibn 'Ali, at Karbala, one of the most outrageous massacres in Muslim political history. Husayn was a man of peace who had declared to Mu'awiya in a written contract his decision to renounce the caliphate, provided he be allowed to live in safety with his family. A poet, he celebrated the women he adored: Rabab, his wife, and Sukayna, his daughter. After the death of

Mu'awiya, when he refused to swear allegiance to Mu'awiya's son, Husayn was killed at Karbala in the midst of his family, including Sukayna.[5] It happened on the Day of Ashura (the Day of Atonement), October 10, AD 680. All her life Sukayna harbored feelings of contempt, which she never hesitated to express, for the Umayyad dynasty and its bloody methods. She attacked the dynasty in the mosques and insulted its governors and representatives every time she had the opportunity, even arranging occasions for this purpose.[6]

She made one of her husbands sign a marriage contract that officially specified her right to *nushuz*, that rebellion against marital control that so tormented the *fuqaha*. She claimed the right to be *nashiz*, and paraded it, like her beauty and her talent, to assert the importance and vitality of women in the Arab tradition. Admiring and respectful, the historians delight in evoking her family dramas – for instance, the case that she brought against one of her husbands who had violated the rule of monogamy that she had imposed on him in the marriage contract. Dumbfounded by the conditions in the contract, the judge nevertheless was obliged to hear the case, with his own wife attending this trial of the century and the caliph sending an emissary to keep him *au courant* with the course of the trial.[7]

You can imagine my surprise when I was accused of lying at a conference in Penang, Malaysia in 1984, where I presented Sukayna as a type of traditional Muslim woman for us to think about. My accuser, a Pakistani, editor of an Islamic journal in London, interrupted me, shouting to the audience: "Sukayna died at the age of six!" Trying to snatch the microphone away from me in a vindictive rage, he kept repeating: "She died at Karbala with her father! She died at Karbala!" Then smugly assuming the role of *qadi*, he demanded that I name the sources where I found my version of Sukayna's history. I furnished him a list on the spot – in Arabic obviously. He looked at it with disdain and told me it was very scanty. In fact, it contained the names of Ibn Qutayba, Ibn 'Abd Rabbih, Ibn 'Asakir, al-Zamakhshari, Ibn Sa'd, Ibn al-Ma'ad, al-Isbahani, al-Dhahabi, Al-Safadi, Al-Washaa, al-Bukhari – in short, the great names of Muslim historiography. I learned later that this important editor, whose journal claims to contribute to a better understanding of the Muslim world, neither speaks nor reads Arabic.

Sukayna died in Medina at the age of 68 (year 117 of the Hejira). Other sources have her dying at the age of 77 at Kufa. This is extremely unlikely, as she liked neither Iraq nor the Iraqis: "You killed my grandfather ['Ali], my father [Husayn], my uncle [Hasan, another son of 'Ali], and my husband," she told them, referring to her widowhood. Mus'ab Ibn al-Zubayr, the husband whom she loved the most, was killed by a fifth Umayyad caliph, 'Abd al-Malik Ibn Marwan (685–705).[8]

In any case, that verbal aggression that I was subjected to and that attempt to obliterate the memory of Sukayna by a modern Muslim man who only accepts his wife as veiled, crushed, and silent remains for me an incident that symbolizes the whole matter of the relationship of the Muslim man to time – of amnesia as memory, of the past as warping the possibilities of the present. Jean Genet, who has thought long about the subject of memory, describes so well in *Le Captif amoureux* that strange power of reminiscence that gushes forth in the present and metamorphoses it:

> Every memory is true. A gust of fresh air gives fleeting life to a moment that is past, definitively past. Every memory, perhaps something less than a drop of perfume, brings the moment to life, portrayed not according to its living freshness in this period, but otherwise, I mean, reemerging from another life.[9]

What a strange fate for Muslim memory, to be called upon in order to censure and punish! What a strange memory, where even dead men and women do not escape attempts at assassination, if by chance they threaten to raise the *hijab* that covers the mediocrity and servility that is presented to us as tradition. How did the tradition succeed in transforming the Muslim woman into that submissive, marginal creature who buries herself and only goes out into the world timidly and huddled in her veils? Why does the Muslim man need such a mutilated companion? According to Jurji Zaydan, the downward slide as far as women are concerned took place under the Abbasid dynasty. That period that is regularly presented to us as the Golden Age (eighth and ninth centuries) was the period of international conquest for the Muslims and also of the arrival of the *jawari* (women slaves) coming from the conquered countries: "Men gave each other *jawari*, Persians, Romans, Turks, etc."[10] With the economic boom and the expansion of the cities, "the Arab woman was completely marginalized; she had lost all her freedom and pride . . . . Then she began to be treated with contempt. She was imprisoned behind locked doors and windows."[11] The *jawari* turned to learning and poetry to better their condition and attract the attention of powerful men who paid well for the company of beautiful, learned women who could provide them with diversion. They gave birth to male children whom they were able to push into positions of power. They accomplished this through intrigue, and many caliphs were sons of *umm walads*, of slaves who rose to the rank of queen. Harun al-Rashid (786–809) is a representative of this "Golden Age," which the *Arabian Nights* has immortalized forever in the fascinating tales in which women and men met and sought diversion in the streets of Baghdad against a background of intrigue and political absolutism.

It remains to be asked why today it is the image of the woman of the "Golden Age" – a "slave" who intrigues in the corridors of power when she loses hope of seducing – who symbolizes the Muslim eternal female, while the memory of Umm Salama, 'A'isha, and Sukayna awakens no response and seems strangely distant and unreal.

The answer without doubt is to be found in the time-mirror wherein the Muslim looks at himself to foresee his future. The image of "his" woman will change when he feels the pressing need to root his future in a liberating memory. Perhaps the woman should help him do this through daily pressure for equality, thereby bringing him into a fabulous present. And the present is always fabulous, because there everything is possible – even the end of always looking to the past and the beginning of confidence, of enjoying in harmony the moment that we have.

Notes

INTRODUCTION

1 Morocco, Ministère de l'Artisanat et des Affaires Sociales, *Les femmes marocaines dans le développement économique et social, décennie 1975–1985*.

2 Al-Bukhari, *Al Sahih* (Collection of Authentic Hadiths), with commentary by al-Sindi (Beirut: Dar al-Ma'rifa, 1978). The Hadith quoted by the schoolteacher is in vol. 4, p. 226.

3 Ibn Hajar al-'Asqalani, *Huda al-sari, muqaddimat fath al-bari*, commonly known as *Fath al-bari*. It comprises al-Bukhari's text with a commentary by al-'Asqalani. The Hadith that concerns us here, on the necessity of excluding women from power, is found on p. 46 of vol. 13 of the edition of Al-Matba'a al-Bahiya al-Misriya (1928), and on p. 166 of vol. 16 of the edition of Maktaba Mustafa al-Babi al-Halabi fi Misr (1963).

4 The Muslim world is divided into two parts: the Sunnis (orthodox) and the Shi'ites (literally, schismatics). Each group has its own specific texts of *fiqh* (religious knowledge), especially as regards sources of the *shari'a* (legislation and laws). The Sunnis are split between four *madhahib* (schools). The Malikis follow Malik Ibn Anas (AD 717–95). The Hanafis follow the school of Abu Hanifa (died in AD 767). The Shafi'is follow al-Shafi'i (died in AD 820). And finally the Hanbalis follow Ibn Hanbal (died in AD 855). The differences between them most frequently relate to details of juridical procedures.

5 Alexandria: Mu'assasa al-Thaqafa al-Jami'iya, 1976.

6 Muhammad Ibn 'Abdallah Ibn Sulayman 'Arafa, *Huquq al-mar'a fi al-Islam*, 3rd edn (n.p.: Al-Maktab al-Islami, 1980), p. 149.

7 Ibid., p. 150.

8 Sa'id al-Afghani, *'A'isha wa al-siyasa*, 2nd edn (Beirut: Dar al-Fikr, 1971).

9 Imam Zarkashi, *Al-Ijaba li 'irada ma istadrakathu 'A'isha ala al-sahaba*, 2nd edn (Beirut: Al-Maktab al-Islami, 1980).

10 Al-Dhahabi, *Siyar al-nubala'*, 2nd edn (Beirut: Dar al-Fikr, 1969).

Notes

11 Al-Afghani, '*A'isha wa al-siyasa*, p. 34.

12 Ibid., p. 142.

13 Ibid., p. 348.

14 Ibid.

15 Ibid., p. 342.

16 Ibid., p. 246.

17 Ibid., p. 8.

18 See Appendix 1, Sources.

19 Ibn Qayyim al-Jawziya, *Al-Manar al-munif fi al-sahih wa al-da'if* (Aleppo: Maktaba al-Matbu'a al-Islamiya, 1982), pp. 213ff. (The author died in year 751 of the Hejira.)

20 Jean Genet, *Le Captif amoureux* (Paris, Gallimard, 1986), p. 495.

CHAPTER 1 THE MUSLIM AND TIME

1 'Abd al-Kabir Khatibi, "Les Arabes entre la post-modernité et la modernité" (paper delivered at the Twentieth Anniversary Meeting of the Middle East Studies Association of North America, Boston, 20–23 November 1986).

2 Muhammad 'Abid al-Jabiri, *Nahnu wa al-tharwa* (Beirut: Al-Markaz al-Thaqafi al-'Arabi, Al-Dar al-Baida, and Dar al-Tali'a, 1980), p. 22.

3 Muhammad 'Abid al-Jabiri, *Taqwin al-'aql al-'Arabi* (Beirut: Dar al-Tali'a, 1980), vol. 1, 1984; vol. 2, 1986. Translating the word *'aql* is such a perilous undertaking that al-Jabiri devotes whole pages of his work to defining what he means by this word, cautioning, moreover, against confusing it at all costs with *fikr* (thought).

4 Jabiri, *Taqwin al-'aql*, vol. 1, p. 63.

5 Serge Moscovici, "Le temps et l'espace social," interview in *L'Espace et le temps aujourd'hui* (Paris: Editions du Seuil, 1983), p. 262.

6 Ibid., p. 264.

7 Jean-Pierre Rioux, "A la recherche de la mémoire," *Pénélope*, no. 12 (1985).

8 Marshall McLuhan and Quentin Fiore, *The Medium is the Message* (New York: Bantam, 1967), pp. 153–4.

9 Jabiri, *Nahnu wa al tharwa*, p. 22.

10 Ibid.

11 'Ali Umlil, *Al-Islahiya wa al-dawla al-wataniya* (Casablanca: Al-Markaz al-Thaqafi al-'Arabi, 1985), pp. 31ff.

12 Ibid., p. 151.

CHAPTER 2 THE PROPHET AND HADITH

1 Al-Tabari, *Mohammed, Sceau des prophètes*, trans. by Herman Zotenberg (Paris: Sindbad, 1980), p. 251.

Notes

2 Ibid., p. 61.

3 Ibid., p. 65.

4 Ibid.

5 'Ali Ibn Ahmad al-Wahidi al-Nisaburi, *Asbab al-nuzul*, ed. Abu al-Hasan (Beirut: Dar al-Kutub al-'Ilmiya, 1978), p. 7. (The author lived in the fifth century of the Hejira.)

6 Qatada Ibn Di'ama al-Sadusi, *Kitab al-nasikh wa al-mansukh* (Beirut: Mu'assasa al-Risala, 1984), p. 52. (The author died in year 117 of the Hejira.)

7 Ibid., p. 9.

8 See the introduction by 'Abd al-Qadir Ahmad 'Ata to the book by al-Suyuti, *Asrar tartib al-qur'an* (Cairo: Dar al-I'tisam, 1978), p. 25. And in al-Suyuti's text itself, see pp. 69ff. (Al-Suyuti died in year 849 of the Hejira (fifteenth century AD).) See also al-Nisaburi, *Asbab al-nuzul*, p. 2.

9 It is not possible to calculate equivalent dates between the Muslim calendar and the Christian calendar by adding on the difference (that is, 622), because the Muslim calendar month is lunar and thus shorter than that of the Christian calendar. The year 1990 corresponds to the year 1410–11 of the Hejira. Every year the Muslim calendar gains a few days on the Christian calendar, and every century it gains three years. See Marshall G.S. Hodgson, *The Venture of Islam: Conscience and History in a World Civilization* (Chicago: University of Chicago Press, 1974), vol. 1, p. 52, 'The Islamic Calendar.'

10 The goddesses are mentioned in verses 19 and 20 of sura 53. See the commentary of al-Tabari, *Tarikh al-umam wa al-muluk* (Beirut: Dar al-Fikr, 1979), vol. 2, p. 226. See also the excellent summary by William Montgomery Watt in *Mohammed at Mecca* (Oxford: Oxford University Press, 1953), pp. 103ff.

11 Tabari, *Mohammed, Sceau des prophètes*; Tabari, *Tarikh*, vol. 2, p. 231; Ibn Hisham, *Al-Sira al-nabawiya* (Beirut: Dar Ihya' al-Tharwa al-'Arabi, n.d.), vol. 2, p. 63.

12 Ibn Hisham, *Sira*, vol. 2, p. 60; Tabari, *Tarikh*, vol. 2, p. 229.

13 Ibn Hisham, *Sira*, vol. 2, p. 70.

14 Tabari, *Mohammed, Sceau des prophètes*, p. 104.

15 Ibn Hisham, *Sira*, vol. 2, p. 71.

16 Ibid., p. 83; Tabari, *Tarikh*, vol. 2, p. 237.

17 Al-Suyuti, *Lubab al-nuqul fi asbab al-nuzul* (Beirut: Dar Ihya' al-'Ilm, 1984), p. 69.

18 Ibn Hisham, *Sira*, vol. 1, p. 262.

19 See the excellent study by Saad Eddin Ibrahim, "Anatomy of Egypt's Militant Islamic Groups," *International Journal of Middle East Studies*, 12, no. 4, 1980, pp. 423–53.

20 Note the numerous papers read at conferences each year in the Muslim world on the right of the modern individual to question, to criticize, to take the initiative. See, in particular: "*Tahdith al-fikr al-'Arabi*," special issue of *Al-Wahda*, no. 1, October 1984; and "*Al-tharwa wa al-'amal al-siyasi*" ("Patrimony and Political Action"), in *Al-Majlis al-qawmi li thaqafa al-'Arabiya*, 1984.

21 Muhammad Abu Zahra, *Malik* (Cairo: Dar al-Fikr al-'Arabi, n.d.), p. 146.

22 Ibid.

23 Tabari, *Mohammed, Sceau des prophètes*, p. 352. See also Ibn Hisham, *Sira*, vol. 4, p. 314.

24 Tabari, *Mohammed, Sceau des prophètes*, p. 234.

25 Ibn Hisham, *Sira*, vol. 4, pp. 303ff; Ibn Sa'd, *Al-Tabaqat al-kubra* (Beirut: Dar Sadir, n.d.), vol. 3, pp. 171ff.

26 Tabari, *Mohammed, Sceau des prophètes*, p. 349.

27 Ibid., p. 350.

28 Ibid., p. 351; Tabari, *Tarikh*, vol. 3, p. 199; Ibn Sa'd, *Al-Tabaqat*, vol. 3, p. 186.

29 Tabari, *Tarikh*, vol. 3, p. 51.

30 Ibid., p. 192.

31 Ibid., p. 51.

32 Ibn Sa'd, *Al-Tabaqat*, p. 192.

33 Al-Mas'udi, *Muruj al-dhahab* (Beirut: Dar al-Ma'rifa, 1982). Translated by A.C. Barbier de Meynard and A.J.B. Pavet de Courteille as *Les Prairies d'or* (Paris: Société Asiatique, 1971). See also Tabari, *Tarikh*, vol. 5, p. 16.

34 Tabari, *Tarikh*, vol. 3, p. 33.

35 Ibid., vol. 5, pp. 113ff.

36 Ibid., p. 203.

37 Mas'udi, *Muruj*, vol. 3, pp. 649 and 667.

38 Ibid., p. 683; Tabari, *Tarikh*, vol. 6, p. 83.

39 Bukhari, *Sahih*, vol. 1, p. 1; 'Asqalani, *Fath al-bari*, vol. 1, p. 261.

40 Bukhari, *Sahih*, vol. 1, p. 1.

41 Ibid., p. 3. We will see further on in al-'Asqalani's commentary on al-Bukhari (*Fath al-bari*) that he eliminates still more repetitions and reduces the *Sahih* of al-Bukhari to less than 2,000.

42 Joseph Schacht, *An Introduction to Islamic Law* (Oxford: Clarendon Press, 1964).

43 'Asqalani, *Fath al-bari*, vol. 1, p. 265.

44 Ibid.

45 Abu Zahra, *Malik*.

46 Ibid., p. 148.

47 Ibid.

48 Taha Husayn, *Fi al-adab al-jahili*, 10th edn (Cairo: Dar al-Ma'arif, 1969), pp. 149–50.

49 Abu al-Faraj al-Isbahani, *Kitab al-aghani* (Beirut: Dar Ihya' al-Turath al-'Arabi, 1963), vol. 1, p. 23. Al-Isbahani was born in Ispahan in year 284 of the Hejira (tenth century AD).

50 Ibid.

51 Ibn al-Kalbi, *Kitab al-asnam* (Cairo: Maktaba Dar al-Kitab, 1924), p. 18.

52 Taha Husayn, *Fi al-adab al-jahili*, p. 152.

Notes

CHAPTER 3 A TRADITION OF MISOGYNY (1)

1 Bukhari, *Sahih*, vol. 4, p. 226. See also the edition published by Al-Matbaʻa al-Bahiya al-Misriya, 1928, vol. 13, p. 48; and the edition published by Maktaba Mustafa al-Babi al-Halabi bi Misr, 1909, vol. 16, p. 166.
2 ʻAsqalani, *Fath al-bari* (Cairo: Al-Matbaʻa al-Bahiya al-Misriya, n.d.), vol. 13, p. 46.
3 See Hodgson, *Venture of Islam*, vol. 1, p. 199.
4 See note 2.
5 On this dilemma and the division that it occasioned, see ʻAsqalani, *Fath al-bari*, vol. 13, p. 49. On the political implications and the philosophical debates that the Battle of the Camel aroused, see the extraordinary description by Tabari in his *Tarikh*, vol. 5, pp. 156–225.
6 Ibn Saʻd, *Al-Tabaqat*, vol. 3, p. 159.
7 Ibid.
8 ʻAsqalani, *Fath al-bari*, vol. 13, p. 622 (see note 2 for full details).
9 Ibn al-Athir, *Usd al-ghaba fi tamyiz al-sahaba* (n.p.: Dar al-Fikr li al-Tibaʻa wa al-Tawziʻ, n.d.), vol. 5, p. 38.
10 Ibid., vol. 4, p. 578.
11 See Chapter 3, "Sex and Marriage Before Islam," in my book, *Beyond the Veil: Male-Female Dynamics in Modern Muslim Society*, 2nd edn. (Bloomington: Indiana University Press, 1987), pp. 65–85. I give there some references on this question, particularly the works of Gertrude Stern and Robertson Smith on the texts of religious history. See also the analysis by Ahmad al-Hawfi of the situation of the wife and mother in pre-Islamic Arabia as depicted in poetry, *Al-Marʼa fi al-shiʻr al-jahili* (Cairo: Dar Nahdat Misr, 1970), pp. 74–314. See also vol. 10, "Bedouin Social Structures," in Salih Ahmad al-ʻAli, *Muhadarat fi tarikh al-ʻArab* (Baghdad: Maktaba al-Muthanna, 1960), 6th edn, pp. 134 ff.
12 Ibn al-Athir, *Usd al-ghaba*, vol. 5, p. 38.
13 Masʻudi, *Muruj*, vol. 2, p. 380; and the French translation of this work, *Les Prairies d'or*, vol. 3, p. 646.
14 Tabari, *Tarikh*, vol. 5, p. 182.
15 ʻAsqalani, *Fath al-bari*, vol. 13, p. 46 (see note 2 for full details).
16 Ibid., vol. 13, pp. 50 and 51 for the first version, and p. 44 for the second.
17 See the analysis of Hamied N. Ansari, "The Islamic Militants in Egyptian Politics," *International Journal of Middle East Studies*, 16, no. 1, 1984, pp. 123–44.
18 Tabari, *Tarikh*, vol. 5, p. 179.
19 ʻAsqalani, *Fath al-bari*, vol. 13, p. 46 (see note 2 for full details).
20 Masʻudi, *Muruj*, vol. 2, p. 378; and the French translation, *Les Prairies d'or*, vol. 2, p. 644.
21 Tabari, *Tarikh*, vol. 5, p. 221.
22 Ibid., p. 188.

Notes

23 Bukhari, *Sahih*, vol. 4, pp. 221ff.

24 Mas'udi, *Les Prairies d'or*, vol. 2, p. 645.

25 Tabari, *Tarikh*, vol. 5, p. 190.

26 'Asqalani, *Fath al-bari*, vol. 13, pp. 51ff (see note 2 for full details); Mas'udi, *Muruj*, vol. 3, pp. 4ff; and Tabari, *Mohammed, Sceau des prophètes*, vol. 6, p. 95.

27 'Asqalani, *Fath al-bari*, vol. 13, p. 56 (see note 2 for full details).

28 For assistance with the research for this chapter, I am indebted to Professor Ahmed al-Khamlichi, Chairman of the Department of Private Law, Faculté de Droit, Université Mohammed V, Rabat.

29 Ibn 'Abd al-Barr, *Al-Intiqa' fi fadl al-thalath al-a'imma al-fuqaha* (Beirut: Dar al-Kutub al-'Ilmiya, n.d.), pp. 10 and 16. The author of this book died in year 463 of the Hejira (eleventh century AD). One of the values of this book is its concision: the biographies of the three imams, Malik, al-Shafi'i, and Abu Hanifa, are condensed into 200 pages.

30 Ibid., p. 16.

31 Ibid.

32 Ibid., p. 15.

33 Ibn al-Athir, *Usd al-ghaba*, vol. 5, p. 38.

34 'Umar Ibn al-Khattab institutionalized the recourse to capital punishment for fornication; his contemporaries were not at all in agreement with his position. See Bukhari, *Sahih*, vol. 4, pp. 146ff. We will learn more about 'Umar Ibn al-Khattab in Part II of this book; he was the instigator of the wearing of the veil and was in complete disagreement with the Prophet about the way to treat women.

35 'Asqalani, *Fath al-bari*, vol. 13, p. 47 (see note 2 for full details).

CHAPTER 4 A TRADITION OF MISOGYNY (2)

1 Bukhari, *Sahih*, vol. 1, p. 99.

2 Imam Zarkashi, *Al-Ijaba*, p. 52.

3 Ibid.

4 Imam Nasa'i, *Al-Sunan*, with commentary by Al-Suyuti and notes by Imam al-Sindi (Cairo: Al-Matba'a al-Misriya, n.d.), vol. 1, p. 242.

5 Concerning the first Hejira (migration), when some Companions of the Prophet decided to go to live in Ethiopia, see Ibn Hisham, *Sira*, vol. 1, pp. 344ff.

6 Tabari, *Mohammed, Sceau des prophètes*, p. 135. See also Imam Nasa'i, *Sunan*, vol. 1, p. 242.

7 Concerning the denigrating attitude of the orientalists toward Muhammad, see William Montgomery Watt, "Criticisms of the Claim to Prophethood," in *Bell's Introduction to the Koran*, revised and enlarged by William Montgomery Watt (Edinburgh: Edinburgh University Press, 1970), pp. 17ff. See also his summary of the orientalists' studies on the Koran, and especially the problems

they face as non–Muslims: "The Qoran and Occidental Scholarship," ch. 11 of the above book, pp. 173ff.

Concerning the way in which some orientalists have analyzed Muhammad's relationship with the Jewish community of Medina, see the following works, in which the political and ideological choices of the man doing the analysis can be seen threaded throughout his work: William Montgomery Watt, *Mohammed at Mecca*, Excursus B, "Arabian and Judeo-Christian Influences," pp. 158–61; Maxime Rodinson, *Mahomet*, ch. 3, "Naissance d'un prophète" (Paris: Seuil, 1961), p. 61; and H.A.R. Gibb, *Islam*, ch. 2, "Mohammed" (Oxford: Oxford University Press, 1969).

8 Tabari, *Tafsir*, Dar al-Fikr edn, vol. 24, p. 90.
9 Imam Nasa'i, *Al-Sunan*, vol. 1, p. 211.
10 Ibid., vol. 2, p. 62.
11 Bukhari, *Sahih*, vol. 1, p. 199.
12 Ibn Hajar al-'Asqalani, *Al-Isaba fi tamyiz al-sahaba* (Cairo: Maktaba al-Dirasa al-Islamiya Dar al-Nahda, n.d.), vol. 8, p. 18.
13 Ibid., vol. 7, p. 427.
14 Marmaduke Pickthall, *The Meaning of the Glorious Koran* (New York: Dorset Press, n.d.), sura 27, "The Ant," verses 22, 23, and 24.
15 'Abd al-Mun'im Salah al-'Ali al-'Uzzi, *Difa' 'an Abi Hurayra*, 2nd edn (Beirut: Dar al-Qalam; and Baghdad: Maktaba al-Nahda, 1981), p. 13.
16 'Asqalani, *Isaba*, vol. 7, p. 426.
17 Ibid., p. 434.
18 Ibid., p. 441.
19 Imam Zarkashi, *Al-Ijaba*, p. 118.
20 'Asqalani, *Isaba*, vol. 7, p. 440.
21 Imam Zarkashi, *Al-Ijaba*, p. 112.
22 Ibid.
23 Ibid., pp. 112 and 113.
24 Ibid., p. 111.
25 Ibid., p. 115.
26 Nasa'i, *Sunan*, vol. 1, p. 155.
27 Ibid., p. 152.
28 Ibid., p. 147.
29 Bukhari, *Sahih*, vol. 3, p. 243.
30 Imam Zarkashi, *Al-Ijaba*, p. 113.
31 Bukhari, *Sahih*, vol. 3, p. 243.
32 The biography of 'Abdallah Ibn 'Umar can be found in 'Asqalani, *Isaba*, vol. 4, pp. 182ff.
33 Bukhari, *Sahih*, vol. 4, p. 137.
34 Imam Zarkashi, *Al-Ijaba*, pp. 37 and 38.
35 Ibid., p. 32.
36 Ibid., p. 31.
37 Zahiya Kaddura, *'A'isha, umm al-mu'minin* (Beirut: Dar al-Kitab al-Lubnani, 1976).

38 Imam Zarkashi, *Al-Ijaba*, p. 116.
39 'Asqalani, *Isaba*, vol. 8, p. 17.
40 Imam Zarkashi, *Al-Ijaba*, p. 120.
41 See note 15.
42 Al-'Uzzi, *Difa' 'an Abi Hurayra*, p. 7.
43 Bukhari, *Sahih*, vol. 1, p. 34.
44 Al-'Uzzi, *Difa' 'an Abi Hurayra*, p. 122.
45 Ibid.
46 Abu Zahra, *Malik*, p. 146.
47 'Asqalani, *Isaba*, vol. 7, p. 440.
48 Abu Zahra, *Malik*, p. 145.
49 'Asqalani, *Isaba*, vol. 7, p. 432.
50 Bukhari, *Sahih*, vol. 1, p. 34.
51 Ibid.
52 Ibid.
53 'Asqalani, *Isaba*, vol. 7, p. 517.
54 Ibid.

CHAPTER 5 THE *HIJAB*, THE VEIL

1 All the writers agree on the year, but the month varies: Ibn Sa'd, *Tabaqat*, vol. 8, p. 174; Tabari, *Tarikh*, vol. 3, p. 42; Tabari, *Mohammed, Sceau des prophètes*, pp. 221ff; and Ibn Hisham, *Sira*, vol. 3, p. 237.
2 Pickthall, *The Meaning of the Glorious Koran*, p. 305.
3 Tabari, *Tafsir*, Dar al-Ma'rifa edn, vol. 22, p. 26.
4 Tabari, *Mohammed, Sceau des prophètes*, p. 337.
5 Ibn Hisham, *Sira*, vol. 11, p. 364.
6 Tabari, *Mohammed, Sceau des prophètes*, p. 150.
7 Ibid., p. 156.
8 Ibn Hisham, *Sira*, vol. 2, p. 285.
9 Tabari, *Mohammed, Sceau des prophètes*, p. 154.
10 Ibn Hisham, *Sira*, vol. 2, p. 372.
11 Tabari, *Mohammed, Sceau des prophètes*, p. 191.
12 Ibid., p. 201.
13 Ibn Hisham, *Sira*, vol. 3, pp. 64–112.
14 Tabari, *Mohammed, Sceau des prophètes*, p. 209.
15 Al-Suyuti, *Lubab al-'uqul fi asbab al-nuzul*, 4th edn (Beirut: Dar Ihya' al-'Ilm, 1984), p. 13.
16 Ibid., p. 15.
17 *Encyclopedia of Islam*, 2nd edn, section on "*Hidjab*."
18 There is no fifth caliph in orthodox Islam. There are only four: Abu Bakr, 'Umar, 'Uthman, and 'Ali. Mu'awiya, who took power using an unacceptable method, a rigged arbitration, represents a break in the transmission of

power. I am only using the number five to help the reader to clarify the historical sequence.

19 *Encyclopedia of Islam*, 2nd edn, section on *"Hidjab."*
20 Titus Burckhardt, *Introduction aux doctrines ésotériques de l'Islam* (Paris: Dervy-Livres, 1969).
21 Al-Hallaj, *Diwan*, trans. Massignon (Paris: Le Seuil, 1981).
22 Al-Darqawi, *Lettres d'un maître sufi*, trans. Titus Burckhardt (Milan: Arché, 1978).
23 *Encyclopedia of Islam*, 2nd edn, section on *"Hidjab."*
24 Pickthall, *The Meaning of the Glorious Koran*, p. 340.
25 Tabari, *Tafsir*, vol. 24, p. 92.
26 Ibid.
27 'Ali Ibn Ahmad al-Nisaburi, *Tafsir ghara'ib al-qur'an wa ragha'ib al-furqan*, published as an annex to Tabari, *Tafsir al-qur'an* in the Dar al-Ma'rifa edn, vol. 11, p. 18.
28 Ibn al-Jawzi, *Kitab ahkam al-nisa'* (Beirut: Al-Maktaba al-'Asriya, 1980).
29 Ibid., p. 200.
30 Ibid., p. 251.
31 Ibid., p. 144.
32 Ibid., p. 330.
33 Ibn Taymiyya, *Fatawa al-nisa'* (Cairo: Maktaba al-'Irfan, 1983), p. 5. (The author died in year 728 of the Hejira.)
34 Muhammad Siddiq Hasan Khan al-Qannuji, *Husn al-uswa bima tabata minha allahi fi al-niswa* (Beirut: Mu'assasa al-Risala, 1981). (The author died in year 1307 of the Hejira, that is, around the turn of the last century.)
35 Bukhari, *Sahih*, vol. 3, p. 254. The verse quoted is verse 53 of sura 33, given at the beginning of this chapter.
36 Bukhari, *Sahih*, vol. 3, p. 254; Ibn Sa'd, *Tabaqat*, vol. 8, p. 173.

CHAPTER 6 THE PROPHET AND SPACE

1 Tabari, *Mohammed, Sceau des prophètes*, p. 67; Tabari, *Tarikh*, vol. 2, pp. 209ff; Ibn Hisham, *Sira*, vol. 1, pp. 245ff.
2 Tabari, *Tarikh*, vol. 2, p. 207.
3 Tabari, *Mohammed, Sceau des prophètes*, p. 68.
4 William Montgomery Watt argues the opposite in his book, *Muhammad, Prophet and Statesman* (London: Oxford University Press, 1961), p. 159. However, his argument seems unconvincing to me, since all the Muslim sources speak of the Prophet's "love at first sight" for Zaynab.
5 Tabari, *Mohammed, Sceau des prophetès*, p. 222.
6 Ibid.
7 Tabari, *Tarikh*, vol. 3, p. 80; Tabari, *Mohammed, Sceau des prophètes*, p. 248.
8 Tabari, *Mohammed, Sceau des prophètes*, p. 325; Mas'udi, *Les Prairies d'or*, vol. 3, p. 527.

9 Ibn Hisham, *Sira*, vol. 2, p. 137.

10 Ibid.

11 Ibid., vol. 2, p. 140.

12 Ibid.

13 Ibid. In one of Tabari's versions, the land had a date grove and a cemetery on it; see Tabari, *Mohammed, Sceau des prophètes*, p. 112.

14 Ibn Hisham, *Sira*, vol. 2, p. 141.

15 Ibid.

16 Ibn Sa'd, *Tabaqat*, vol. 8, p. 167; Ibn Hisham, *Sira*, vol. 2, p. 143.

17 Ibn Sa'd, *Tabaqat*, vol. 8, p. 166. The *minbar* is the wooden pulpit in the center of the mosque, where the imam stands in order to have maximum visibility while he leads the prayers.

18 Ibid.

19 Ibid.

20 Ibid.

21 Ibid.

22 Ibid.

23 Tabari, *Mohammed, Sceau des prophètes*, p. 6.

24 Watt, *Muhammad at Mecca*, p. 141.

25 Tabari, *Mohammed, Sceau des prophètes*, p. 103.

26 Ibn Sa'd, *Tabaqat*, vol. 8, p. 166.

27 Ibid., p. 167.

28 Ibn Hisham, *Sira*, vol. 2, p. 143.

29 Ibid., vol. 2, p. 150, note 4.

30 Although everyone agrees about the day and month of the Prophet's death, there is no unanimity about the year. Some say that it was year 10 of the Hejira (AD 632), others that it was year 11 (AD 633): Ibn Hisham, *Sira*, vol. 4, p. 291; Tabari, *Tarikh*, vol. 2, pp. 188ff. But al-Mas'udi in his *Muruj al-dhahab* lists all the various versions of the date and does a critical evaluation of them (vol. 2, p. 297 of the Arabic text of this work, and vol. 3, p. 575 of the French translation, *Les Prairies d'or*). For the correspondence of dates between the Muslim calendar and the Christian calendar, I rely on either the *Encyclopedia of Islam* or Montgomery Watt.

31 Tabari, *Mohammed, Sceau des prophètes*, p. 341. The Arabic text of this event differs slightly from the French translation (based on Bal'ami's Persian version): it states that the Prophet emerged from the room and walked toward the *minbar* "while dragging his feet" (Tabari, *Tarikh*, vol. 2, p. 196). See also Ibn Hisham, *Sira*, vol. 4, p. 302.

32 Ibn Hisham, *Sira*, vol. 4, p. 302.

33 Ibid., vol. 4, p. 297.

34 Ibid., vol. 4, p. 302.

35 Ibid.

36 See Tabari, *Tarikh*, vol. 3, p. 195; and Ibn Hisham, *Sira*, vol. 4, p. 303.

Notes

1 Pickthall, *The Meaning of the Glorious Koran*, sura 87, verse 9.
2 'Asqalani, *Isaba*, vol. 8, p. 224.
3 Ibid.
4 Ibid., p. 223.
5 Ibid.
6 Ibid.
7 Ibid.
8 Tabari, *Mohammed, Sceau des prophètes*, p. 198.
9 Ibn Hisham, *Sira*, vol. 3, p. 96.
10 'Asqalani, *Fath al-bari*, vol. 8, p. 141.
11 Tabari, *Mohammed, Sceau des prophètes*, p. 286.
12 Ibn Hisham, *Sira*, vol. 4, p. 47; Tabari, *Tarikh*, vol. 3, p. 121. See also Ibn 'Asakir, *Tarikh madinat Dimashq (History of the city of Damascus)*, ed. Sakina Shihabi (Damascus: n.p., 1982), p. 437.
13 See note 10.
14 Tabari, *Tafsir*, vol. 22, p. 10.
15 Ibid.
16 Pickthall, *The Meaning of the Glorious Koran*, sura 33, verse 35.
17 Tabari, *Tafsir*, vol. 22, p. 10.
18 Pickthall, *The Meaning of the Glorious Koran*, sura 4, verse 37.
19 Tabari, *Tafsir*, vol. 8, p. 107.
20 Ibid.
21 On the subject of slaves and prisoners of war, see the following: Tabari, *Muhsan*, ed. M.M. Shakir (Cairo: Dar al-Ma'arif, n.d.), vol. 8, pp. 151ff; Ahmad Muhammad al-Hawfi, "*Al-sabaya wa al-ima*'" (*Prisoners of War and Slaves*), in *Al-mar'a fi al-shi'r al-jahili* (Woman in Pre-Islamic Poetry), 2nd edn (Cairo: Dar al-Nahda, 1970), pp. 464–524; the chapters by Salah Ahmad al-'Ali on Bedouin social structures in his *Muhadarat fi tarikh al-'Arab* (Papers on Arab History), 6th edn (Baghdad: Maktaba al-Muthanna, 1960), vol. 1; Jurji Zaydan, *Tarikh al-tamaddun al-Islami* (*History of Muslim Civilization*) (no publisher or date given); Fu'ad 'Abd al-Mun'im Ahmad, "The Problem of Slavery and the Principle of Equality in Islam," in *Mabda' al-musawa fi al-Islam* (*The Principle of Equality in Islam*) (Alexandria: Mu'assasa al-Thaqafa al-Jami'iya, 1972).
22 'Asqalani, *Isaba*, vol. 8, p. 258.
23 Tabari, *Tafsir*, vol. 9, p. 255.
24 Ibid., vol. 8, p. 105.
25 Pickthall, *The Meaning of the Glorious Koran*.
26 Tabari, *Tafsir*, vol. 8, p. 107.
27 Ibid., vol. 8, p. 113. A trace of this constraint on women still exists in Muslim family laws, namely, the *khul'* option offered to a woman who wants a

divorce: she agrees to pay a sum to her husband if he consents to give her her freedom.

28 Pickthall, *The Meaning of the Glorious Koran*.
29 Tabari, *Tafsir*, vol. 9, p. 255.
30 Ibid., vol. 8, p. 235.
31 Ibid.
32 Ibid., vol. 9, p. 255.
33 Pickthall, *The Meaning of the Glorious Koran*, sura 6, verse 12.
34 Ibid., sura 4, verse 5.
35 Tabari, *Tafsir*, vol. 7, p. 561.
36 Ibid., vol. 7, pp. 562–3.
37 Ibid., vol. 1, pp. 293–5; vol. 3, pp. 90 and 129; vol. 6, pp. 57–60.
38 Ibid., vol. 3, pp. 90 and 129.
39 Ibid., vol. 6, p. 57.
40 Ibid., vol. 7, pp. 560ff.
41 Ibid., p. 565.
42 Ibid., p. 567.
43 See the biography of 'Umar in 'Asqalani, *Isaba*, vol. 4, p. 588.
44 Tabari, *Tafsir*, vol. 8, p. 266.
45 Pickthall, *The Meaning of the Glorious Koran*, sura 4, verse 32.
46 Tabari, *Tafsir*, vol. 9, p. 256.
47 Ibid., vol. 8, p. 261.
48 See note 21.
49 Maurice Lombard, *L'Islam dans sa première grandeur* (Paris: Flammarion, 1971), pp. 212ff.
50 Mas'udi, *Les Prairies d'or*, p. 612.
51 Ibid., p. 614.
52 Ibid.
53 Tabari, *Mohammed, Sceau des prophètes*, p. 309.
54 Ibid.
55 Tabari, *Tafsir*, p. 261.
56 Pickthall, *The Meaning of the Glorious Koran*, sura 48, verse 30.
57 Tabari, *Mohammed, Sceau des prophètes*, p. 97.
58 Ibid., p. 290.
59 Ibid. See also the detailed account of this battle and the taking of Ta'if in Ibn Hisham, *Sira*, vol. 4, pp. 80–141; and Tabari, *Tarikh*, vol. 3, pp. 165ff.
60 Tabari, *Mohammed, Sceau des prophètes*, p. 296.
61 Ibid.
62 Ibid.
63 Ibid.
64 Ibid.
65 Ibid., p. 299.
66 Ibid., p. 300.
67 Ibid.

68 Ibid.

69 Ibid., p. 301. See also the Arabic text of the *Tarikh*, vol. 2, pp. 136ff.

70 See the chapter on "The Affair of the Possessions and the Women and Children Prisoners of War of the Hawazin," in Ibn Hisham, *Sira*, vol. 4, pp. 130ff.

71 William Montgomery Watt, *Muhammad at Medina* (Oxford: Oxford University Press, 1956).

72 Pickthall, *The Meaning of the Glorious Koran*, sura 49, verse 13.

73 Tabari, *Mohammed, Sceau des prophètes*, p. 320.

74 Ibid. For more details see Tabari, *Tarikh*, vol. 3, p. 245.

75 Tabari, *Mohammed, Sceau des prophètes*, p. 321.

76 Mas'udi, *Les Prairies d'or*, vol. 3, p. 321.

77 Ibid., p. 594.

78 Tabari, *Mohammed, Sceau des prophètes*, p. 321. For more information on the personality of Musaylima, see Ibn Hisham, *Sira*, pp. 223ff and pp. 247ff; Tabari, *Tarikh*, vol. 3, pp. 243ff; and Mas'udi, *Muruj*, vol. 2, p. 310.

CHAPTER 8 'UMAR AND THE MEN OF MEDINA

1 'Asqalani, *Isaba*, vol. 4, p. 588; Ibn Hisham, *Sira*, vol. 8, p. 366.

2 Ibn Hisham, *Sira*, vol. 8, p. 367.

3 Ibid., p. 366.

4 Mas'udi, *Muruj*, vol. 2, p. 313; Mas'udi, *Les Prairies d'or*, vol. 3, p. 595.

5 Tabari, *Tarikh*, vol. 5, p. 27.

6 Mas'udi, *Muruj*, vol. 2, p. 313; Mas'udi, *Les Prairies d'or*, vol. 3, p. 596.

7 Tabari, *Tarikh*, vol. 5, p. 27.

8 Bukhari, *Sahih*, vol. 3, p. 258; French trans. by Houdas, p. 587.

9 Ibid.

10 Ibid. See also Ibn Sa'd, *Tabaqat*, vol. 8, p. 186.

11 Ibn Sa'd, *Tabaqat*, vol. 8, p. 180.

12 Tabari, *Tarikh,*, vol. 4, p. 51.

13 Ibn Sa'd, *Tabaqat*, vol. 8, p. 180.

14 Bukhari, *Sahih*, vol. 3, p. 258; French trans. by Houdas, p. 588.

15 In accordance with tradition, al-Tabari devotes several paragraphs to a physical description of the Prophet in the Arabic original of his *Tarikh* (vol. 3, pp. 185ff). He speaks of his magnificent head of hair, his long neck, his energetic walk, but he omits the smile that is described at some length in the Persian version that I cite: *Mohammed, Sceau des prophètes*, p. 377.

16 Tabari, *Tafsir*, ed. Shakir, vol. 4, p. 409.

17 Pickthall, *The Meaning of the Glorious Koran*.

18 Tabari, *Tafsir*, vol. 4, p. 405.

19 Ibid., p. 400.

20 Ibid., p. 402.

21 Ibid., pp. 413ff.
22 *Encyclopedia of Islam*, 2nd edn, section on "'Abd" (Slave).
23 Ibid.
24 Pickthall, *The Meaning of the Glorious Koran*.
25 Tabari, *Mohammed, Sceau des prophètes*, p. 33.
26 Ibid., p. 328.
27 Ibid., p. 338.
28 *Encyclopedia of Islam*, 2nd edn, section on 'Abd'.
29 Ibid.
30 Tabari gives a long account of the slavegirl in connection with the idea of *muhsan*, a concept connected to marital status. See his *Tafsir* in Shakir's edition, vol. 7, pp. 151ff. There are decisions concerning individual cases in the following biographies of the Companions: Ibn Sa'd, *Tabaqat*; 'Asqalani, *Isaba*; and Ibn al-Athir, *Usd al-ghaba*. But obviously the information is scattered throughout these works. There are some excellent analyses, such as that of al-Hawfi, who examines the position of prisoners of war and slaves in the light of pre-Islamic literature and especially poetry, which played as important a role at that time as the media do today: *Al-mar'a fi al-shi'r al-jahili*, pp. 464–524. See also the chapters by al-'Ali on bedouin social structures in his *Muhadarat fi tarikh al-'Arab*. Finally, Jurji Zaydan's book, *Tarikh al-tamaddun al-Islami*, is not only full of information but a pleasure to read. Zaydan gives a thorough description of slavery during the so-called "Golden Age" of Islam, the eighth and ninth centuries, the Abbasid period.
31 Ibn Hasan al-Maliki, *Al-hada'iq al-ghana' fi akhbar al-nisa'* (Tunis: Al-Dar al-'Arabiya li al-Kutub, 1987), p. 73. (The author died in the twelfth century.)
32 Ibid.
33 Ibid.
34 Bukhari, *Sahih*, vol. 4, p. 271.
35 Ibn Sa'd, *Tabaqat*, vol. 8, p. 174.
36 Pickthall, *The Meaning of the Glorious Koran*, sura 49, verses 4 and 5.
37 Ibid., sura 49, verse 2.
38 Mas'udi, *Les Prairies d'or*, p. 595.
39 Pickthall, *The Meaning of the Glorious Koran*, sura 4, verse 34.
40 Al-Tabari explains to the believer that the rules governing his relations with a free woman are different from those regulating his relations with a slave girl: "[women slaves] do not have the same rights with regard to you as free women." He makes this statement in his commentary on verse 3 of sura 4 on the subject of polygyny (Tabari, *Tafsir*, ed. Shakir, vol. 7, p. 540).
41 Pickthall, *The Meaning of the Glorious Koran*, sura 4, verse 34.
42 Tabari, *Tafsir*, vol. 8.
43 Ibn Sa'd, *Tabaqat*, vol. 8, p. 205.
44 Tabari, *Tafsir*, vol. 8, p. 299.
45 Ibn Sa'd, *Tabaqat*, vol. 8, p. 204.
46 Bukhari, *Sahih*, vol. 3, p. 259; French trans. by Houdas, p. 589.

47 Ibn Sa'd, *Tabaqat*, vol. 8, p. 204. The word used is *fasadna*, with a connotation of sexual disorder. It means a disturbance of the ethical order that governs sexuality.
48 Ibid.
49 Ibn Hisham, *Sira*, vol. 1, p. 369.
50 Ibid.
51 Ibn Sa'd, *Tabaqat*, vol. 8, p. 179.
52 Tabari, *Tarikh*, vol. 5, p. 16.
53 Ibn Sa'd, the author of the *Tabaqat*, died in year 230 of the Hejira (about AD 845) and al-Tabari in 310 (about AD 922).
54 Ibn Sa'd, *Tabaqat*, vol. 8, p. 204.
55 Tabari, *Tafsir*, vol. 8, p. 290.
56 Ibid., p. 302.
57 Ibid., p. 304.
58 Ibid.
59 Ibid., p. 308.
60 Ibid., p. 309.
61 Ibid., p. 313.

CHAPTER 9 THE PROPHET AS MILITARY LEADER

1 Tabari, *Tarikh*, vol. 3, p. 49.
2 Ibid., p. 54.
3 Régis Blachère, *Le Coran* (Paris: Maisonneuve et Larose, 1980), p. 180.
4 Ibn Sa'd, *Tabaqat*, vol. 2, p. 355.
5 Al-Suyuti, *Asrar tartib al-qur'an*, 2nd edn (Cairo: Dar al-I'tisam, 1978).
6 Ibn Hazm, *Al-nasikh wa al-mansukh* (Beirut: Dar al-Kutub al-'Ilmiya, 1986); al-Suyuti, *Asrar tartib al-qur'an*.
7 Ibn Hazm, *Al-nasikh wa al-mansukh*, p. 69. See also the commentary by Sulayman al-Bindari to this new edition, and especially his chronological ordering based on the classical ordering.
8 The fifth month, taking Muharram as the first month of the Muslim calendar. The Muslim year has 12 months, of which the first is Muharram and the last Dhu al-Hijja. Ramadan is the ninth month. The Muslim month is determined by the appearance of the new moon. This means that the same month can have a different number of days according to the year, and in the same year according to the geographical location of the spot where you are. It is easy to imagine how this sometimes creates confusion about dates.
9 Ibn Hisham, *Sira*, vol. 3, p. 220.
10 Tabari, *Mohammed, Sceau des prophètes*, p. 205.
11 Ibid., p. 219.
12 Pickthall, *The Meaning of the Glorious Koran*.
13 Ibid., sura 4, verse 102.
14 Ibn Hisham, *Sira*, vol. 3, p. 231; Tabari, *Tarikh*, vol. 3, p. 46.
15 Ibn Hisham, *Sira*, vol. 3, p. 225; Tabari, *Tarikh*, vol. 3, pp. 44ff.

Notes

16 Ibn Hisham, *Sira*, vol. 3, pp. 226 and 235, Tabari, *Tarikh*, vol. 3, p. 44.

17 Tabari, *Mohammed, Sceau des prophètes*, p. 224.

18 Ibid., p. 225.

19 Pickthall, *The Meaning of the Glorious Koran*.

20 Ibid.

21 Tabari, *Mohammed, Sceau des prophètes*, p. 225.

22 Ibn Hisham, *Sira*, vol. 3, p. 243; Tabari, *Tarikh*, vol. 3, p. 51.

23 Tabari, *Mohammed, Sceau des prophètes*, p. 228.

24 Ibn Hisham, *Sira*, vol. 3, p. 233; Tabari, *Tarikh*, vol. 3, p. 47.

25 Tabari, *Tafsir*, vol. 22, p. 40. The verse referred to is verse 53 of sura 33, "The Clans."

26 See the commentary on the Koran by al-Nisaburi, *Tafsir ghara'ib al-qur'an*, accompanying the *Tafsir* of Tabari, 2nd edn (Beirut: Dar al-Ma'rifa, 1972), vol. 22, p. 27.

27 Ibid.

28 'Asqalani, *Isaba*, vol. 4, p. 768.

29 Al-Nisaburi, *Tafsir ghara'ib al-qur'an*, vol. 22, p. 27; 'Asqalani, *Isaba*, vol. 4, p. 768. The Prophet's fears were not unfounded.

30 Tabari, *Tafsir*, vol. 22, p. 41.

31 'Asqalani, *Isaba*.

32 Tabari, *Tafsir*, vol. 22, p. 27.

33 'Asqalani, *Isaba*, vol. 7, p. 258 (the biography of Rawda). If the Prophet used to free his slaves, one might ask how it was that he had one. Apparently the process of freeing slaves was neither rapid nor automatic. It set in motion a whole train of negotiations that allowed for a certain balancing of interests between the old and the new masters and everybody who was concerned by such a bouleversement in the traffic in human beings.

34 Ibn Sa'd, *Tabaqat*, vol. 8, p. 174.

35 Ibid., p. 176.

36 Pickthall, *The Meaning of the Glorious Koran*.

37 Tabari, *Tafsir*, vol. 22, p. 47.

38 Pickthall, *The Meaning of the Glorious Koran*.

39 Tabari, *Tafsir*, vol. 22, p. 50.

40 Verse 28 of sura 33 has an economic connotation, while verse 51 definitely regulates sexual discontent.

41 See the commentaries in Ibn Sa'd, *Tabaqat*, vol. 8, p. 196; Tabari, *Tafsir*, vol. 21, pp. 155ff, and vol. 22, p. 26.

42 Tabari, *Mohammed, Sceau des prophètes*, p. 337.

43 Ibid.

44 Tabari, *Tafsir*, vol. 21, p. 157.

45 Ibid.

46 On the subject of Zayd and Zaynab, see verse 37 of sura 33, as well as Tabari's commentaries on this verse in *Tafsir*, vol. 22, pp. 16ff.

47 Tabari, *Tafsir*, vol. 22, p. 45.

48 Tabari, *Mohammed, Sceau des prophètes*, p. 253.

49 Ibid., p. 255.

50 Tabari, *Tarikh*, vol. 3, pp. 92ff and p. 178.

51 *Umm walad* is a slave with whom a master officially maintains sexual relations, and who cannot be sold. The children born from such a union are free and enjoy all the rights of legitimate filiation, especially the right to the father's name and inheritance. For further details, see *Encyclopedia of Islam*, 1st edn. See also Ibn Sa'd, *Tabaqat*, vol. 2, p. 117.

52 Tabari, *Tarikh*, vol. 3, p. 180.

53 Ibn Sa'd, *Tabaqat*, vol. 2, p. 116.

54 On the legal aspect of *umm walad*, see Sakanya Ahmad al-Bari, *Ahkam umm walad fi al-Islam* (Cairo: Al-Dar al-Qawmiya li Tiba'a, 1964).

55 Tabari, *Mohammed, Sceau des prophètes*, p. 238. See the long passages devoted to this incident in Ibn Hisham, *Sira*, vol. 3, p. 309; Bukhari, *Sahih*, vol. 4, p. 174; and finally Isbahani, *Aghani*, vol. 4, p. 157.

56 Tabari, *Mohammed, Sceau des prophètes*, p. 239.

57 Ibid., p. 240. The slanderers were flogged, in accordance with the new divine laws revealed on this matter.

CHAPTER 10 THE *HIJAB* DESCENDS ON MEDINA

1 Ibn Sa'd, *Al-Tabaqat*, vol. 8, p. 176. In this chapter I am only going to cite specific references from Ibn Sa'd, but the same material is discussed, with only minimal differences, by al-Tabari, al-Bukhari, and others when they touch on the subject of the veil and the verses concerning it. I cite Ibn Sa'd alone for one simple reason: I like him. I like his turn of mind, his style, his subtlety, his sensitivity, his incredible attention to detail. Besides being a scholar, he is a man who does not treat women with scorn. I cannot say this of the others. But, to ease my conscience, I will give here once and for all the references to the *hijab* in the other classic sources used in this work: Tabari, *Tafsir*, vol. 22, pp. 45ff; Bukhari, *Sahih*, vol. 3, pp. 254ff.

2 Ibn Sa'd, *Al-Tabaqat*, vol. 8, p. 176.

3 Pickthall, *The Meaning of the Glorious Koran*. This verse dates to the Medinan period.

4 Ibid.

5 'Asqalani, *Isaba*, vol. 7, p. 517 for the biography of Umayma; vol. 8, p. 119 for the biography of Musayka under her real name, Mu'ada.

6 'Asqalani, *Isaba*, vol. 8, pp. 120–1.

7 Ibn Sa'd, *Tabaqat*, vol. 8, pp. 176–7.

8 Bukhari, *Sahih*, vol. 3, p. 248; French translation by Houdas, p. 566. I discussed this text in my book *Beyond the Veil*. But when I wrote that book I did not ask the key question concerning that text: What was the social origin of the women who practiced these kinds of marriages? To find the answer one would have to systematically go through the biographies of the first Muslims.

Notes

We have at our disposal a huge literature about them, which up until now has been given little analysis.

9 See Adam Metz's chapter on sexual mores in the fourth century of the Hejira (twelfth century AD), especially the development of the use of eunuchs, pederasty, and the institutionalization of prostitution in his *Al-hadar al-Islamiya fi al-qarn 'Arabi al-hijri* (Cairo: Maktaba al-Khanji, n.d.).

10 Al-Nisaburi, *Tafsir ghara'ib al-qur'an*, vol. 22, p. 9.

11 Ibn Sa'd, *Tabaqat*, vol. 8, p. 177.

12 Ibid.

13 Pickthall, *The Meaning of the Glorious Koran*, sura 33, verse 59.

14 See the excellent study by Ignace Goldziher, "The Arab Tribes and Islam," in his *Muslim Studies* (Chicago: Aldine, 1966).

CONCLUSION

1 Tabari, *Mohammed, Sceau des prophètes*, p. 282. See also the wonderful description by Ibn Sa'd, *Tabaqat*, vol. 2, p. 137.

2 Tabari, *Mohammed, Sceau des prophètes*, p. 286.

3 Salih Ahmad al-'Ali, "*Al tanzimat al-ijtima 'iya 'inda al-badw*" (Bedouin Social Structures) in his *Muhadarat fi tarikh al-'Arab* (Baghdad: Maktaba al-Muthanna, 1970). On p. 139 the author uses Koranic verses to demonstrate that the origin of *wa'd* (infanticide) is religious (see verses 132 and 140 of sura 6). He also explains that it is ridiculous to make of that an indication of the humiliating and degraded situation of women, "because certain goddesses were women." In this he is correct.

4 Isbahani, *Aghani*, vol. 16, pp. 168–9.

5 On the murder of Husayn, see Tabari, *Tarikh*, vol. 6, pp. 251ff; Mas'udi, *Les Prairies d'or*, vol. 3, p. 749. On Sukayna and her experience of the event, see the biography by 'Abd al-Rahman, *Sakayna, bint al-Husayn* (Beirut: Dar al-Kitab al-'Arabi, n.d.), pp. 58ff.

6 Isbahani, *Aghani*, vol. 16, p. 143.

7 For biographical information on Sakayna, see the following, which, however, is far from being an exhaustive list: Ibn Sa'd, *Tabaqat*, vol. 8, p. 475; Isbahani, *Aghani*, vol. 3, pp. 361ff; vol. 16, pp. 138ff; vol. 17, pp. 43ff; and vol. 19, pp. 155ff; Ibn 'Asakir, *Tarikh madinat Dimashq* (Damascus: n.p., 1982), pp. 155ff. (The author died in the eleventh century.); Ibn Hasan al-Maliki, *Hada'iq*; Ibn Habib al-Baghdadi, *Kitab al-muhabbar* (Beirut: Al-Maktaba al-Tijariya, n.d.), pp. 439ff. (The author died in year 245 of the Hejira, the ninth century.)

8 See the sources cited in the previous note.

9 Genet, *Le Captif amoureux*, p. 404.

10 Zaydan, *Tarikh al-tamaddun al-Islami*, vol. 5, p. 76.

11 Ibid., p. 77.

Appendices

Appendix 1
Sources

For this study I have used not only the Koran, the key text of the religious literature, but also the historical information on the context in which the development of the sacred in Islam, as a written text, took place, especially the ten years of the Prophet's life in Medina – the period during which the revelation of the majority of the texts concerning women took place. In this Appendix I list only the works that I used the most. As for the others, they will be found in the Notes.

THE KORAN

The English translation of the Koran used is the following: Marmaduke Pickthall, *The Meaning of the Glorious Koran* (New York: Dorset Press, n.d.).

The Tafsir (*commentary on the Koran*) of Tabari

The *Tafsir* of the Koran is a commentary that takes each verse separately and elucidates it by placing it in its historical context and subjecting every single word to a systematic linguistic and grammatical analysis. Most of the revelations, the divine words inspired by God in the Prophet, were intended to resolve real-life problems that the Prophet confronted or questions that the new converts asked him. So the explication of a verse consists of making it comprehensible through an investigation into the circumstances of its revelation as well as its grammatical nuances and linguistic complexities.

Al-Tabari, who died in year 310 of the Hejira (AD 922), occupies an eminent position as *mufassir* (commentator on the Koran; more precisely, he who explicates) and also as a historian. His work is a masterpiece of religious literature and he is a scholar without equal – one of impeccable clarity and rigor.

I have used various editions of his commentary. Since I am not an expert in religious scholarship, I need an edition of Tabari that is carefully edited and commented on by a contemporary writer. As ill luck would have it, the ideal edition for me, that by the impressive Mahmud Shakir, is incomplete. Shakir died before finishing the gigantic work that he had undertaken, namely, to comment on and clarify the 30 volumes of Tabari's commentary on the Koran.

Anybody used to buying old Arabic books knows the importance of the competence of the editor, and his reputation often makes the price of the edition double that of others, or even more. Since these are books that were written centuries ago, only the editor can give you the indispensable grammatical and historical information you need to master the text.

For the volumes that Shakir did not do a commentary on, I used two other versions where the commentaries are less adequate. So the following are the three editions I used:

> Al-Tabari, *Tafsir, jami' al-bayan 'an ta'wil ayi al-qur'an*, edited by Mahmud Muhammad Shakir (Cairo: Dar al-Ma'arif, n.d.). Fifteen volumes have been published, but I was only able to use nine of them.
>
> Al-Tabari, *Tafsir, jami' al-bayan 'an ta'wil ayi al-qur'an* (Beirut: Dar al-Fikr, 1984).
>
> Al-Tabari, *Jami' al-bayan fi tafsir al-qur'an*, with the commentary of al-Nisaburi, *Tafsir ghara'ib al-qur'an wa ragha'ib al-furqan*. (Beirut: Dar al-Ma'rifa, 1972).

The only translation of al-Tabari I have used is the part covering the biography of the Prophet translated by Zotenberg from the Persian version of the *Tarikh: Mohammed, Sceau des prophètes* (Paris: Sindbad, 1980).

Treatises on the causes of the revelations: Asbab al-nuzul

In addition to the commentaries on the Koran, there are treatises in which the *fuqaha* (religious scholars) try to identify for each sura the circumstances that caused its revelation. The experts on this subject emphasize the necessity of distinguishing the explanations and causes for each verse. Nevertheless, one very often finds the same historical references. The special usefulness of these works is that they are a sort of very concise summary of dozens of volumes of commentary and are usually in just one volume. This makes them extremely valuable to the non-specialist. I have used the following ones:

Al-Suyuti, *Lubab al-nuqul fi asbab al-nuzul*, 4th edn (Beirut: Dar Ihya' al-'Ilm, 1984).

Al-Nisaburi, *Asbab al-nuzul* (Beirut: Dar al-Kutub al-'Ilmiya, 1978).

Treatises on the Koranic verses that, according to some experts, were nullified by later contradictory revelations: the nasikh *and the* mansukh

Although the *fuqaha* are far from being in agreement concerning this, these treatises are useful because for each sura they give a list of the verses which, according to the experts on *nasikh* and *mansukh* (that which abrogates and that which is abrogated), were replaced by later revelations. For example, they list all the verses in which tolerance toward non-Muslims, particularly Jews and Christians, was nullified by a later verse that instituted total war against all "infidels." These documents were very useful in connection with this book in that they clarified the chronology of the revelations, which one needs to know in order to show that a later verse nullified such and such a verse. This is far from being a simple matter, because the order of the suras that we have today is not that of the time of revelation.

Most of the new editions of the ancient texts concerning *nasikh* and *mansukh* have been edited by excellent contemporary scholars who give extremely useful information about the chronology of the suras in their commentaries and references. This is much needed, because in the same sura there may be verses belonging to different periods. Another advantage of these works is their concision. They bring together in a few dozen pages information drawn from huge works comprising dozens of volumes, some of which still only exist in manuscript form:

Qatada Ibn Di'ama al-Sadusi, *Kitab al-nasikh wa al-mansukh* (Beirut: Mu'assasa al-Risala, 1984). The author died in year 117 of the Hejira (eighth century AD). The editor is Salih al-Dhamin.

Appendices

Ibn Hazm, *Al-nasikh wa al-mansukh* (Beirut: Dar al-Kutub al-'Ilmiya, 1986). The editor is Sulayman al-Bindari.

Ibn al-Jawzi, *Min 'ilm al-nasikh wa al-mansukh* (Beirut: Mu'assasa al-Risala, 1984). The author died in year 597 of the Hejira (thirteenth century). The editor is Salih al-Dhamin.

Ibn al-Barizi, *Nasikh al-qur'an wa mansukhuh* (Beirut: Mu'assasa al-Risala, 1983). The author died in year 738 of the Hejira (fifteenth century AD). The editor is Salih al-Dhamin.

HADITH

For Hadith I have used the texts of al-Bukhari and al-Nasa'i:

Al-Bukhari, *Al-Sahih*, with commentary by al-Sindi (Beirut: Dar al-Ma'rifa, 1978). In some cases I have used the French translation by O. Houdas: al-Bukhari, *Traditions islamiques* (Paris: Imprimerie Nationale, 1908). The volume I have used most often is volume 3, which contains the "Livre du mariage."

In addition to al-Bukhari's *Sahih*, I have also used a version commented on by the brilliant Ibn Hajar al-'Asqalani, *Huda al-sari, muqaddimat fath al-bari*, commonly known as *Fath al-bari* (Cairo: Maktaba Mustafa al-Halabi, 1963). Al-'Asqalani was born in year 773 of the Hejira and died in year 852 (fifteenth century AD). He does for Hadith what al-Tabari does for the Koran. He takes each Hadith, dissects it, identifies the chain of transmitters and the circumstances of the Hadith, and describes the debates that the Hadith aroused. Al-Bukhari's four volumes are thus studied and examined under a microscope in 17 volumes of commentary in which al-'Asqalani produces a veritable staging of each Hadith. He sets the historical scene and places in it each of the transmitters; he gives us the motives, whether admitted or not, and then sends that character offstage before bringing on another. It is an extremely vivid account which reads like part-detective story, part-epic. The great advantage of this book, like most of the old texts of Muslim literature, is that it has an extremely detailed index (of places, persons, tribes, battles, etc.) that makes it possible to easily find the Hadith you are seeking.

Imam al-Nasa'i, *Al-Sunan*, with commentary by al-Suyuti and notes by Imam al-Sindi (Cairo: Al-Matba'a al-Misriya, n.d.).

Sources

BOOKS OF RELIGIOUS HISTORY

For the devotee of religious history, the large number of Muslim sources, their diversity and the quality of their narrative make them a rich treasure. The personality of the historian sets the tone, despite the repetitiousness of the events, the same in each work, that are being described.

First of all there is the *Sira*, biography of the Prophet, which recounts his public and private life and his expeditions.

Another extremely useful historical genre is the biographies of the Companions, which give a detailed genealogy of each of the Companions of both sexes, their contributions, and the significant events of their private and public lives.

Finally, there are the books of general history that recapitulate the main events, often in chronological order. This is what al-Tabari does. His book lists events year by year. In general, the very detailed indices, which often fill a whole volume, help the non-specialist reader to find his or her way through the three principal themes of religious history: the life of the Prophet, the lives of the Companions, and historical events.

Sira, *biography of the Prophet*

Ibn Hisham, *Al-sira al-nabawiya* (Beirut: Dar Ihya' al-Tharwa al-'Arabi, n.d.). Ibn Hisham died in year 218 of the Hejira (AD 833).

Biographies of the Companions

Ibn Hajar al-'Asqalani, *Al-Isaba fi tamyiz al-sahaba* (Cairo: Maktaba al-Dirasa al-Islamiya, n.d.). Al-'Asqalani died in year 852 of the Hejira (fifteenth century AD).

Ibn al-Athir, *Usd al-ghaba fi tamyiz al-sahaba* (Beirut: Dar al-Fikr, n.d.). The author died in year 630 of the Hejira (thirteenth century AD).

Ibn Sa'd, *Al-Tabaqat al-kubra* (Beirut: Dar Sadir, n.d.). Ibn Sa'd died in year 230 of the Hejira (AD 845). Volume 8 of this work is devoted to biographies of the women Companions.

Appendices

General history

Al-Tabari, *Tarikh al-umam wa al-muluk* (Beirut: Dar al-Fikr, 1979). I cite this work as *Tarikh*, followed by the number of the relevant volume. For the part of this work that concerns the biography of the Prophet, I have quoted the French translation of the Persian version: Tabari, *Mohammed Sceau des prophètes*, trans. Herman Zotenberg (Paris: Sindbad, 1980).

Al-Mas'udi, *Muruj al-dhahab* (Beirut: Dar al-Ma'rifa, 1982). Al-Mas'udi died in year 346 of the Hejira (AD 956). I have also used the excellent French translation of this book by A.C. Barbier de Meynard and A.J.-B. Pavet de Courteille, *Les Prairies d'or* (Paris: Société Asiatique, 1971).

Appendix 2
Chronology

This chronology is intended to give the reader the key dates needed to contextualize the events referred to in this book. Often I have indicated the date according to both the Muslim and Christian calendars. To establish the correspondence between the two calendars I have used the following sources: *Shorter Encyclopedia of Islam* (Ithaca, New York: Gibb and Kramers); Richard Bell, *Bell's Introduction to the Koran*, revised and enlarged by William Montgomery Watt (Edinburgh: Edinburgh University Press, 1970); and especially Marshall G.S. Hodgson, *The Venture of Islam: Conscience and History in a World Civilization* (Chicago: University of Chicago Press, 1974).

What must be kept in mind is that 1990 corresponds to the year 1410–11 of the Muslim calendar. This is because that calendar begins with the Hejira, the emigration of the Prophet from Mecca, his native city, to Medina, which took place in AD 622. Because the Arab month is lunar, and thus shorter, it is not possible to shift from one calendar to the other by adding or subtracting 622. Each century the Arab calendar gains some months.

Around AD 570: Birth of the Prophet.
AD 579: Death of the great Persian emperor, Khusraw Anushirvan. His empire becomes embroiled in war with the other great power of the region, the Roman empire. It is in the shadow of these two great powers that Islam is born.
AD 595: Muhammad marries Khadija.
AD 610: Muhammad receives his first revelation.
AD 610–14: Reign of Heraclius, who reorganizes the Roman empire.
AD 613: Muhammad begins to preach publicly in Mecca.

AD 613: The first emigration of Muslims persecuted in Mecca to Ethiopia. Muhammad, however, remains in his native city and continues to preach and confront the Meccan polytheists.

AD 619: Death of Khadija and Muhammad's uncle, Abu Talib, chief of Banu Hashim, the Prophet's clan. The Prophet, feeling himself in danger, tries to leave Mecca.

AD 619: The Persians occupy Egypt.

AD 621: Muhammad's first contact with the Medinese.

AD 622: **The Hejira**. Muhammad leaves Mecca for Medina. He is 40 years old, according to some sources; 43 according to others. The first year of the Hejira is the first year of the Muslim calendar.

AD 624: Battle of Badr. Attacked by the Meccans and their allies, the Muslims succeed in routing the enemy, despite the latter's numerical superiority.

AD 625: Battle of Uhud. The Meccans return to the charge against Muhammad, determined to make him capitulate. They attack at Uhud, a mountain near Medina. Muhammad and his men are routed. This is the disaster of Uhud.

AD 627: (year 5 of the Hejira): The Battle of the Trench. The Meccans besiege Muhammad in Medina itself.

AD 628: Treaty of Hudaybiyya. Muhammad signs a truce with Mecca.

AD 630: (year 8 of the Hejira): Muhammad occupies Mecca and sends a first expedition to Mu'ta near the Syrian border.

AD 632: Death of the Prophet. He dies on June 8, AD 632, 13 *Rabi' al-awwal* of year 10 of the Hejira. He lived ten years in Medina, the period that concerns us for this book.

Abu Bakr: *the first orthodox caliph*. After the death of the Prophet, the most powerful men of Medina got together to name his successor. The first caliph of Islam was Abu Bakr. He was very close to the Prophet, who had married his daughter 'A'isha. He died in August AD 634 (year 13 of the Hejira).

'Umar: *the second orthodox caliph*. 'Umar Ibn al-Khattab, like Abu Bakr, had given his daughter (Hafsa) in marriage to the Prophet. But Hafsa, unlike 'A'isha, had a very retiring personality. 'Umar was elected caliph after the death of Abu Bakr and remained in that position until November AD 644 (year 23 of the Hejira). He was assassinated while in the mosque.

'Uthman: *the third orthodox caliph*. 'Uthman Ibn 'Affan was named caliph in AD 644 (year 23 of the Hejira) after the assassination of 'Umar, and he remained in that position until AD 655 (the end of year 35

of the Hejira), when he also – in his own house – was killed by a crowd of discontented citizens who besieged him.

'Ali: the fourth and last orthodox caliph. The choice of 'Ali Ibn Abi Talib as the fourth orthodox caliph in June AD 656 (year 35 of the Hejira) was challenged, and his reign was inaugurated by the troubles that led to civil war and to a bizarre arbitration that put an end to his caliphate and to the "orthodoxy" of political power in February AD 658 (year 37 of the Hejira).

The Muslim world was forever after divided into two parts – the Shi'ites (schismatics), the unconditional supporters of 'Ali, and the Sunnis, who accepted the result of the fraudulent arbitration and the nomination of Mu'awiya as caliph. While 'Ali was the Prophet's cousin and like him belonged to Banu Hashim, one of the clans of Quraysh tribe, Mu'awiya belonged to a rival branch of that tribe, the clan of the Bani Umayya. From this comes the name of the Umayyads, the dynasty inaugurated by Mu'awiya. There is no fifth orthodox caliph. With the choice of Mu'awiya, the orthodox sequence of caliphs was broken – that is, caliphs selected by agreement among a small group of the ruling elite. With Mu'awiya political Islam became a dynasty. 'Ali was assassinated in January AD 661 (year 40 of the Hejira).

Index

Index

Ibn al-Jawzi, 98
idda, 52, 182
al-ifk (affair of the necklace), 177–8
isnad, 9, 35

al-Jabiri, Muhammad, 15–16, 20
jariya (pl. *jawari*), 151, 195
al-Jawziya, Ibn Qayyim, 9
Juwayriyya Bint al-Harith, 149–50

Khadija Bint Khuwaylid, 27–8,
30, 102–3, 116
Khandaq, Battle of the, 167–70
Kharijites, 41–2
Khatibi, 'Abd al-Kabir, 15

mansukh, 165, 219–20
Mecca, conquest of, 189–91
Moscovici, Serge, 17
Mu'awiya, 41–2, 151, 191, 192–3,
225
Muhajirun, 30, 37–8, 106, 111
Muhammad, The Prophet, 8, 25–
34, 37, 65–8, 86–92, 102–8,
112–13, 115, 117–18, 135–8,
145, 153–7, 159–60, 161–4,
165–78, 187, 189
munafiqun see Hypocrites
Musaylima, 139, 140

nasikh, 165, 219–20
nushuz, 156, 158, 193
nuzul, 93, 219

qibla, 64, 65, 69

Safiyya Bint Huyayya, 176–7
Sajah Bint al-Harith Ibn Suwayad,
139
salat al-khawf (prayer of fear), 164,
165, 166–7
Shakir, Mahmud, 159
Shi'ites, 41, 196, 225
slavery, 121, 148–53, 178–9, 180–2,
183, 186, 209, 211
sodomy, 146–8
sufism, 95, 96
Sukayna, 192–4
Sunnis, 41, 196, 225

ta'arrud, 180, 182
al-Tabari, 8, 126–8, 142, 146, 147,
156–9, 162
Trench, Battle of the (*see* Khandaq,
Battle of the)

Uhud, Battle of, 91, 165, 166
'Umar Ibn al-Khattab, 33, 34–40,
60–1, 79–80, 113, 114, 130,
141–5, 155–7, 162, 184–6, 188
Umm Kajja, 121–2
Umm Kulthum, 142
Umm Salama, 103, 104, 105, 115–
16, 118–19, 132, 144, 145, 154,
162–3, 186
umm walad, 195, 212
Usama, 150
'Uthma Ibn 'Affan, 33, 34–40

Zarkashi, Imam, 77
Zaynab Bint Jahsh, 86–7, 104, 163,
175
Zayd Ibn Haritha, 104, 150, 175
zina, 60–1, 180, 183, 186

4/22